it's
beginning to
look a lot like
Christmas

Chicken Soup for the Soul: It's Beginning to Look a Lot Like Christmas
101 Tales of Holiday Love & Wonder
Amy Newmark

Published by Chicken Soup for the Soul, LLC www.chickensoup.com
Copyright ©2019 by Chicken Soup for the Soul, LLC. All Rights Reserved.

The publisher gratefully acknowledges the many publishers and individuals who granted Chicken Soup for the Soul permission to reprint the cited material.

Front cover illustration courtesy of Shutterstock.com/MarinaMarkizova (©MarinaMarkizova)
Back cover and Interior photo courtesy of iStockphoto.com/catinsyrup (©catinsyrup)
Photo of Amy Newmark courtesy of Susan Morrow at SwickPix

Cover and Interior by Daniel Zaccari

Distributed to the booktrade by Simon & Schuster. SAN: 200-2442

Publisher's Cataloging-In-Publication Data
(Prepared by The Donohue Group, Inc.)

Names: Newmark, Amy, compiler.
Title: Chicken soup for the soul : it's beginning to look a lot like
    Christmas : 101 tales of holiday love & wonder / [compiled by] Amy
    Newmark.
Other Titles: It's beginning to look a lot like Christmas : 101 tales of
    holiday love & wonder
Description: [Cos Cob, Connecticut] : Chicken Soup for the Soul, LLC,
    [2019]
Identifiers: ISBN 9781611599916 | ISBN 9781611592917 (ebook)
Subjects: LCSH: Christmas--Literary collections. | Christmas--Anecdotes. |
    Gratitude--Literary collections. | Gratitude--Anecdotes. | LCGFT:
    Anecdotes.
Classification: LCC GT4985 .C455 2019 (print) | LCC GT4985 (ebook) | DDC
    394.2663/02--dc23

Library of Congress Control Number: 2019939672

it's beginning to look a lot like Christmas

101 Tales of Holiday Love & Wonder

Amy Newmark

Chicken Soup for the Soul, LLC
Cos Cob, CT

Changing your world one story at a time®
www.chickensoup.com

Table of Contents

❶

~It's Time to Count Our Blessings~

❷

~Christmas Angels~

❸
~Feeling that Christmas Spirit~

❹
~Family Fun~

❺
~Best Gift Ever~

❻

~Getting Creative~

❼

~Through the Eyes of a Child~

8

~The Joy of Giving~

9

~Perfectly Imperfect~

10

~Homemade Holidays~

⓫

~It Takes a Village~

Chapter 1

It's Time to Count Our Blessings

Christmas Oranges

*In every conceivable manner, the family is link
to our past, bridge to our future.*
~Alex Haley

E very Christmas, my mom would fill our stockings with little treats so my siblings and I could get up at the crack of dawn and my parents could sleep for a few extra hours. We were allowed to play with anything in our stockings as soon as we got up, but we had to wait for my parents to open our gifts from Santa and the family.

Our stockings were always overflowing with small toys and candies. At the very tip of the stocking, the very last thing that we would pull out was an orange. For years, I hated the tradition. It was disappointing to pull an orange out of my stocking after uncovering so many fun and delicious treats. An orange wasn't special. I could eat one any time of year, and it was just taking up room that could have been filled with more candy.

When I was thirteen, I finally asked my mother why she put oranges in our stockings. She sat down with me at the kitchen table and explained that my grandfather had grown up very poor. His father had a brain tumor that left him blind and unable to work, so his mother relied on welfare and donations from the church to take care of her seven children. Every Christmas, a local church donated a basket of fruit to their family. This was my grandfather's favorite day of the year because it was the only day he could eat fresh fruit. The oranges were his favorite because they tasted like sunshine. When he grew up, he always made sure to have a bowl of oranges around at Christmastime so he could share his favorite Christmas memory with his children.

When my mom finished telling the story, I felt ashamed. In my rush to collect as much candy as possible, I had forgotten to be grateful. Now the orange at the bottom of my stocking is a reminder to be grateful for the beautiful Christmases that my parents gave me and for the hard work they did that ensured I could have an orange any day of the year.

— Erinn C. —

The Coat Off My Back

*Christmas is the season for kindling the fire
of hospitality in the hall, the genial flame
of charity in the heart.*
~Washington Irving

I t was Christmas Eve, and we'd just begun the drive home from my parents' house in Pennsylvania. Our two children were bundled under coats and blankets in the back seat, singing along to Christmas carols on the radio, entertaining their daddy while he drove.

Visions of lasagna danced through my head. Tomorrow, my parents would make the one-hour journey to join us for lunch. I reviewed everything I needed to do before I could lay down my head for a much-needed rest. Homemade sauce had to go into the Crock-Pot. Wine had to go in the refrigerator. The kids would cuddle in front of holiday movies until they couldn't keep their eyes open or until the Santa Tracker said he was close. Once they were tucked into bed, I'd spring into action: sweeping the main floors, scrubbing the bathroom, and setting out the good china—all before Santa arrived. I had a lot to do to make it a perfect Christmas.

Barely five minutes into our ride, it began to snow. The heat in our truck was never quite enough, so I reminded the kids to snuggle under the extra blanket between them.

I zippered my heavy-duty outdoors vest. I slipped my hands into my pocket to get my mittens and hat. My fingers wrapped around something papery, and I mentally scolded myself as I slipped on my gloves. I never left cash in my pockets for fear of forgetting it.

"We've just got to take it slow," Dan remarked, carefully watching the road.

It was one more obstacle on our way to a perfect holiday. *Why couldn't it wait until we got home?* I asked myself silently.

As we came up to a turn, out of the corner of my eye I saw a man standing next to a gas station alongside the road and holding a large piece of cardboard.

"It's not the kind of night to be stuck outside," my husband remarked.

The snow was falling heavily now, and the man was barely visible as we drove past.

Somewhere deep inside me, something instinctive and hurting rose up. I was doing the holiday all wrong; my priorities were completely out of whack.

"Turn around!" I shouted suddenly. The children went quiet. "Right now, turn around."

My husband, having never heard me speak so firmly, carefully pulled into an empty parking lot and drove back.

I didn't know what I was going to do or say, but all my worries seemed insignificant as I got out of the car.

My husband reached into his pocket. "Give him this. It's all I have with me."

I nodded and hurried along as I walked in front of the headlights of our truck.

The snow was coming down hard, and I was sure, even with the roar of the truck engine and the bright lights behind me, that the man was unable to hear me approach.

As I tapped him on the shoulder of his worn, thin hoodie, he turned. He was a young man, probably in his mid-twenties. His wispy blond hair blew about in the wind, and his skin was red and chapped. Yet through all the snow, I could make out his kind, bright blue eyes.

"Are you okay?" I felt stupid. Of course, he wasn't okay. If he were, he wouldn't be standing outside in this weather.

For a moment, the cold, the wind and even the wet snow all

disappeared. The world stood still.

"My wife and I are spending the night at the homeless shelter. She's pregnant, and we are just trying to get home," he explained. "Our car broke down, and we're stuck."

I knew he was only a few blocks from the shelter. I also knew that in weather like this, they would soon be accepting only women and children, as the space was very limited. I am not cynical by nature, and something deep inside told me his story was true.

I handed him the money my husband had given me. "I hope this helps."

Then I took off my vest and put it over his shoulders. "You shouldn't be out on a night like this. I'm sorry for your situation. I only wish I could do more."

"I can't take your coat," he protested.

"But you will, and you will take my hat and gloves as well." I placed them in his trembling hands. "You need them far more than I do. Please take care of yourself. Merry Christmas!" Hugging him, I hurried back to the truck.

I felt him watch us leave. I am sure those items meant more to him than they ever could to me.

My kids handed me a blanket, and we all sat quietly listening to the radio. The atmosphere was more reflective than jovial.

I thought about everything that had seemed important just moments before. It didn't really matter how perfect everything was; we had each other. It was okay if the floors weren't swept, and if the bathroom was tidied but not scrubbed. It would be okay if Christmas lunch were served on paper plates.

When we stopped for coffee and treats, no one was disappointed when I realized that I'd left all the cash we had on us in the pocket of my vest.

"They needed it more than us, Mommy," my son said maturely. "I hope they make it home."

"We all do," my husband replied.

— Nicole Ann Rook McAlister —

The Grinch Came to Visit

*To us, family means putting your arms around
each other and being there.*
~Barbara Bush

Last December, the Grinch came to visit. We were caught unaware because from all appearances, it was going to be a fine Christmas. Our two daughters and their families, from Wisconsin and Chicago, would be with us in Ohio, and preparations were mostly finished. The tree was up, the house decorated, and presents wrapped and under the tree.

The day before the Grinch arrived, Christmas was still five days away, and we were completing the planning for the nine people who would be here. By the end of the day, we were ready. That was Tuesday. On Wednesday, the Grinch was the first of our guests to arrive.

He arrived at 10:00 p.m. when my wife Kathy, heading for bed, complained of a little bloating and pains in her stomach. An hour later, she was in the bathroom on her knees for the first of dozens of visits the rest of the night. It continued all Wednesday night and into Thursday, when we called our kids to tell them not to come. We didn't want the little ones catching whatever she had.

Susan, the one farthest away in Wisconsin, decided not to chance it and kept her family home. It was a wise decision.

Missy, however, still planned to come from Chicago because her family also had plans for Christmas with her husband's family in Toledo. We reserved a hotel room for them, thinking that staying away from us "most of the time" would be somewhat of a flu-prevention method. On Friday night, I met them at the hotel and took them out to dinner, while Kathy stayed home alone, staring at a paper plate of food she didn't want to eat.

The next day was Christmas Eve. I returned to the hotel in the morning to take them to visit my mother, who was recovering from hip surgery. We arrived home that afternoon to find Kathy was still sick. Missy and I managed to make dinner preparations for our Christmas Eve dinner, and things appeared to be proceeding satisfactorily.

But late in the afternoon, I, too, began feeling pains in my stomach and became bloated. Within an hour, I began my own series of visits to the bathroom. By dinnertime on Christmas Eve, I sat beside Kathy with a few untouched bites on my own paper plate.

Then things deteriorated further. The Grinch launched a second attack, and everyone fell like flies. Throughout Christmas Day, more and more headed for bathrooms or to bed. By the time we tried to serve lunch on the day after Christmas, the only ones still standing were two grandchildren — thoroughly enjoying having access to all the desserts. The rest of us stared at the tiny portions we had put on our plates. Ultimately, the two "well" grandchildren didn't escape either. One of them fell ill on the turnpike halfway back to Chicago the next day, and the other got hit the moment she got home.

In the middle of all this, we managed to sit around the tree and open presents. The Grinch couldn't steal Christmas! We had laughter and joy and somehow enjoyed being miserable together. The joy of Christmas never left, even though we sometimes had to remind ourselves we would enjoy it more later when we'd tell the story year after year.

The Grinch never had a chance. He gave us his best shot, but he couldn't destroy our Christmas.

The only one disgruntled was our daughter Susan who stayed in Wisconsin and missed it all. "Boy! It sounds like you guys had a really good time. I wish we had been there and gotten sick with you!" We had learned, once again, that Christmas has nothing to do with presents and big meals — and everything to do with love and being together.

— Lynn Gilliland —

Chicken Soup for the Soul

The Best Christmas Turkey that Never Was

*Open your presents at Christmas time but be thankful
year round for the gifts you receive.*
~Lorinda Ruth Lowen

We were approaching our first Christmas in Maine, and I was determined to make it spectacular. My nine-year-old daughter, Lily, and seven-year-old son, Jasper, decorated our towering evergreen. My husband strung sparkly white lights. I had been sneaking the kids' presents in for weeks, and I couldn't wait to wrap them.

Relatives were coming to town, and packages arrived almost daily. I was certain we could even check "White Christmas" off our list since the prediction was for eight to ten inches of snow on Christmas Day.

I loved this time of year — the beauty and lights, the carols sung in high voices, the cozy warmth inside, all the anticipation. And the holiday food! I covered entire pages with grocery store lists for our menus — homemade cannelloni, from-scratch hot chocolate, warm and gooey cinnamon rolls, pavlovas with lemon curd, bourbon cocktails, hearty red wines and lots of champagne.

I planned our menus weeks ahead of time. I planned when I should have been writing. I planned in my dreams. Christmas Day was the most important. Should I make an egg casserole the night before so we could just pop it in the oven Christmas morning? Would turkey breast be perfect for Christmas dinner? Should we try a new citrus-rum punch?

For me, the magic in this season was feeding people I loved.

My daughter and I had agreed we'd make a turkey breast and mashed potatoes. She loved to make divine, buttery potatoes. And we all drooled over leftover-turkey sandwiches.

As Christmas Day approached and the news stations predicted a blizzard, everyone said, "Be prepared!" And I was nothing if not prepared. I planned for deliciousness. I planned for yummy leftovers, game playing, cocktail drinking, and napping—holiday comfort at its finest.

A week before Christmas, we learned that a young, single mom we knew and her three little boys were struggling financially. "Christmas is hard when I can't pay my bills," the mom said to me one day.

That night, I didn't dream about which kind of roast to cook, but rather a home with no tree or presents to wrap. I pictured not being able to give gifts to my kids. I imagined the mailman skipping our house and no Santa in sight. There were no fresh mandarins or charcuterie platters, no cookies shaped like candy canes—only an empty refrigerator, an empty dinner table, and hungry tummies.

The next day, I said to my husband, "I think we should shop for this family for Christmas, if it's okay with the mom. I know it might be difficult for our kids because they wouldn't be buying anything for themselves, but I think we should do this."

He agreed immediately, so off to Target we flew. We filled the cart with toys for each boy: new *Star Wars* T-shirts and winter hats, fun snacks, milk, cereal, bread, and vegetables. I even picked out an easy option for them for dinner—a three-pound turkey breast that would go directly from freezer to oven and cook in its bag—super easy, super delicious, and warm and comforting for all those bellies.

My husband and I loaded up the car and delivered the gifts to the mom a few days before Christmas while the kids were at school. When we left her dilapidated subsidized-housing unit, it was all I could do to keep my tears from flooding the car due to the absolute squalor the family lived in.

I realized, in that moment, how much I took for granted.

When Christmas Day arrived, as we opened presents and drank hot tea, we were pummeled with more than fourteen inches of snow. It was a beautiful white Christmas indeed. Late in the afternoon, as I poked around in the fridge to get our turkey breast so I could prep it, my heart fell. There on the bottom shelf wasn't our eight-pound turkey breast, but the three-pound one I had intended to give the other family.

I was so mad at myself. I had unintentionally given her the large turkey. I didn't even know if she knew how to cook it. And the one in my hands — this "freezer-to-oven" magic — had been thawing in my refrigerator for at least four days because I had stupidly swapped them. All my careful, delicious planning for the perfect Christmas dinner was for nothing.

I looked out at the glittering snow, the magical white blanket, and I talked myself down from the ledge. "It's just a smaller, thawed turkey breast that's easy to cook, so let's do this." I gave myself a pep talk, but honestly, I was still angry and disappointed. It was the part of Christmas I looked forward to most, and I had ruined it. No big, delicious turkey breast for us. No leftover turkey sandwiches slathered with mayo and seasoned salt.

I crankily cut the turkey out of the bag it was supposed to cook in, placed it over some carrots and onions in my glass baking dish, slathered it with butter, and put it in the oven. About twenty minutes into the baking, I opened the oven to add white wine to keep the turkey juicy. As I poured the cold wine, the glass dish exploded in the oven into millions of shards — all over the turkey, the oven, and the floor.

"Oh, my God!" I screamed and jumped back.

My dad and my husband heard the crash and the swearing and ran into the kitchen. "It exploded," I said, still staring at the mess. Suddenly, like popping a balloon, all my anger and disappointment drained out of me, too. "I guess we're not meant to have turkey for dinner tonight," I sighed.

"Nope, I guess not," my husband said.

They helped me clean up the mess, and we threw together a quick version of chicken saltimbocca with a few leftover chicken breasts I quickly thawed. And, along with my daughter's mashed potatoes, it was delicious.

The truth was, while we didn't have the best turkey breast ever, we did not want for anything. We had a scrumptious meal, and we were all safe and warm together. Most importantly, my children had a chance to do something precious for other children. As I sat down at the table, I was truly thankful for so much — my healthy kids, the wonderful, generous people in my life, financial stability, and a dinner table full of food — even if it wasn't exactly the meal I had planned. And when I remember my favorite holiday meals, I will always remember this one, and the best Christmas turkey that never was.

— Sara Ohlin —

A Light in Darkness

Happiness can be found in the darkest of times,
if one only remembers to turn on the light.
~J.K. Rowling, Harry Potter
and the Prisoner of Azkaban

"Everyone! Everyone, it's time to do Santa Lucia!" I have heard this announcement nearly every year of my life on December twenty-third. It's usually declared by one of my aunts during the annual family Christmas party at my grandmother's that has happened every year for as long as I can remember. To me, the Santa Lucia processional is the ultimate and most enduring expression of the holiday spirit.

Growing up in Southern California, my Christmases were never like the ones on greeting cards or in Thomas Kincaid paintings. Christmas meant palm trees, sunny skies, and a balmy seventy degrees most years. But Santa Lucia was different; it brought us the magic of a dark, winter night I never knew but always imagined.

For those unfamiliar, Santa Lucia is a Scandinavian tradition. My grandfather's family emigrated from Sweden and brought it with them, and we can thank the American Girl doll company for bringing it into popular culture with the story of Kirsten Larson. The traditional tale goes something like this: Lucia was an early Christian martyr who delivered food to oppressed and starving believers forced to live in the catacombs. Legend says she wore a wreath of candles on her head to light the way through the dark, and eventually, she was made a saint for the sacrifice she made for those driven underground.

St. Lucia's Day, traditionally, is celebrated on the shortest day of the year. Santa Lucia processionals in Scandinavia feature young women in white dresses, red sashes, and wreaths of holly and candles on their heads. Attendants carry candles while the person representing Santa Lucia leads fellow participants in the darkness and brings trays of cookies and saffron buns to the congregations and families that gather to remember the special role she played.

In our family, after dinner was over and the sun had set, my aunts would corral the young girls in the family to the back bedroom of my grandmother's house and open up the cedar chest. There, we would find long white dresses, red sashes, candles, and the wreath with electric candles. We alternated who got to lead the processional each year, handing out desserts to aunts, uncles, cousins, and grandparents. As the older cousins grew up, younger ones took their place. Eventually, the older cousins had daughters who took part; so the tradition lives on with each and every family Christmas party.

One Christmas, a few years ago, I was seated on my grandmother's couch waiting for Santa Lucia to begin. As the lights throughout the house were turned off, I reflected on my year. It had been difficult, and I found myself thinking about all the things that had gone wrong. The Christmas season's former joys seemed empty in light of the reality of life, with all of its setbacks, complications, and obstacles. My mind turned to the legend of St. Lucia. I considered the early Scandinavians, searching for meaning in a world full of both personal and physical darkness — no wonder they created a festival of light surrounding the ancient Lucia. Even her name's origins signify light. I wondered if those early Christians, too, felt the unsettling squeeze of despair in the darkness those many years ago.

I sank further into my unhappy thoughts. Then, someone started humming "Silent Night." Someone else started singing the words. Within a few moments, everyone was quietly singing "Silent Night." It wasn't planned or formal, but it was beautiful. I felt something loosen in my chest — something that had been tightening and hurting me through months of depression — and I barely dared to sing along as my eyes watered. Instead, I pictured the joyous images of this traditional Christmas song and contemplated the alleluias of heavenly beings, the light of pure love, radiant beams, and dawns of redeeming grace.

As soon as the song was over, the traditional chorus heralding the entry of Santa Lucia started up from someone's phone. In came the happy faces of my younger sisters and cousins' children in a line, dressed in the familiar white dresses and red silk sashes, holding candles. They made their way around the room. Santa Lucia offered sweets, as she always did, but the procession had never looked so beautiful as it did now. I thought about those white dresses, representing the pure and unadulterated love of God, and looked at the red sashes, representing the blood of charitable sacrifice. I realized that what made the moment so perfect was the light that allowed me to make those connections and see those symbols of the holiday, literally and figuratively.

In that brief moment, I understood what ancient Christians felt hiding away in the catacombs, waiting for relief brought by a young girl with a wreath of candles to light the way. I understood what beleaguered Scandinavians—perhaps my own ancestors—felt during short, cold days and nights of interminable darkness. I understood the intercessory peace brought by St. Lucia, who faced a world more dangerous, more painful than my own.

The whole event lasted no longer than ten minutes, but it felt like hours' worth of change had been wrought upon me. The procession circled the room twice and then slowly shuffled out, led by the glow of candles and the promise of redemption from the soul's dark, winter night.

—Emily Olson Shipley—

The Celebration

Gratitude is the fairest blossom which springs
from the soul.
~Henry Ward Beecher

In our family, Friday night dinners were the same as any other night except that there was no school the next day. Before the last bite was swallowed, my brothers, my sister and I would race out the front door and scatter in different directions to find our friends.

Both my brothers had bar mitzvahs, but we did not attend Friday night or Saturday morning services regularly. Holiday dinners, however, were another matter. It was a reason to gather the family: brothers, sisters, aunts, uncles and cousins.

One Hanukkah, in particular, was very special. That was the year my parents spent every spare penny they had saved to sponsor my father's niece, Mitzi, her husband, Jacob, and their four-year-old daughter, Ruth, from Siberia and bring them to Canada.

They arrived at our house on an icy December afternoon in Montreal's Outremont district. It would be years before I realized their desperate condition. I saw them at the time only as pale and tired, in neat but worn clothing.

My brother Harry and I were crouched on the floor in the living room. He was teaching me the fine art of gambling while playing dreidel. Slowly but surely, he relieved me of all my chocolate coins wrapped in gold paper as he won each spin. Then we were called to dinner, and at the table, my big brother gave me back all the chocolates I had lost to him.

There wasn't an extra inch of room around the table. The English speakers sat on one side. My mother and father sat at the end closest to the kitchen while my brothers, my sister and I shared one side of the table. The foreigners — Mitzi, Jacob and Ruth — sat across from us.

My father stared at his niece — his newfound family. They spoke Rumanian with the odd Yiddish word thrown in when my father couldn't remember or understand a word or two of the language he had left behind so many years before. It was the only time I ever saw a tear slide down his cheek, and he brushed it aside with a flick of his thumb. I wondered what was wrong, but a smile remained as he talked, his eyes never straying from the face so much like his older sister who had been lost in World War II.

While everyone talked, my mother, already exhausted from preparing the feast, trekked from the kitchen to the dining room table with plates of roasted chickens. Steaming bowls of mashed potatoes, boiled carrots, parsnips and peas, all drizzled with melted butter, followed. There were also platters of crispy potato latkes with side dishes of sour cream and applesauce and a special treat of Rumanian-style roasted eggplant, mashed with onion and green pepper and splashed with olive oil.

Mitzi just stared at the food. Her eyes slowly filled with tears. She thanked my father in Rumanian, Yiddish and, finally, in the few words of English she knew. Her family's years of starvation were over. They were now living in the land of plenty — the land of freedom and opportunity. Jacob put his hand on her shoulder while she wept.

Perhaps it took all the intervening years for me to discover the meaning of the war, the suffering of other people, and my own experiences of growing up before I could really understand the significance of that special dinner.

Until the day he died, Mitzi was my father's connection to all he had left behind. She was a constant companion and the family historian for those lost in the war or concentration camps.

I never saw another tear on my father's cheek, but I will never forget the one I saw that day, and what I learned from it.

—Joei Carlton Hossack—

Turkey, Pumpkin Pie, and Enchiladas

Travel and change of place impart new vigor
to the mind.
~Lucius Annaeus Seneca

Thanksgiving was always Grandma's holiday. And boy, did she go all out. Every year, she would invite the whole family to her country club to be served a five-course meal by waiters in bow ties.

It was refined. It was classy. I hated it.

I didn't exactly have a mature palate, so the caviar appetizers were not appreciated. Even the mashed potatoes tasted too "fancy." Also, I had to wear an itchy skirt, and the adults separated all of us cousins at the table, so we couldn't even talk to each other.

But I did have someone to commiserate with: my mom.

While I was complaining about my stiff Mary Jane shoes, she was muttering about her heels. While I was complaining that even the butter had herbs in it, she was insisting we stop for French fries on the way home.

We'd put on polite smiles at the table, and then laugh about the stuck-up country-club members in the car.

"Why, yes, indubitably, I do love the horse races, Bernard," I'd say in my best English accent.

"Quite right, Gwendolyn, right after a morning of croquet."

We sounded like an Oscar Wilde play.

We did this every year. That is, until the summer I was twenty-three, when Grandma passed away.

Mom took the loss hard that year, and I missed Grandma, too. But it didn't really hit me until Thanksgiving approached.

Usually, at that time of year, we'd be rolling our eyes at the first thought of the country club. It was the first year we hadn't started discussing how we should sneak pizza rolls and Tater Tots into our purses so we could have "real food."

Instead, that year we avoided the subject for weeks. As the days passed, I started to wonder what would happen. Maybe there wouldn't be a Thanksgiving. After all, it was always Grandma who arranged the holiday celebration. She was the one who planned the event and made the reservations. I understood how Mom and the rest of the family felt that we couldn't go on business-as-usual without Grandma, especially since we only went to the country club because she liked it. But we also weren't ready to start new traditions; it felt like moving on too fast.

Suddenly, I started to miss our Thanksgivings a lot. I didn't appreciate them at the time, but it was sort of fun to have one "fancy" night a year, and it always made my grandparents so happy. Plus, there was always really great pumpkin pie. It made me miss not only my grandma, but our tradition.

One day, in the middle of November, my mom called me at work.

"I just saw a commercial for a sale on direct flights to Puerto Vallarta. We should go."

I thought that sounded great, of course. We needed something fun to look forward to.

"Let's leave on the twenty-third."

"Of this month?" I looked at my calendar. "But that's right before Thanksgiving."

"Exactly."

It took a few minutes, but eventually I understood what she was thinking. It all made sense. Instead of spending the holiday struggling through a forced meal, missing Grandma, we could skip it all with a conveniently timed trip. We'd be leaving the rest of the family to figure it out while we were far away on a beach. And Mexico, of course, doesn't have Thanksgiving.

It was the perfect plan.

I agreed to the trip. I knew my mom was missing Grandma, and if it would help her forget about her grief, I wanted to do it. And besides, we would have a ton of fun.

So, late November, the rest of our family was planning trips to my grandpa's house for Thanksgiving, and Mom and I were boarding a plane to Mexico.

To our surprise, the plane was packed with other families escaping home for the holidays. One newlywed couple told us that they couldn't decide whose parents' house to go to, so they decided they wouldn't choose at all.

We got to our resort, a beach paradise with all-inclusive food and drink and an infinity pool right outside our room. It was a perfect escape for Mom to clear her head and for the two of us to spend some time together.

Every day, we ate a ton of Mexican food and had margaritas on the beach. We had so much fun hiking and renting kayaks.

But something felt off.

As Thanksgiving Day approached, it was sad to think that we wouldn't have a Thanksgiving with Grandma again. But it was also disappointing to know we wouldn't be seeing our family for the holiday, that we wouldn't have a Thanksgiving at all. I wondered, on the morning of Thanksgiving Day, if maybe we should have stayed at home. It would have been awkward and a little sad, but at least we'd be together. At least we'd have had a Thanksgiving. In Mexico, there were no celebrations, no turkey carving, no pumpkin pie, and I missed it all.

Thanksgiving night, we had dinner at one of the restaurants at the resort, but the dining room was nearly empty. Over enchiladas, Mom and I wondered where the other guests had gone. Had all the Americans visiting the resort gone home for the holiday? It didn't make sense. As we were leaving dinner, we heard music and followed some other hotel guests to one of the ballrooms. Inside, there were dozens of tables dressed in orange and yellow, a band, and buffet tables of turkey and gravy, mashed potatoes, and pumpkin pie. It was a Thanksgiving party!

Somehow, just seeing the celebration made me feel like we were home. It was a lot different from what we were used to, but somehow that was just fine.

Mom and I stayed for a long time talking to other families, listening to music, and eating pumpkin pie.

As it turned out, we didn't skip Thanksgiving after all. Maybe it wasn't our usual tradition, and maybe we weren't making new traditions that we'd share the next year back home, but it was just what we needed. It was fun and different, and I appreciated the time to spend with my mom and wipe the slate clean. It was an opportunity to honor our memories and to make room for new ones.

And even though we were thousands of miles from the rest of our family at home, I felt like Grandma was there with us, somehow, celebrating.

—Jilly Pretzel—

December Morn

Concentrate on counting your blessings,
and you'll have little time to count anything else.
~Woodrow Kroll

A fresh white blanket of snow draped my favorite pine tree in our front yard. A smattering of snowflakes lingered in the air as daylight began. In the back yard, our Golden Retriever romped in the crisp snow and stopped briefly to let a couple of the flakes tickle her nose.

It was morning, just three weeks before Christmas Day.

I couldn't sleep so I got up early with the dog and took in the serene beauty of the first snowfall of the holiday season.

I stretched the kinks out of my fifty-year-old body, and then I turned on the lights of our two Christmas trees. I admired the beauty of the decorations and the memories they represented. These were memories that my wife, daughter and I had created. On one tree, we had ornaments from our various travels and favorite places. The other tree had a variety of ornaments made by our daughter. The scent of fresh pine lingered on each tree.

Below our neatly decorated fireplace mantel sat a red poinsettia plant. I laughed to myself as I thought that it was already a Christmas miracle that this plant had survived since Thanksgiving. My wife and I have a reputation for killing plants in record time.

I started a pot of coffee and took in the aroma of fresh hazelnut. I peeked out at the dog to see how she was doing. As I glanced outside,

I saw a bright red cardinal land on a pinecone birdfeeder. A streak of sunshine grazed the cardinal and made its red feathers seem even more brilliant. It was a simple snapshot of nature's beauty, and I felt lucky to see it.

I sat waiting for the dog and began thinking of the upcoming weeks and sighed. No gifts had been wrapped; half of them still needed to be purchased. The cookies had not been baked or iced. Christmas cards still needed to be filled out and mailed. Final decorations and planning had to be finished. Work projects would need to be completed before the end of the year. It was all a bit overwhelming.

Thankfully, the dog barked at the back door and helped me erase those thoughts of the upcoming tasks. I let her in, and she sat obediently so I could dry off her paws.

I petted her, and she wagged her tail as if to say thanks. She was ready for her favorite moment of the day. After she was released, she rumbled back to our bedroom to greet my wife and daughter who had snuck into bed with us. The dog jumped onto the bed and licked them both as if to say, "Good morning," and "I love you." From my spot in our bedroom doorway, I watched the proceedings and smiled. It may have been cold outside, but I had a warm feeling on the inside.

The three things I loved most in life were all in one spot. My wife, daughter and dog all seemed content on this early December morning.

In three weeks, it would be a morning of chaos. Wrapping paper would be strewn everywhere. We would be unwrapping and examining gifts, running around trying to decide what to wear to the afternoon gatherings, cooking last-minute dishes and who knows what else. It would be yet another hectic Christmas Day.

As for me, my Christmas gift had come early. Money can't buy gifts like a fresh white blanket of snow, a bright red cardinal or an unexpected quiet moment when I could cherish the memories that our Christmas trees represent. The gifts of unconditional love from my dog and the security of knowing my wife and daughter had slept warmly in their bed and woke up happy on a crisp and beautiful December morning were far better than anything one could find at a store.

Maybe I'm becoming a sentimental fool, but I know what I want for Christmas every year. I don't need the songs or the gifts or the cookies. Well, maybe a couple of cookies... What I really need is a quiet and beautiful December morning — the time when everything is just right and those who are closest to me are there to share my moment. That can always be my Christmas gift — a gift that costs nothing but means everything in the world to me.

— David Warren —

The Grateful Girls

My idea of Christmas, whether old-fashioned or modern, is very simple: loving others. Come to think of it, why do we have to wait for Christmas to do that?
~Bob Hope

Christmas was a week away, but I wasn't feeling that holiday spirit. My daughter Anne and I were living with my mother because my husband and I had separated. As my mom and I cleaned up the breakfast dishes, she asked, "Do you want to go over to church with me to help with the Christmas giving?"

"Sure," I said, thinking maybe it would help me feel better about the impending holiday.

In the church basement, we chatted and laughed with many of my mom's friends as we organized the packages of food and toys for families whose names were on a list. All day long, people came and picked up their gifts. Late in the day, just before we left, I noticed a woman struggling with five bags, taking two out, leaving them on the sidewalk, and then returning for the others.

"Do you need help? Do you have a car?" I asked.

"No, I don't have a car."

"Could I drive you home?"

She hesitated, and then agreed. We loaded the bags into my car, and she told me where she lived. I chatted on the way, telling her a little about my present situation and my children. She limited her conversation to a few brief comments.

"I have four little girls," she said. "When they get older, I'm going back to school."

I told her I thought that was a good idea. I also asked her if we had their entire Christmas in my car.

"Yes, this is it. I can't afford to get them anything. Here's my place." She pointed to a house. I pulled up to the curb in front of a two-story wooden structure with many concrete steps in front. As we unloaded the bags, an animated little girl around seven years old ran down the stairs to greet us.

"Hi, Mama," she said. Standing on tiptoe, she jumped up and down, trying to look into the bag her mother held. She hollered back to another little girl standing in the doorway. "Michelle, there's a present in here for you! I can read your name on it."

The woman gently held the little girl back while she gathered up two other bags and started up the steps. I followed with the remaining two bags. As we walked into the living room, we were met by the rest of the family: three little girls around four, five and six years old. The living room was spotless, and I could smell the faint scent of pine disinfectant. I felt that I had stepped into a fairy tale complete with four little elves scurrying around, doing chores.

"Take the food into the kitchen, girls," she said to the two oldest as I handed the bags to them.

"Mama, we did the dishes, made the beds and cleaned up," announced a little girl who was around five and clutching a broom.

While the woman put the food bags into the kitchen, I took a quick glance around the room and saw that life was not easy for her. A worn sofa and a sagging, overstuffed chair were the only pieces of furniture in the room. Old linoleum covered the floor. Taped to the wall between the living room and the kitchen was a large brown paper cutout of a Christmas tree adorned with yellow stars and colorful swags of construction-paper chains.

"Mama, can we open our presents now?" another excited voice chimed in, this time from the oldest girl.

"Please, please?" the youngest begged.

"No, you have to wait until Christmas Day. Put them under the tree."

The children responded, all chattering excitedly, while they placed the four wrapped gifts on the floor under the paper Christmas tree.

As I turned to leave, I wished them a Merry Christmas.

"Merry Christmas!" their voices chirped in unison.

I drove back to the church with tears running down my face. This Christmas would be sparse for us also, but I knew it was temporary until I found a writing job. I thought back to past Christmases and all the gifts my children had received, and of how happy those little girls were to be receiving just one gift each. My first thought was to drive, then and there, to a toy store and buy at least one more gift for each child, using my credit card.

Once I got myself together, I decided that with no job, I shouldn't put myself in debt. The next two Christmases, after I began working again, a friend and I provided three gifts for each of the girls in that family. On the third Christmas, I requested the family's name again for the gift giving, but was told that she had not called the church.

As Christmases come and go, I look back on that day with warm feelings, knowing how blessed I was to meet that peaceful mother and her four sweet girls. I will always remember that admirable, courageous woman and her grateful little daughters.

— Kathleen Cox Richardson —

Chapter 2

Christmas Angels

Two Little Stoves

Appreciation is a wonderful thing. It makes what is
excellent in others belong to us as well.
~Voltaire

It was late Christmas Eve, and Mom and Dad had plenty left to do. Gathering the remaining presents from their hiding places, Mom set them on the couch in the front room while Dad collected his tools and the two boxes that contained the toy stoves that my sister and I were hoping to receive.

Bursting with holiday spirit, my mother flitted about like a Christmas elf while she fussed with the stockings and artistically arranged packages under the tree. Meanwhile, Dad carefully spread the contents of each box on the floor, side by side.

After Mom had joyfully crossed everything off her list, she headed over to help my father clean up and put the stoves in their place. Much to her surprise, she found that Dad had not yet started.

Now, my father wasn't exactly what you would call a "handy" kind of guy. However, he had sworn he could assemble the stoves without any trouble. They were toys — how difficult could it be? It was obvious by the puzzled expression on his face that it was a lot harder than he expected.

"Don't the instructions tell you what to do?" my mother asked quietly.

"No. They make no sense whatsoever," my father answered, shaking his head. He handed the pamphlet over to my mother, who pored over the pages and arrived at the same conclusion. Now what would they do?

Together, they tried to decipher the directions and work on the stoves. But as the hours crept by, they felt helpless. When my father announced that it was already 1:00 a.m., it occurred to my parents that they might not finish the task before my sister and I woke up.

Then, the doorbell rang. I'm sure that my father hoped that Santa had arrived to help. After all, who else would be outside at one in the morning on Christmas Day? Surprisingly, it was a couple that lived down the street.

"Merry Christmas!" the husband said. "I'm Arnold, and this is my wife Doris. We were taking a stroll through the snow and enjoying the Christmas lights when we saw you through your front window. We didn't mean to peek, but you looked flustered with whatever you're working on, so we thought you might like a little help."

"Please, come in," my parents said, feeling blessed and moved beyond words by this generous offer. They could not believe these kind people had stopped to lend a hand, especially in the middle of the night.

As my parents explained their dilemma, Arnold, who happened to be an engineer, assured my parents that they'd have the stoves finished in a jiffy. Yet even Arnold found the directions worthless and the construction challenging.

When it became obvious that it would take Arnold longer than he had expected, my parents didn't feel right taking up more of the couple's time. However, Arnold and Doris insisted on staying until they had completed both stoves. After all, they couldn't disappoint two little girls on Christmas morning.

As the two couples worked together, they had a blast. It took them until four in the morning to finish, but by that time they had become the best of friends. They cheered as they placed the two little stoves in front of the fireplace where my sister and I would discover them a few hours later.

As my parents watched Arnold and Doris walk home through the snow that Christmas morning, their hearts overflowed with gratitude for the help and newfound friendship that had come their way.

While my sister and I have fond memories of cooking on our little stoves, we had no idea how much love and time had gone into them. Throughout the many years, my mother has never forgotten the true meaning of giving that filled our home when she and Dad opened the door and found the neighbors that night. Arnold and Doris's gift of kindness to our family remains in Mom's heart as the most memorable and favorite Christmas of her entire life.

—Jill Burns—

Unexpected Angel

Wherever there is a human being,
there is an opportunity for a kindness.
~Lucius Annaeus Seneca

A few days before Christmas 2012, I found myself in Walmart. It was the last place I wanted to be, especially during the chaos of last-minute Christmas shopping and all that Christmas spirit. It had been a little more than a month since Hostess closed its doors and my husband was laid off.

I was immensely grateful for our community that year. The school my kids attended asked if we needed help for Christmas, and we accepted. If not for them, our kids would not have had Christmas gifts under the tree.

My children were with me that day at Walmart. Our cupboards were bare, and I had only eighty dollars to feed a family of six for a week. It's not impossible to accomplish, but certainly not comfortable. It leaves little room for extra anything. Yet, it was Christmas, and my kids asked if they could buy a present for their dad. How could I say "no"? I found a gift box of their dad's favorite cologne and hoped I could afford it; lucky for me, my husband doesn't have expensive taste.

My husband worked very hard to provide for us, and I stayed home. It wasn't by choice. Having two children on the autism spectrum makes it difficult for me to work. Doctors' appointments, therapy schedules, and school meetings make it near impossible to maintain a regular work schedule. So, when he was laid off, things got very tight quickly. He wasn't without a job long, but the absence of income for a couple of weeks certainly put a strain on our family. It's not easy to play catch-up on your bills in the month of December.

As I chose my groceries, I kept a running total in my head. As my cart filled, my anxiety rose. The more I thought about it, the less likely it was that I would be able to buy a Christmas gift for my husband.

When I went to the checkout, I set aside the cologne gift box. My kids protested, but I didn't have much of a choice. I held out hope that my math was wrong and I'd somehow be able to afford it. My heart sank when the grocery total was indeed too high for us to buy the gift, but an angel was waiting in the wings.

What happened left me speechless, and being the talkative type, speechless is rare for me. A man who had seen the whole thing approached us, thrust four twenty-dollar bills into my hand and happily exclaimed, "Merry Christmas!" He left so fast I didn't even have a chance to say, "Thank you."

A wave of emotion came over me as I added the cologne gift set to the belt. My kids were thrilled, the cashier was thrilled, and my husband had a Christmas present. But I received the best gift of all, a blessing only an angel could provide — I had found my Christmas Spirit.

— HM Cook —

12

A Christmas Eve Taxi Fare

Christmas waves a magic wand over this world, and
behold, everything is softer and more beautiful.
~Norman Vincent Peale

T his story took place sometime in the early 1980s on a Christmas Eve. I didn't know any of the people involved, but I know what I saw.

I was attending college at the time and driving a cab evenings and weekends. As the Christmas break approached, I decided not to go home, but to stay throughout the holidays and make some extra money.

Christmas Eve arrived, and I was working. I must mention just how beautiful the city was that evening — the lights of the city, snow-covered trees, office towers dressed in Christmas lights. It was very quiet and heartwarming.

My cab number came over the car's radio. I answered the dispatcher and headed toward the address he gave me. Upon arriving, I saw a young man standing in front of his apartment building waiting for me. He got in and read an address from a crumpled piece of paper in his hand. I turned the cab around and we set off.

After a few blocks, I sensed something wasn't quite right with this fellow. His fidgeting, mumbling and sighing told me he was struggling. He said he was also a student and was from the East Coast. He desperately wanted to go home and be with his family and friends for Christmas, but it was on the other side of the country. He couldn't afford the trip, and he was hopelessly homesick. He couldn't sleep; he couldn't sit still; he couldn't concentrate on his studies; he couldn't think. "I'm a complete mess," he told me as I kept driving toward the address he had given me.

Now I was thinking, *I'm a pretty compassionate guy, but I'm not going home for Christmas either. I've got family and friends I'd like to see, and things I'd rather be doing than working on Christmas, especially Christmas Eve. But, you know, I'm not going off the deep end like him.* So I was beginning to think this fellow had to grow up in a hurry and learn to live with the ups and downs that life sometimes throws at us. After all, he was a university student, not in junior high. I have to admit I found him somewhat pathetic.

He repeated the address from the crumpled piece of paper he had been holding, which turned out to be a page torn from the local telephone directory. I noticed him staring at the page, and he said, "They have the same last name as me."

I said, "What do you mean?"

"Where you're taking me," he said.

"They have the same surname, so they're relatives of yours?" I asked.

"Nope, never met them," he replied. He went on to tell me that he went to the phonebook and looked up his surname, finding several listings. Then he decided to call the one at the top of the column.

I couldn't help myself. "For God's sake, what did you say?" I asked.

He said, "I told the lady who answered the phone the same thing I've been telling you. That I'm at my wit's end over Christmas, homesick, lonely, the whole nine yards. And I only contacted her because she was in the phonebook at the top of the column with the same name as mine."

"What did she say?" I asked.

"She said I couldn't have phoned at a better time as her whole family was just sitting down for Christmas Eve dinner, and I should get over there right away before everything got cold. And that's when I phoned a cab — and that's where we're going."

It wasn't long before we arrived in an older neighbourhood with gorgeous, snow-laden trees along each boulevard. He was looking eagerly out the window at each home. I pulled up to the address he had given me. Through a picture window, I could see several people sitting down at what appeared to be a large dinner table and no doubt a huge Christmas feast.

My passenger thanked me, paid his fare and got out of the cab. I watched him walk toward the house, and through the window I could see a lady at the dinner table leap from her chair. The next thing I knew, she was coming out the front door of her home and walking toward this poor soul with outstretched arms. They met on the sidewalk, and she hugged him instantly. I looked back at the home, and I could see the rest of the people getting up from the table and streaming out the front door to meet him. The women hugged him. The men shook his hand. And all of them obviously welcomed him to their home. They gathered around him in front of the home for a few minutes exchanging greetings, and then they all filed back into the house.

I stayed a bit and watched from my cab through their picture window while they found him a spot at their table. I could now see my passenger laughing and smiling at their table, and it made me feel good. I realized he was far from being pathetic; he was actually quite courageous!

Then I turned my cab around and drove off that Christmas Eve to pick up another fare.

— Greg Cameron —

13

Bring Her Home

May the spirit of Christmas bring you peace,
the gladness of Christmas give you hope, and the
warmth of Christmas grant you love.
~Author Unknown

When I was five, our Christmas season was filled with more than the normal amount of anticipation. Besides the pressure of writing the perfect letter to Santa Claus, my mom was expecting a baby, the sixth in our family, and it was on Christmas Day! I was excited to become a big sister again.

When the nights got colder, Dad began building fires in the hearth every night. We children brought our sleeping bags out to the living room, enjoying the warmth and festivity. On December 18th, we slept beside the tree, watching the lights twinkle. I loved the old-fashioned manger we had under the tree, especially the Baby Jesus, with his deep blue eyes and soft white swaddling. His arms were outstretched, as if he were reaching toward me.

That night I nestled my pillow close to the Baby Jesus and dreamt of my new little sibling. During the night, I woke up to a gush of cold wind that made the embers of the fire flare to life as the door opened and closed.

"Go back to sleep, Katie," my older sister said. "Dad took Mom to the hospital."

"Is the baby coming early?" I asked.

"Dad says it will be born tonight." She smiled. "Now go back to sleep."

I was so excited but I managed to go back to sleep. When I woke up, Dad wasn't home. Later, he called and told us we had a new baby sister, but she was not coming home that day. Mom wasn't ready to leave the hospital and wouldn't be for a few days.

The wait seemed endless. The second day passed slowly, and then a third. We five young children felt a hole in the family where Mom should have been. Waiting for her and the new baby felt so long that we even altered our Santa letters to ask for our mom and baby to be our Christmas gift. Another day passed, and they still had not come.

Finally, we had a chance to visit the hospital. I jumped for joy! I was sure we were going to bring them home.

We rushed past the holiday decorations in the hospital as we headed to Mom's room. But at the door, a worried nurse hushed us. Before allowing us in, she instructed us to carefully wash our hands.

The hospital room was shadowy. The monitors and machines beeped. Mom couldn't get up when we came. We weren't even allowed to touch her. She had a massive infection. The doctors couldn't trace it, and the antibiotics weren't working. No one knew if her body could fight it off.

For a few minutes, I held our sweet, new sister, loving the way she smelled and the adorable noises she made. She had sky blue eyes and a flash of bright red hair. The precious little one was kept in the nursery and fed from a bottle because Mom was too sick to care for her. To my dismay, we left the hospital without Mom or our sister.

That night was heartbreaking. I slipped on the flannel nightgown that Mom had made last Christmas and hugged it close to me. Its softness comforted me, reminding me of her. Being so young, I didn't realize the gravity of the situation until Dad told us how bad things really were.

"I'm sorry, kids. We are going to have a really rough Christmas. I'm not sure if you know that I lost my job at Thanksgiving. We don't have insurance, and Mom staying at the hospital so long will be very expensive for us. We've been lighting fires to keep the heating bills low, but it won't help very much. We just don't have extra money for anything."

His blue eyes teared up with discouragement, the responsibility of a young family bowing his shoulders. He explained that he had no luck finding a new job. There would be a few small gifts from Grandma, just things we needed, but no toys. Not even a proper holiday dinner.

"There's nothing more I can do." He sighed.

We children were somber and thoughtful for a few minutes before my sister got up and stood beside Dad.

"It's okay, Daddy." My sister patted his shoulder. "We don't need any of that stuff. We just need Mom to come home."

"And the baby, too," I added.

Together, we knelt and prayed for a miracle. We prayed morning and night! I made a special petition to the beautiful Baby Jesus as he reached toward me from his porcelain bed.

The next day, a man in a dark suit came to the house and introduced himself to my dad. "Sir, I'm a pastor for a local church," he said. "One of our members is a friend of your wife. She asked me to stop by."

Dad shook his hand. "That's nice of you. Please come in and sit a while."

He and Dad talked for a long time. Dad explained the dire situation of our family. The pastor looked thoughtful as he left.

The next day was Christmas Eve. Dad went to the hospital around noon. About sundown, the fresh snow blanketing the street was disturbed by a large gathering of people on our lawn singing Christmas carols. My older sister opened the door.

At once, the house was crowded with people. Holiday scents filled the air. Sweet honey ham, fresh baked bread, and cinnamon Christmas cookies were placed on the table. Boxes of food were stacked in the kitchen. Mounds of presents appeared under the scantily decorated fir tree, burying the manger scene entirely. Santa himself pushed through the crowd, ho-ho-hoing all the way.

We children were ecstatic! We leapt and spun, giggling and smiling.

"Come here, little girl. Santa's got a gift for you."

Santa scooped me onto his lap and reached for his bag. He pulled out a red-haired doll and placed it in my arms.

"Just like Mom's new baby." I scooted down from Santa's lap and hugged my doll, salty tears stinging my eyes. How I wished Mom could be here, too!

The crowd parted when the door opened again. Dad rolled Mom in on a borrowed wheelchair, cradling the baby in her arms.

Food and gifts were forgotten as we held each other close and gave our thanks to God. What more could we ask for? Even without the presents or the food, we had all we needed.

I found out later that those good people had decided to gather food and gifts to give to a family in need, even though they didn't have one in mind. Besides the gifts and food, they gathered funds to pay the bills, even Mom's large hospital bill. I'll always be thankful for that Christmas Miracle.

—Kate E. Anderson—

14

Angel or Alien?

I love Christmas, not just because of the presents
but because of all the decorations and lights
and the warmth of the season.
~Ashley Tisdale

"**M**om! I made an angel for the top of our Christmas tree!" my five-year-old daughter exclaimed as she pulled the treasure she had made in kindergarten from her backpack. Then she held it up for me to admire.

It consisted of a six-inch cardboard cone spray-painted gold, very much resembling a metallic gold, upside-down ice-cream cone. To that base, white pipe cleaners had been glued on the sides and bent so that they came together in front. There, they were also glued to a small rectangle-shaped paper so as to appear to be holding sheet music. In the back, a lacy doily had been glued. These, I assumed to be wings.

Up to that point, it wasn't so bad, but its head looked like something out of a science-fiction movie. It was a rather large white Styrofoam ball in which my sweet daughter had stuck large, colorful pins to make its facial features. The pins for eyes had been stuck through small, round metallic gold papers. The papers were not glued down, and thus did not rest against the round Styrofoam ball. They sort of stuck out all around the pin eyeballs, looking a bit more like fins than eyes. This caused the angel's eyes to look like insect eyes.

Its hair was a series of yellow pipe cleaners that had been cut short and individually stuck in the head. They were bent so they hung down rather than sticking straight out, thank goodness. Its halo was another yellow pipe cleaner that had been stuck in the very top of the Styrofoam ball head and then bent into a circle around it. Since she had used the same pipe cleaners as the hair, it sort of looked like one piece of hair had gotten wind-blown and messed up. I had to fight the urge to smooth it down along with the other hair.

But my daughter was so proud! What's a mother to do?

Of course, I told her the strange looking thing she held in her hand was beautiful, and I climbed on a chair and placed it on top of my tree.

And there it remained, and was placed again, year after year after year. It peered down on us Christmas after Christmas, looking more like a space alien than an angel. And every year, as I placed it on the tree, I tried to assess my daughter's level of attachment to it, always hoping we could finally laugh at it and declare it for what it was — a five-year-old's funny attempt at making an angel. But each year, my daughter smiled and admired it when it came out of the Christmas box. Many times, she excitedly placed it in my hand and exclaimed, "My angel! Here, Mommy, put her on top of the tree." (I suppose the angel was a "her." It was hard to tell, but my daughter seemed to think it was.)

One year when my daughter was in middle school, as I was taking the angel out of the box of decorations, the angel's head fell off and rolled onto the family room floor. I jumped at the opportunity, quickly suggesting that perhaps it was time to get a new angel for our tree.

My daughter's face immediately registered disappointment. Even though she was close to being a teenager, she still held affection for this strange item that bordered on being a monstrosity. "Or... I could try gluing the head back on and see if it stays," I suggested quickly. This pleased my daughter, so her alien angel once again graced our tree... for many more years.

I was beginning to wonder if I would have to have that bug-eyed thing topping my tree forever! I would see beautiful trees in stores, magazines and other people's houses, but not mine. My tree was forever doomed to be decorated with homemade ornaments that my three sons and one daughter had brought home to me through the years. And it would forever have this insect-like alien with messed-up hair sitting on top of it!

Then, one Christmas morning when my daughter was in high school, she handed me a gift. I opened it, and there before my eyes was a beautiful, elegant, store-bought angel tree topper! I have never been so happy to receive a gift in my life! She and the whole family burst out laughing when they saw how happy I was.

Today, my tree is a mix of homemade ornaments and purchased ones. But sitting on the very top is a lovely angel holding tiny candles that light up. She has normal looking hair and eyes and an elegant halo. She looks down at us in a gentle, smiling sort of way, instead of peering at us through bulging insect eyes.

And the other, much-loved angel of days gone by rests in the bottom of the decoration box in two parts — body and head — because her head came off again. Every year, I look at it and laugh... but I think I miss her a little. I love her too much to throw her away. She is a treasure in her own way.

My daughter is grown now with a child of her own. One year, I offered to glue her angel's head back on and let her use it for her own Christmas tree. She politely declined, and we both burst out laughing. Better she keep that spot open anyway, as she's undoubtedly going to receive her own strange, handmade tree topper one day.

— Harriet E. Michael —

15

Genuine Kindness

Kindness is igniting a light in someone else for no
reason other than to watch them enjoy the glow.
~Author Unknown

It was Christmastime. We had been struggling through some hard times, and I was disappointed that I couldn't buy a Christmas tree for our house. No matter how I budgeted, it looked like we would either have a tree or gifts, but not both. I still wanted to do something special for my kids, so I used a staple gun to fashion a tree outline out of a string of lights on the entry-hall wall of our home. The kids thought it was clever and even commented on my creativity.

The day after Christmas, though, I went out to catch the after-Christmas sales in hopes of finding an artificial tree so we would never have another tree-less Christmas. Waiting for the store to open, I shared my story with two ladies who also had plans to take advantage of the sales. We talked about the economy and hopes for the future. They asked about my kids, and I shared that my husband and I have seven, including two sets of twins.

When we went in the store, everyone waiting at the door went first to check out the deals on the artificial trees. I found the one I wanted, grabbed a tag, and continued to browse. As I was heading to the register, the two ladies stopped me. They handed me a receipt and told me that my tree was waiting for me by the register. They were so touched by my story and what I had done to make the holiday special for my kids that they wanted to do something special for me! That artificial tree was a reminder of some very special genuine kindness for many years to come.

— Ginger M. Galloway —

Snow Angel

None of us knows what might happen even the next
minute, yet still we go forward. Because we trust.
Because we have faith.
~Paulo Coelho

I accompanied my daughter Elizabeth to my grandson Jacob's appointments on that frigid December day in 2010. I watched and waited with her as a legion of nurses and doctors poked and prodded the five-year-old's abdomen. They drew blood before requiring him to drink a canister of vile white liquid for the CT scan. Sensing the concern of the adults around him, Jacob complied without a whimper, entertaining himself by drawing pictures of army men, not comprehending he was facing his own battle.

I was with them when a doctor stated that Jacob had a Wilms' tumor, a rare form of cancer, and it had spread to his lungs. The recommended treatment at the University of Iowa Hospital was immediate surgery, followed by radiation and months of chemotherapy.

My fourteen-year-old daughter Emily and I stayed at the Ronald McDonald House during those first difficult days after the surgery so we could help Elizabeth. We took turns watching Jacob as he struggled to talk around a breathing tube, a silent plea in his pain-filled eyes.

One evening, after a long day at the hospital, Emily and I collapsed on the couch of the living area, staring at the Christmas tree. Gifts labeled "boy" or "girl" were piled underneath. I knew from a sign on the wall that Santa Claus would be visiting each room on Christmas Eve, dispersing gifts to anyone unlucky enough to be spending Christmas there. Emily and I would be going home, but I could hardly bear the thought that my son-in-law Ben and their two other children would remain behind.

Suddenly, an idea came to me. Wouldn't it be way more personal, even magical, if Santa Claus not only knew their names, but could choose something meaningful for each one?

"I want to help Santa," I told Emily. "I'll make up a list of what Ben and the children would like, and then help pay for the personalized gifts."

Emily wasn't convinced.

"No, Mom. You don't have money for that."

I promised her I'd wait until morning to decide. I fell asleep praying about it and woke up even more determined to make a little Christmas magic happen for my daughter and her family. Emily remained skeptical as I jotted down notes. Ben was religious and needed spiritual strength, so a men's Bible or devotional would be appropriate. Elizabeth loved stationery. Jacob loved *Toy Story* and army guys. Oldest daughter Becca liked Littlest Pet Shop toys. Two-year-old Joe could spend hours playing with toy cars. I scrutinized the list, wondering what amount would cover a volunteer's personalized shopping. David and I had promised to always discuss any purchases over fifty dollars with each other, but I hadn't had a chance to talk to him.

Emily eyed the list, clearly distraught. "I don't think you should do this. You don't have the money. You've already spent so much at the hospital on food."

She was correct. We didn't have the extra cash, but there was so little I could do to help, and this Christmas was going to be difficult enough for Elizabeth's family. I hesitated only briefly before writing out a forty-five-dollar check. Tears pooled in Emily's eyes when she leaned over and saw the amount.

"Mom, you can't afford that."

"Don't worry. I need to do this." I was reassuring myself as much as her. "Just wait. You'll see. The money will come back to me in some way, and maybe more."

She looked dubious. I hugged her before adding my list and the check to an envelope marked "Santa's Elves." I left it on the front desk before we headed back to the hospital.

We spent most of the day in Jacob's hospital room. It was dark by the time we returned to the Ronald McDonald House, and fresh snow was falling. My oldest son Dan and daughter Rachel were driving eighty miles to share an evening meal with us before visiting their sister and nephew. My cell phone rang just as we'd given up on their arrival.

"Could you come outside and flag me down?" Dan asked. "I must be missing the turn-off, and I can't find it in the dark."

Emily and I hurried outside, forgetting to grab our coats. We hadn't realized how cold it had gotten. We hugged our arms to our sides to keep warm as we slogged through the deepening snow. We climbed atop a snowy bank in view of the highway. We laughed a little, imagining how silly we must look to passing cars as we wildly waved our arms back and forth each time we spotted a vehicle that looked like Dan's.

I felt a tap on my shoulder and turned to see a stranger standing in the snow behind us.

"Are you staying at the Ronald McDonald House?" she asked. When I nodded, she pressed something into my palm.

"Merry Christmas," she said, as Emily and I stared down at the carefully folded bills I clutched in my hand. When we looked up again, the woman had disappeared.

"Where'd she go? Where are her footprints?" Emily asked in bewilderment. "And why did she give you money?" I could only shake my head in response.

"How much is it?"

Numb with shock and cold, my fingers fumbled with the crisp twenty-dollar bills. One. Two. Three. A total stranger had just handed me sixty dollars. Emily's eyes widened as she drew in a sharp breath.

"There it is. You just got it back, and a little more."

It took a few seconds for her words to register. I felt a distinct prickle at the back of my neck as it dawned on me. Hadn't I told Emily that morning not to worry? Didn't I predict that my generosity would come back to me in some way? I certainly hadn't expected anything so soon, or from a stranger in the snow.

I often think back to that Christmas, the year I encountered an angel on a cold winter night, and the money that covered the check I'd written out in faith that morning. And then some.

—Mary Potter Kenyon—

The Best Christmas Ever

The best and most beautiful things in the world
cannot be seen or even touched.
They must be felt with the heart.
~Helen Keller

My children were raised in the Uintah Basin, Utah, amid all the turmoil and ups and downs of the oil field. This particular year, the oil industry had crashed, leaving all the Basin in economic disaster. It could have been our worst Christmas ever, but it turned out to be one of the best.

We had a tradition that the whole family loved. On December twenty-sixth a plain glass jar was placed in a prominent place in the house where everyone could reach it. During the year, pocket change and pennies found in the washer and in parking lots were added to the jar. Sometimes, Mom, Dad or the older kids would drop in $10 or even $20. Often, the younger kids would pay their tithing, and then all the rest of their allowance went into the jar. It was all by choice, each adding what they could, when they could.

Then, eleven months later, on Thanksgiving weekend, we would count the money in the jar. There would be excited cries around the table. "Wow! It's going to be *amazing* this year!" "Just think of all the stuff we can buy!" "I had no idea this jar could hold so much!"

And then the hunt would be on for a special family — the family that would be the recipients of our shopping with all that money. We would sneak up to their house and leave everything that we had bought for them.

This particular year, little Jonathan was the most excited. All year, the older kids had been talking about how they would each carry something. Everyone would sneak up to the unsuspecting home, carefully put their armload on the porch, and then quietly sneak back into the dark. One of the oldest would linger just a few moments, and then ring the doorbell and run! This year, Jonathan would finally be allowed to help carry presents to the doorstep.

But there was a problem. It was the weekend after Thanksgiving, time to count the money and pick a family. But my husband and I kept putting off what we knew we had to do. We had to tell the children that this year would be different.

Finally, we called them all together. My husband explained that the year had really taken its toll on our family business. We were barely surviving financially. We could not pick a Christmas family this year. In fact, if we were going to buy presents for our family, we would have to use the money in the jar. There were audible gasps from around the room and cries of "No!"

Christmas was always a simple event for us anyway. We didn't believe in lavish amounts of money being spent on presents. We liked to keep the spirit of Christmas centered on Christ. Lots of expensive presents just didn't support that idea. Helping the Christmas family was what made the season really special. And here we were, taking that away.

One by one, the kids left the room quietly. My husband and I looked at each other; the anguish on his face was evident. I squeezed his hand and said, "We didn't have any choice." The pain was tangible.

A short time later, we were surprised by all five kids silently filing back into the room as a group. They stood before us, with something clearly on their minds. Harold Junior, the oldest, spoke up. "We have been talking and, well, Jonathan has a plan he wants you to hear." He gently nudged his little brother forward and kept his hands on Jonathan's shoulders.

"We want to do the Christmas family!" Jonathan pleaded. He told us they wanted to use the money for another family like we always did.

In confusion, I looked at all the kids. They all had huge smiles and were nodding in agreement. "But I said that if we do that, you won't have any presents."

"Oh, but we will!" exclaimed Mark.

"Yes!" cried Seth. "We will make each other coupons!"

"Love coupons!" cried out Kami as she bounced up and down.

"Please!" pleaded Jonathan.

My husband and I looked at each other. Tears streamed down my cheeks. He was dabbing at his eyes. "Well," he said. "I guess we better get the money in that jar counted and get to finding a family!" Shrieks of joy and wild dances erupted in our living room as all of us made a beeline for the Christmas jar.

Our traditional Christmas Eve activities were a little different that year. Supper was ground-beef stew because we couldn't afford the normal turkey. But it didn't matter. The air was tinged with excitement. We acted out the birth of Christ with each of the kids taking one or two parts to cover the whole story. Harold Junior was still nursing his ankle — the one he had twisted as he fell in a ditch running away from the Christmas family's house — so all the kids catered to him, bringing him a tray with paper and crayons so he could make his coupons. There were giggles as each of us hid our papers from certain family members as we created our masterpieces.

Christmas morning dawned at the usual bright and early time. But this time, it wasn't just the little ones who were awake early; it was *all* of us. We were all eager to watch each other unwrap the gifts that we had made. There was no frantic tearing into packages. We all wanted to see the expressions on the faces of the recipients as they read the things we had promised to do for them on the coupons.

So the presents were opened one by one as the rest of the family looked on. Some coupons were serious: "I will wash the dishes for you when it is your turn to do them." "I will carry the buckets of water to the horse trough for you."

Some were funny. "I will pick up your stinky socks for you before

Mom sees them." "I will fix your hair for you" (from a brother to his sister).

Some were loving: "I will give you a hug on demand." "I will give you a foot massage when you get home from work."

The rest of the day was spent playing favorite games, eating popcorn and laughing together.

It was the best Christmas ever!

— Diana Traeger —

Blessing in Disguise

*Faith consists in believing when it is beyond
the power of reason to believe.*
~Voltaire

It was a warm winter day in San Diego. Thanksgiving had just passed, and I was trying to wrap my mind around a sermon I had heard in church: "Thank God for Everything." It wasn't the typical Thanksgiving message when people are encouraged to make a list of all the good things they're grateful for. No, this year our pastor challenged us to thank God for *everything*, even the bad. "Sometimes, bad things happen for a good reason," he said. "And even when they don't, God can still bring good out of a bad situation."

This Thanksgiving challenge was easy at first, even with Christmas approaching. Because we weren't used to having much for the holiday, my eight-year-old daughter Desirée and I were content with what we had on my meager income. My daughter received one main gift each year, along with a stocking full of knickknacks and trinkets that gave her the excitement of having a lot to unwrap.

I went into the Christmas season with a grateful heart. But as I was making our holiday plans, an unexpected bill arrived, and I realized I wouldn't be able to get Desirée the only thing she wanted — a $69 portable stereo. *My sweet little Desi will have nothing but the junk I pass off as presents,* I thought. As the guilt set in, my eyes filled with tears. I was just about to start sobbing aloud when I remembered what the pastor said, "Thank God for everything."

As difficult as it was, I thanked God for the bill, but found something good to be grateful for as well. I remembered the old camcorder I had bought years before when I had a little extra money. "I could create a video for Desirée, a priceless gift she could treasure forever," I reassured myself. "The memories will mean more to her than any stereo — someday, anyway."

I jumped up, grabbed a stool and pulled down the camcorder from the top shelf in my apartment. It was one of the first personal video cameras that came out. It had been a while, but I could still remember laughing sarcastically when I bought it "on sale" because it also required the purchase of an expensive battery — not included — that was almost as big as the camera itself. *And the salesman talked me into purchasing the extended warranty. What a sucker I was,* I thought. *Oh, well. No use in letting that get me down now.*

I pulled the video camera out of the box to see if I had any room on the videotape inside. But when I went to check, I realized that the camera wasn't working. I couldn't believe it. *Just my luck,* I thought. *Why are these things always happening to me?*

Just when I was about to start my pity party, I remembered Pastor's sermon.

"Thank you for breaking my video camera, God," I shouted halfheartedly up to the sky. *And thank God I had the wisdom to buy the warranty,* I smirked to myself.

I jumped into my beat-up, old Corolla, picked up Desirée from school, and took the video camera back to Circuit City to be repaired. As we walked back to the customer service department, there it was, right in our faces — the $69 boom box Desirée wanted for Christmas. She ran right up to it, knelt down on her little knees, and enthusiastically inspected every aspect of the shiny silver stereo. It just killed me.

I couldn't pull her away, so I let her look at it while I stood in the long line waiting to be helped. The longer I watched her, the bigger the lump grew in my throat. Finally, it was my turn. I handed the camera to the clerk, who took it to the back. Just when I thought my heart couldn't sink any lower, he came back with it. "We can't fix this," he said. "The part that needs to be replaced isn't available. They don't make these older models anymore."

"No!" I gasped. "So what good is the warranty then? You guys talked me into getting it in the first place."

As I continued my rant and my voice began to carry across the store, I noticed I was getting sympathy from everybody except the clerk. His straight face just angered me all the more, and I felt no guilt for the tongue lashing I was giving him.

After I catastrophized my situation to its fullest and ran out of things to say, the unsympathetic clerk continued, "But what we can do is replace it for you."

"Oh," I said under my breath, turning my face away from my supporting audience.

The clerk continued, "And we can give you store credit for the battery you bought. The newer video cameras come with their own."

"Store credit for a battery? What can I get with that — gum?" I asked. "What's it even worth?"

"Sixty-nine dollars," he said. "Plus tax."

— Adrienne A. Aguirre —

Chapter 3

Feeling that Christmas Spirit

Christmas Spirit? Aisle Five

*The Christmas spirit whispers softly in my ear
to be of good cheer.*
~Richelle E. Goodrich, *Being Bold*

It had been a long, busy day at work. Not a bad day, just one of those days when getting those 10,000-plus steps on the old Fitbit was child's play.

I was sink-into-the-couch-in-a-trance tired. All I wanted was to get home, feed the dogs, slip my feet into my magically soothing fuzzy house shoes, and enjoy a little quiet time.

Oh, wait. The humans should eat, too.

That whole food-for-the-humans thing meant my plans for a fast track to the welcoming cushions of our couch had to take a little detour — actually, a not-so-little detour to the behemoth known as Walmart. But I had a list, and I would stay focused, navigating the crowds with my mad cart-handling skills. I'd be in and out of there in a flash.

As I was speeding through the aisles, slaloming through the other shoppers at what had to be a gold-medal pace, I caught sight of something that stopped me in my tracks. It was a bin full of Christmas teddy bears strategically placed like a mogul on a downhill course. Ah, the marketing genius of Walmart.

Those Christmas teddy bears almost proved to be the kryptonite to my speed-shopping mission. I was mesmerized, reaching out to run my fingers through the soft fuzz of a big white bear wearing a Santa hat and a bright red sweater.

My mom had always had a huge soft spot for teddy bears, amassing quite a collection in her day. Little bears wearing elaborate handmade costumes and hats. Colorful big bears with shiny button eyes and big, squishy bodies perfect for grandkids to hug. And holiday bears. Mom specifically loved Christmas bears.

Each year, as Christmas would draw near, a new bear would show up on display in my parents' house. Dad would shake his head and wonder why Mom needed all those bears. Mom would just smile and give each bear a little pat. "Oh, Papa," she'd say, using the nickname the grandkids had given him, "no bear should be left behind at Christmas."

One hand on my cart, one hand still on the big, white bear, I smiled at the memory, but then snapped back to the task at hand. Food for the humans — get home to Jim, the dogs, the magic house shoes, and the couch.

Bears were a thing of the past — a happy memory to cherish from the past. Now, go!

I resumed my well-planned trek through the store, zipping to my last stop for milk before the sprint to find the shortest checkout line.

Just as I was pulling my cart into the most promising queue, I saw Barbara. Ah, Barbara, my favorite Walmart employee of all time.

Barbara is something special. One glance, and it's easy to see she has joy buried deep in her soul, and it just can't help but bubble to the surface on a regular basis. She is the Walmart Old Faithful of joy.

I got to know Barbara a couple of weeks before Thanksgiving. She was my cashier, and I couldn't help but admire her fancy, fall-themed, self-crafted headband. She had autumn leaves and flowers sprouting all over the crown of her head. It was not subtle — and perhaps not Paris-runway fashionable — but it was 100-percent awesome.

"Oh, just you wait," she said with a laugh. "It will grow. I add something to it every day until Thanksgiving Day." Her eyes were sparkling with the obvious fun of it all. "Then, the day after Thanksgiving, I start all over again for Christmas. You should watch for me."

I promised her I would, and I did. True to her word, the day after Thanksgiving, I saw her again, and she had one little sprig of holly fastened to an otherwise bare headband.

Now, a few weeks into the Christmas season, Barbara's headband was starting to really take shape again. And, as people smiled and commented on her decoration, she was beaming.

Suddenly, I wasn't so tired. My mission for home and couch seemed a little less urgent. And the holiday-infused craziness of the crowded store didn't seem quite so daunting.

Barbara was working the checkout at Walmart during one of the busiest, most chaotic times of the year. She could have chosen to be grumpy, or harried, or stressed. She could have chosen to just put her head down, scan and bag items, and push from one customer to the next.

But she didn't. She chose joy. Barbara unfailingly chose to greet each customer with a huge smile and a giant dose of good cheer.

Without a second thought, I surrendered my prime spot in the line and wheeled back to the bin of holiday bears. The big white bear was lying there on his back, his black eyes blank and fixed on the ceiling, his arms and legs flung out as if in surrender to his plight.

No bear likes to be left behind at Christmas, right?

I picked up the big bear, gave him a good test hug, and placed him in my cart on the seat where a small child would perch. Then I took him for a ride through the store to check out the other Christmas decorations.

Finally, with a few extra bright and shiny items added to my cart of essentials, I made my way back to the checkout line — Barbara's checkout line.

It was no longer the shortest line. I didn't care. I wanted more joy to bubble my way. Barbara, with greenery, poinsettias, and other foliage sprouting from her hair, nodded approvingly at my prized Christmas bear as the most wonderful grin bloomed across her face.

I admired her headband, and she once again assured me it would get better. I told her I knew it would, and that I would be following her progress. Then we both turned back to our duties. Mine to get home.

Hers to get customers through checkout while spreading her special brand of joy — and I may have that in the wrong order.

I placed my bear in the passenger seat, safety belt fastened snugly around his plump, squishy belly, and pointed the car toward home.

Isn't it funny, I mused to my new friend, how the Christmas spirit can find you in places and moments when you least expect it? It's just a matter of recognizing it and choosing to accept it. Mr. Bear's eyes shone in agreement.

Every year, there seems to be a great debate about whether Christmas has been trampled by a stampede of commercialized hustle and bustle, or if there is still true wonder and meaning to be found in the season. Barbara taught me that it's all about making a choice.

So, I choose joy and teddy bears — and Barbara.

I now have a new Christmas tradition for as long as Barbara chooses to work at Walmart. I can't wait to make a trip back there on Christmas Eve to see the evolution of her headpiece.

I know, without a doubt, it's going to be spectacular.

— Nancy Gallimore —

20

Our Own Christmas Pageant

Love is what's in the room with you at Christmas
if you stop opening presents and listen.
~Author Unknown

"Should we drive to California or take the train this year?" I asked Hal as we packed away the last Halloween decorations. "Time to make plans for the holidays."

"We need to stay home this year," Hal said as he closed up a box. "Time for our own family traditions."

"Stay in Portland? Everyone will be so disappointed." Every year, we celebrated Christmas in Los Angeles with my parents. Mother's health didn't allow for them to come to us. Our oldest, Tami, was now eight, Benjamin four and Joel two. That was a lot of Christmas Eves singing Christmas carols and listening to Mother tell the Christmas story, her voice ringing out as she read from the Bible. My sister and her family always joined us on Christmas Day for dinner. Not to mention that in Los Angeles I could count on sunshine instead of Oregon drizzle.

"We'll have a great time. You'll see. We can go to Los Angeles to see your folks this summer," Hal assured me. "I have a couple of big photo shoots lined up around Christmas."

I couldn't argue with scheduled photo shoots. It was such good news for his new photography business. But as the holidays drew near, I couldn't muster my usual enthusiasm. Both Hal and I had always enjoyed creating things, and made many Christmas gifts for family and friends. Now Hal worked on a wooden truck to go with the Fisher-Price farm for Joel and a chest for Ben's large collection of LEGOs, whistling as he applied a final coat of paint. The kids and I crafted our usual gingerbread house out of graham crackers and frosting. They were adjusting better to staying home than I was. Sometimes, I blinked back tears as I sewed Raggedy Ann and Andy dolls for Tami and Ben.

Two weeks before Christmas, I was preparing a tuna casserole when Tami wandered into the kitchen. "What are we doing for Christmas Eve?" she asked. "Can I have Emily over?"

My stomach clenched. "Christmas Eve is a family time," I explained, thinking about the irony of not visiting her grandparents this year. Sitting back on my heels, I pushed a wisp of blond hair from her forehead. "We could have Emily over another day."

"What if we invited her whole family?"

I looked into Tami's blue eyes and got an idea. Suppose we did have Emily's family over? When I was growing up, my family went to the home of my mother's widowed best friend and her three children every Christmas Eve. We ate dinner together, sang Christmas carols, and exchanged gifts. I had loved sharing that special night with another family.

"We could invite them for dinner," I said, "and sing Christmas carols afterward."

"And you could read everybody the Christmas story like Grandma always does. Please, Mama?"

"Or what about this. Emily has five brothers and sisters, doesn't she? And you three. With the fathers, we have enough for our very own Christmas pageant."

"Can I be Mary?" Tami's eyes shone with excitement.

I pictured the smug expression on our husbands' faces when I asked them to be wise men because they fit the roles so well. We were going to have fun.

Emily's mother enthusiastically accepted the invitation and offered to bring whatever she could find that might be useful props for our little drama.

When Christmas Eve arrived, I bustled around in my green apron with the holly-leaf appliqué, pulling a ham from the oven and dressing the salad. Hot apple cider with cinnamon and nutmeg simmered in a Crock-Pot. Emily's mother set out sweet potatoes and rolls she'd brought. Christmas carols played on the stereo, everything from "Silver Bells" to "Joy to the World," as the children trooped into our family room to play, and the two men settled on the living room couch to chat.

After dinner, we sang "Jingle Bells" and "Silent Night." Then I cleared my throat. "Ready, everyone? Time for the Christmas story."

Emily's mother and I set out the props we had gathered and assigned roles. As expected, the men exchanged a chuckle when I asked them to be the wise men. Hal wrapped a Navajo blanket around his shoulders and brought out my jewelry box from our bedroom. "Is this wise enough?" he asked as he fashioned a headdress from an embroidered dresser scarf.

"Absolutely." I kissed his cheek.

"And Joseph also went up from Galilee... unto the city of David, which is called Bethlehem... to be taxed with Mary his espoused wife," I read from the Gospel of Luke.

Tami, dressed in a white satin choir robe with a wide blue sash from our dress-up trunk and a blue wool shawl draped over her shoulders, made a lovely, beaming Mary. Emily's fourteen-year-old brother, dressed in a beige karate jacket and a cream-colored dishtowel headdress, made a blushing Joseph.

"Take hands," I prompted, and they stepped forward shyly.

"And she brought forth her firstborn son, and wrapped him in swaddling clothes, and laid him in a manger; because there was no room for them in the inn," I continued.

Joel, swaddled in a turquoise striped beach towel, refused to lie down on the scrap-wood manger. "I'm not a baby," he insisted, fists balled at his sides. He did agree to stand between Mary and Joseph, and Mary placed a protective and gently restraining hand on his shoulder.

"And there were in the same country shepherds abiding in the field, keeping watch over their flock by night." Bathrobes and dishtowels tied with scarves turned three of Emily's brothers into shepherds. Two held craggy, wooden walking sticks I'd found in the garage. Ben made an adorable sheep on his hands and knees, a piece of cream-colored fleece tied to his back. Emily's sister, Ben's age, was similarly attired. "Baa," they chorused, tentatively at first and then louder, as they crawled to their places near Joseph.

"And, lo, the angel of the Lord came upon them, and the glory of the Lord shone round about them." Emily's oldest sister looked truly angelic in another choir robe and a tiara.

I turned to the Gospel of Matthew for the story of the wise men. "Behold, there came wise men from the east to Jerusalem." Hal in his Navajo blanket and Emily's father in a red bathrobe nudged each other and cleared their throats. Both men dropped to one knee before Joel.

The children all giggled, and their eyes sparkled. I winked at Hal.

Enacting the Christmas story with another family or two on Christmas Eve became a treasured tradition we enjoyed for many years. I no longer considered going away for the holidays. Summers, we made the pilgrimage to Los Angeles. Our own Christmas pageant, right at home, filled my heart with the Christmas spirit.

— Samantha Ducloux Waltz —

21

Chicken Soup for the Soul

Christmas in Istanbul

Alone we can do so little; together we can do so much.
~Helen Keller

I was in my mid-twenties and had been in Istanbul for a week when the worst storm in decades stranded an international array of other travelers and me for more than twenty-four hours at the airport. I had gone to Istanbul because I heard it was a beautiful, ancient city with incredible museums. The more pressing reason was that I had been in Ireland for a month before I went to Turkey, and I was frozen solid from the rain and bitter fog that seemed to hang over Ireland constantly. Someone told me Turkey was sunny and warm, and that was all I needed to hear. They were right. It was wonderful; that is, until the storm of the century came thundering through. Apparently, I had brought Ireland's weather with me. The storm was so severe that I began to miss the consistently dreary Irish weather.

Fortunately, the Istanbul airport had all the necessary amenities. Any other day, I would have been happy to lounge around an airport terminal and do some reading, but Christmas changes everything. I was usually good at being alone, but knowing I wouldn't see my parents at Christmas for the first time in my life made being alone much lonelier. The words to that old Christmas carol, "I'll be home for Christmas, if only in my dreams," had never held more meaning.

I made myself as comfortable as possible on the carpet, reading, listening to music and chatting with other stranded travelers. Before long, I was part of an encampment of backpackers exchanging stories about the places we had been. There was Malin from Sweden, Christina from Italy, Lencio from Dubai, Lisbeth from Denmark, and Harlan, a fellow American, from Texas. The conversation meandered but always returned to stories of past Christmases and how much we missed our families. We knew these subjects would just make us more homesick, but we couldn't help ourselves. Harlan was in Turkey on business and had expected to miss Christmas in the States. The rest of us didn't have very far to go, globally speaking, but when stuck in a monster storm, a thousand miles might as well be a million.

We listened hopefully to another announcement over the loud-speaker. The storm was weakening, but our flights wouldn't be cleared for takeoff for another few hours. We groaned accordingly and returned to our conversation. After another excruciating Christmas story, when it seemed sadness might swallow us all completely, I said, "I have an idea. Let's have Christmas here."

Everyone looked at me like I had spent too much time at a hookah lounge.

"I'm serious," I insisted. "We can find something that will pass for a Christmas tree somewhere."

My new friends were all so desperate for some semblance of home that they accepted the challenge. We got our things together and went outside, but finding a decent tree was more difficult than expected. There wasn't a pine tree in sight. There was some foliage in a median where traffic whipped by on both sides, but that wasn't exactly the yuletide mood we were looking for, and we would have gotten soaking wet. In the end, we settled for a large bush in a grassy area with very little foot traffic. There was a cover to keep us dry, but it was bitterly cold, so we had to get our heaviest jackets from our packs. We all gathered around the tree, wondering how we were going to make such a dismal piece of vegetation look spectacular. Harlan and I couldn't help thinking of the tree in *A Charlie Brown Christmas*. For the rest of the evening, he called me Charlie, and I called him Linus.

The next challenge was decorating it. Our only option was to see what the gift shop had. Lencio stayed by the tree and asked Christina to help him with something, but he wouldn't tell us what he was planning. At the gift shop, I bought some candies with brightly colored wrappers. Harlan splurged and bought ten miniature flashlights. Lisbeth bought an extra-large white T-shirt, but Malin had gone missing. She had said to me, "I can't find anything here. I'll meet you back at the tree." When the rest of us returned, we found it already wrapped in strings of popcorn. Apparently, Lencio had a bag in his backpack and a sewing kit to string the popcorn together. He and Christina had worked fast.

I distributed the candies to everyone, crumpled the colorful foil wrappers, and decorated the tree with them. Lisbeth spread the white T-shirt out under the tree for fake snow. Harlan hung his miniature flashlights on branches from their tiny straps and turned them on. Malin returned with a new friend. She had spotted her sitting by herself, wearing five or six necklaces made of colorful Mardi Gras beads she had acquired at a festival that day. When she heard what we were doing, she eagerly contributed the necklaces as garlands for the tree. They were the crowning touch.

It was as humble as could be, but we were proud of our tree. We all sat on the grass admiring it when Christina said, "There's still one thing missing… gifts." We agreed and opened our backpacks, looking for something to give each other — music, books, trinkets we had bought on the road, things that were old and familiar to the giver but new and exciting to the receiver. For those who didn't have six items to give away, hugs were warmly accepted and returned.

We must have been a sight for the mostly Muslim people who walked by. A janitor stopped and was about to say something (presumably "Hey, you can't do that!"), but instead he just smiled, shook his head good-naturedly and went about his work.

Lencio left and came back with a bottle of wine. We all took turns sipping from it and singing Christmas carols. When the wine and our memories for lyrics ran dry, someone suggested we take turns saying the names of the loved ones we missed. What a powerful suggestion that turned out to be. Saying their names out loud made us feel closer to them, but that very closeness only made the actual distance more unbearable. Lisbeth cried, which set off Christina. Our circle closed tighter. A silence fell. We all wished Jesus a happy birthday and prayed for our loved ones and each other. And what started as a silly idea to have fun and kill some time turned into something more, something... sacred.

We said our goodbyes and wished each other well one by one as our flights were called for departure. They weren't easy goodbyes. Within a few hours, we had gone from total strangers to the closest of friends, united by homesickness, faith, and a love of the rituals of Christmas. We missed our families, so we created another, temporary one with each other.

It could have been the worst Christmas Eve of my life, but it turned out to be one of the best, or at least the most unique. It has been almost twenty-five years since that night. I don't know where any of my airport friends are today, but I will always remember their kind faces illuminated by the soft light of our little tree, and how we helped each other through a lonely Christmas Eve in a land far from home.

— Mark Rickerby —

22

Our Christmas Do-Over

The way you spend Christmas is far more important
than how much.
~Henry David Thoreau

When I realized that I had purchased more toys than our children could use that Christmas, I knew things had to change. I had completely lost track of our purchasing and had bought so much that I needed to put toys aside to give our kids on future birthdays.

I seemed to be filling some imaginary quota. It did not seem like enough when I ordered an initial batch of presents online. When I went into stores later that week, I forgot that I had already purchased similar items online. And I was sending my husband out on separate buying missions as well.

When I went home and more items were delivered, the number of gifts for each of our four children seemed uneven. I worried about them counting up gifts and comparing quantities with one another. I worried about their impressions of each item. I worried about their unhappiness. Unhappiness... at receiving mass quantities of gifts? "Is this really what Christmas is about?" I asked myself.

Meanwhile, our kids were also in a frenzied state. The day after Thanksgiving, their wish lists were forming, an endless list of wants, desires and supposed needs. The countdown to Christmas had begun, and it was full of expectations of expensive gifts.

I felt let down and disappointed because the previous month had been spent in reflective thought, considering what we were grateful for each day. We had renamed the month of November, "Thanks-vember." At the end of every day, our kids wrote down something they were grateful for on a Post-it Note. The guidelines were that it had to describe one event, item or person that had touched their lives in a meaningful way that day. Two specific details must be included, and it could not be a repeat from a previous day.

This was a tradition we'd been observing for several years. It was gratifying to watch our children spend time every evening considering what or who had impacted them positively that day. There was the homeless person who taught one child an important lesson, a sibling who gave in during an argument, a teacher who offered a new way of looking at a subject, and the new comforter that provided extra warmth on a chilly night. A couple of weeks into the month, our quest to feel grateful was becoming ingrained, a new habit.

Our special Thanks-vember tradition culminated at the end of the month at our annual Thanksgiving breakfast (which we held in the late morning, purportedly like the pilgrims). Post-it Notes were randomly distributed at each place setting. Before we began to eat, family members read aloud four or five notes in front of them. It was moving to hear each other's grateful moments from the month. Our ten-year-old son read about his dad's gratitude when his outstretched hand was accepted and they walked hand-in-hand the entire way to school. Our daughter read about her younger brother's feeling of gratefulness at being allowed to join her on a special play date that was originally meant for just her and a friend.

However, by December 1st, it seemed that our gratitude was all but forgotten. The kids continuously talked about the new things they expected to acquire at Christmas, and the adults worked to fulfill the unachievable expectations. I interrupted this exasperating cycle by reminding our children that we had decided the gifts they were giving to each other and us parents would be handmade.

With a little extra encouragement and planning, our dining room table was turned into a creation station for the month of December. We threw a huge tarp over the table with the directive to hand-make one gift for every family member. Our kids quickly grew motivated, and their creative process was inspiring. Our six-year-old son took selfies with each family member, altered them in an app, and put them in hand-painted frames. Our seven-year-old made her very own flavored lip balm using tea tree and peppermint essential oils. Our ten-year-old made keychain charms out of clay, monogrammed each one, and attached them to colorful metal key rings. As each gift was created painstakingly from scratch, it brought a feeling of balance to the purchasing that was simultaneously taking place.

Christmas came, and it was like previous Christmases. After an hour of frantic unwrapping, not one of our children seemed satisfied or even happy. We sat around and looked at each other, and the unsaid sentiment seemed to be, "What now?" Our children's handmade gifts were the silver lining of our Christmas morning. These instantly became cherished treasures placed carefully in special nooks near beds and on desks in bedrooms.

A few days later, we were chatting about our New Year's resolutions. Similar to the month of November, we planned to spend an entire month honing our resolutions for the coming year. We were each responsible for developing four resolutions in the categories of:

1. Trying Something New
2. Progressing Something Further
3. Leaving Something Behind
4. I Failed, but I'm Trying Again

As I thought back on our Christmas experience, I realized that it did not align well with our family values. It seemed I had lost track of what brought joy to our children. I had also lost track of what was gratifying to me as a gift giver. I had lost track of simple pleasures and simpler times. I had lost track of the space we had on our shelves, and of the time that existed in a day to use all of the things I had purchased.

We had read about another family's tradition of giving four gifts to their children — within the categories of a want, a need, something to wear, and something to read. We were inspired. We also considered the many children in our city who were enrolled in charity programs to receive exactly one gift on Christmas from a benevolent stranger.

As a family, we made the decision that each child in our family would receive exactly three gifts on future Christmases, no more, no less. The gifts would align with our family values:

1. A Gift to Learn From
2. A Gift that Nurtures a Passion
3. An Heirloom Gift

Each child would also give away three items to a family in need every Christmas. Three in and three out. With these new guidelines, we made the decision to re-do Christmas in January. We returned some of the gifts already received. We pared down the pile, and we sat in long return lines at stores and the post office. It was painful, but it was worth it.

We sat down for our Christmas do-over on January 25th and it was an enlightening experience. Christmas morning slowed down. It was peaceful. There was no mad scramble to rush and tear open everything in view. The three gifts of Christmas were relished. I had time to wrap everything beautifully. There was no waste. Not one gift was left forgotten on the floor, lost under wrapping paper. And every gift was lovingly played with the entire day.

With this new tradition settled, we were finally ready to bring in the New Year.

— Sky Khan —

23

The Strange Thing in the Garden

When you look at your life, the greatest
happinesses are family happinesses.
~Dr. Joyce Brothers

Most people have no idea how or when their family traditions began, and our family was no exception. Both my children were very much attached to what they considered our traditional family Christmas. My detail-oriented son loved selecting and positioning the tree decorations. My daughter had to be lifted up when the ornament hanging was complete to place the angel on the topmost branch.

Before any of this could happen, we had to visit a tree farm and cut down a real Christmas tree. Dressed in our warmest clothes, we would set off into the frozen, snow-covered countryside in search of the perfect specimen. Our careful selection made, it was cut, dragged back to the car park and transported into town strapped to the roof of our family van.

The first order of business upon arriving home was to warm up — lots of mulled wine for the adults and mugs of hot chocolate for the kids. We would then install the tree into its base. Usually, realignment was required once wine was no longer a factor. The unadorned tree was then placed in the centre of our main room window. Decorations came a few days later when friends and family arrived to help hang our festive souvenirs from the branches. Both of my children vowed that no matter where they ended up living, they would pass on the love of our Christmas tradition to their children.

Many years later, my daughter and her husband were assigned to work in Laos. When the opportunity arose to join them at Christmas, I jumped at it. As a new grandfather, this was my chance to not only see my grandson for the first time, but also to pass along some Christmas traditions. I realised that being in Laos would present some difficulty for getting the seasonal props. We certainly would not be driving off into the countryside in search of a tree. I took it upon myself to provide the Christmas tree and the decorations.

The trip to Vientiane was long and tedious, but made more bearable by the reactions I got from airport security personnel along the way. Everyone seemed stunned that I was carrying an artificial Christmas tree as hand luggage. Enthusiasm and understanding for Christmas traditions are not as universal as one might think. There were more than a few surprised comments that the tree I was toting already came decorated with a string of lights. I carried the coloured balls and baubles separately so they didn't present a problem. Everyone's attention was focused on the tree. At one point, a security person asked me to plug in the light socket. He took a step back, seemingly unsure what might happen. The illuminated result even brought some applause from my fellow travellers. If not for the airport "no photos allowed in this area" signs, I would have had some wonderful shots to share. Even I had to smile when I saw the X-ray image of the tree passing through the security conveyor tunnel.

The tree turned out to be a big success in Laos and helped get us into the holiday spirit. The weather was more appropriate to mid-summer than Christmas, but that didn't matter. The rented house was centrally located on a huge property and the main room had a large bay window overlooking a lush tropical garden. We set up my imported Christmas tree outdoors alongside the biggest poinsettia plant I have ever seen. Banana and avocado trees nicely framed the scene.

Each evening, in the week leading up to Christmas, we lit the tree. A colorful but unnatural glow spread out over the garden even as far as the street. It quickly became a local attraction. Parents brought their children to marvel at the odd plastic plant, which for some obscure reason was covered in lights and coloured balls.

On Christmas Eve, we gathered around the tree and sang carols. We must have made an odd sight — a group of people standing in a garden, soaked in mosquito repellant and dressed in T-shirts and shorts, singing about Good King Wenceslas. We were joined by my daughter's friends and a Laotian family that lived next door. As practicing Buddhists, the Lao family didn't know any of the carols, but made valiant attempts to mouth the words they thought we were singing. Local people turned out in droves to watch the spectacle, standing on the road puzzled but fascinated.

During my time in Vientiane, my daughter and her family received word of their reassignment to their next posting — the southern African country of Botswana. Prior to packing their belongings, we held a garage sale. As I had no intention of taking the tree back home with me, it was laid out front and centre.

I was surprised at the interest shown in it by many of the Laotians who came to peruse the sale. It was bought by the family that lived next door.

When I asked why they had bought it, they said that, although they didn't fully understand the meaning of Christmas, they had enjoyed sharing in our celebration. Their children had loved it, especially the idea of a present exchange. Let's face it, what kid would pass up the chance for free gifts?

The large Christmas brunch with mimosas had gone down really well with the adults. I am not entirely sure that the Laotian parents were aware the mimosas were not just bubbly orange juice. I didn't want to get into too much detail as everyone was having such a good time.

The most memorable thing for the Laotian family was seeing all of us standing around the tree on Christmas Eve singing carols. They loved the whole idea of Christmas and fully intended to uphold the tradition, vowing to continue to celebrate around the artificial tree even after my daughter's family had relocated to Botswana.

During my last week in Laos, we visited a local Buddhist temple to have my grandson blessed by the monks. The Christmas tree neighbours were happy to organise the whole thing, providing all of the co-ordination and translations. It seemed to me a good exchange of traditions now that they had adopted ours. The neighbours and the head monk were delighted that we had made the effort to come to the temple and had shown an interest in Buddhist traditions.

In the future, if anyone is travelling in Laos and comes upon a group of Laotians gathered around an artificial Christmas tree singing an odd version of "Good King Wenceslas," then I am afraid that I have to accept responsibility. It is from little seeds like these that new traditions grow — even traditions whose origins may not be fully understood. My daughter still keeps in touch with her Vientiane neighbours. They continue to exchange cards and presents for the children at Christmas. I look forward to next Christmas in Botswana — imagining what I might do to expand, share and even redefine our Christmas tradition yet again.

—James A. Gemmell—

24

Caroling Yoga

Music kindles love and infuses hope.
It has countless voices and instruments.
~S. Sivananda

Our Yoga Ashram is deep in the woods in rural Virginia. Our neighbors think we're a bit odd, and I don't blame them. We're culturally diverse, mostly from cities, and we intentionally honor all spiritual faiths. At the holiday season, we start off celebrating Divali, and then proceed to celebrate Hanukkah, Christmas, and Kwanzaa with equal gusto. We're quiet and respectful, but we don't exactly blend in.

So there was some hesitation a few years ago when I suggested we go Christmas caroling at the homes of our neighbors. I loved to carol as a child. I remembered how exciting it was to walk up to strangers' homes and sing for them. Each open door would glow with a hint of the tree and the festive spirit in the home. I wanted the children in our community to have that experience. But would our neighbors in Virginia welcome us? We decided to give it a try.

Fifteen of us piled into a van and drove to the first house. A couple came outside and listened to our multi-cultural Christmas choir ¾ complete with orange-robed monks, a Jewish drummer boy, and people from all different backgrounds singing together in the cold. We knew this farmer had had a tough year. The holiday spirit floated between us, making us all feel happier. So far, so good.

A couple of big dogs barked to announce our arrival at our next stop, a big Jefferson-style brick house with white columns. Mrs. Taylor sang along with us from her open door. "I've lived in this house for twenty years, and nobody has ever come here to carol. Thank you so much. You all come back when we can have you in for some chocolate," she said, with characteristic Southern hospitality.

At the next house, an older couple listened. As we finished, they asked, "Are you going next door? We'd love our grandson to hear you before he goes to bed." Next door, a young couple came out with their thirteen-month-old son in his mother's arms. The husband disappeared and returned to wrap his babe in a blanket. As we started to sing, a look of shy amazement crept over the baby's face. He broke into a big smile and looked up at his mother as if to say, "Isn't this the best, Mom?" He listened with a sweet expression on his face to the next carol and the next, and smiled after each one. I could have stood there singing all night in the cold just to watch him smile again.

At the next house, the door opened and a tiny dog appeared on hind legs at the screen. He didn't bark, just listened, turning his head to see us all with his little ears bobbing. Occasionally, he disappeared, only to bounce back after a moment and listen again. We sang two carols, but no humans appeared, just this cheerful little dog. But the door didn't close either. So we sang "We Wish You a Merry Christmas" and headed for the van. As we drove around the corner, a young man dashed out the side door of the house and waved. I tapped my horn so he knew we'd seen him. Maybe he was in his PJs when we arrived.

At one of the last houses, the lights were very low, and we waded through a pile of junk on the front porch to knock and signal our arrival. One choir member, Cynthia, was nervous because a dog from that house once chased her on her bike. "I don't think they're home," she said. But a young woman came out alone and stood in the cold, singing along with us. After every carol, she said, "Thank you, thank you for coming." After our last carol, she burst into tears. "Thank you so much for coming. I had such an awful day at work." And Cynthia gave her a hug.

Our last house had a pen full of hunting dogs. They barked and howled along with us the whole time we were singing. I'm sure the family in the doorway couldn't hear much, although they smiled all the same. I started laughing at the doggy choir, and the whole alto section went out in giggles.

It took over two hours to visit a dozen houses, what with loading fifteen singers in and out of the van, and driving between houses. At the end, we were all cold and delighted. "Let's do this again next year!" we all said. I felt so happy I could hardly sleep.

Thank you, neighbors. You gave us so much more than we could possibly have given you.

— Swami Vidyananda —

25

At Sea

Homecoming unites the past and the present.
~Author Unknown

I t had been a dreary patrol for the crew of this Sturgeon-class nuclear-powered attack submarine. We had been put to sea out of Norfolk in the week prior to Thanksgiving. After completing a six-hour surface transit through Chesapeake Bay out to deep water, we dived, headed north and remained submerged and out of touch with the world over Thanksgiving, Christmas, New Year's, and my twentieth birthday.

It was a Cold War-era "northern run" within the territorial waters of the Soviet Union, and the ship had been "rigged for silent running" for more than two months. The living conditions were akin to being entombed because the internal atmosphere was cold and damp owing to the frozen bilge water. We spoke in hushed tones, wore sneakers to cushion our footsteps, and performed our duties in near silence lest we disclose our position to a Soviet submarine or surface craft. Aboard was a special team of Navy linguists whom we referred to as "spooks." They huddled in the radio room to intercept Soviet messages and put out counter-intelligence.

Thanksgiving was okay because we had been submerged for just two weeks, so we still had plenty of fresh food left. Therefore, our traditional meal was enjoyable, complete with sliced turkey and all the fixings, but still not like home. But as soon as we hit the thirty-day mark, the good stuff was gone. By Christmas, it was canned fruit and veggies, powdered milk in our coffee and powdered eggs for breakfast. The crew's morale had slipped a notch, and some guys had been getting a tad grumpy. *If I could just have a glass of fresh milk,* I thought, *and a crispy garden salad, I would be so happy.* But, of course, I couldn't have those common pleasures or others like the warmth of the sun on my face, the wind blowing through my hair, the scent of fresh flowers, a newspaper or TV, a telephone call from home, or receiving Mom's letter in the mail. Submariners led a spartan existence devoid of the simple indulgences of everyday life, so we learned to do without. We lived in the reality of having nothing at all.

There was a noticeable relief and elevation in crew morale after Christmas had passed, fortunate because the riskiest stretch of our mission was still ahead. We were in "enemy territory" and had operated without incident except for encountering frequent surface contacts, prompting us to battle-stations for long shifts. One night, sonar detected a Soviet submarine shadowing us at a distance, but we were able to evade it. Nonetheless, it was a close call.

The trip home was quiet except for the occasional friendly sonar contact. The food was running low, so we were surviving mostly on spuds and canned goods for the final couple of weeks. I perceived that we were getting further south when the bilge water thawed and the internal temperature warmed.

Finally, the announcement came to rig the ship for surface. We were going up. I reasoned that we must be off the coast of Norfolk and the good old USA. So, I made the essential preparations in the torpedo room to surface. After all the compartments had reported, the PA announcement that we all had yearned for came in. "Now surface, surface, surface!" Next, I heard a short burst of 3,000-PSI air hit our ballast tanks, the boat nosed upward, and our speed increased as the hull groaned in response to the decreasing of the enormous sea pressure surrounding us. We ascended from the dark depths toward the sunlight above; we were heading home. Then our bow broke the surface, and we leveled off and settled gently into the sea.

When relieved of my watch, I sprinted up to the control room and was granted my request to visit the bridge. I approached the trunk and felt the cool air drifting downward, and then I started up the ladder. My eyes looked skyward in anticipation as I gulped a blissful breath of fresh Virginia air.

When I reached the top, I poked my head out into the darkness to hear the gentle rumble of the surf as our hull slipped through the chop. Then I climbed out and relished the heavens while the breeze tousled my hair and a blast of frosty wind slapped my face. I gazed out at the sun rising above the sea, illuminating the sky, its rays striking the white-water breaking over our bow and rendering it iridescent against the blackness of the sea. I felt reborn and, with tears rolling down my cheeks, I turned my eyes aft toward our stern and saw the froth of our wake winding a white ribbon upon the sea. I heard the snap of the Stars and Stripes above me as it flapped in the early morning light.

When we made port and had our gangplank to the pier, we sent any sick and injured crewmen over first, and then brought on mail and provisions. Later, I sat patiently in the crew's mess gripping a drinking glass while waiting patiently in anticipation of the mess cook's replenishment of the milk dispenser. Then I began to pour, guzzling the first two glasses in quick succession, and then slowly sipping the next three, savoring them like fine wine. My evening chow would include a crispy garden salad with tomatoes, cucumbers, and green olives. I hoped we had the ones with the pimentos in them.

Families gathered on the pier to reunite with their loved ones, and there were many tears, hugs and kisses. All the guys were looking forward to spending time with their families, but I didn't make it home until mid-February. My mom picked me up at the bus stop and drove me to our house. Upon entering, it seemed quiet, and no one else seemed to be home. But Mom motioned me into the living room where I saw a fully decorated Christmas tree that appeared a bit droopy and brown. Beneath it was a stack of gifts, and my family was there, too. "Welcome home, Jim!" they shouted. What a wonderful surprise because I hadn't expected to see a Christmas tree in February.

Then my mom said, "Now we'll have your Christmas, Jim."

And each holiday season since, I recall that patrol along with my shipmates and the hardships that we endured together as a surrogate family. As I call to mind what it was like to do without, I better appreciate the everyday things in life like the sight of the driven snow, the starlit winter sky, and the twinkle of Christmas lights in a child's eyes. But mostly, I remember that sad-looking Christmas tree with my devoted family welcoming me home from a perilous mission beneath the sea.

— James Fasino —

No Room at the Inn

The holy magic that filled that lonely stable so long ago
still fills the air of Christmas today.
~Mary Hollingsworth

When our children were younger, and all three of my siblings lived within a twenty-mile radius, our annual Christmas tradition started on December 24th. That's when the entire clan would gather at our parents' home in the country.

One year, we left the bright lights of the city, and our two children marveled as usual at the stars that became visible in the dark sky as we drove farther into the country. Margie, age thirteen, and Tim, age eight, were excited to get to their grandparents' home to begin the festivities, including hanging their stockings.

Over and over, I had explained that Santa's presents were nice, but the real reason we reveled in the season was the birth of Jesus. However, it seemed they were focused more on the gifts they would receive than on the original reason for the holiday.

For me, part of the joy of going to Grandma's was that our nuclear family was able to celebrate Mass at St. Joseph the Worker Catholic Church. It's a tiny, picturesque, white-steepled wooden building, nestled between the rolling hills of two small towns on a backcountry road about four miles from Mom and Dad's home. The little church seated eighty to 100 people if they all squished together. I always thought it would be the perfect subject for a Thomas Kinkade painting.

When we arrived at the church that night, we found the recently plowed parking lot completely full and more vehicles parked on both sides of the road. While the kids ran ahead to view the crèche, which included live sheep, my husband and I approached the people gathered on the sidewalk. Someone said, "All the seats are taken inside, and some people are standing behind the last pews. I think we'll be listening to Mass over the PA system."

The words were no sooner out of his mouth than a microphone came alive, and the presiding priest announced, "Due to fire-code regulations, people crowded into the vestibule will have to leave the building." Several families reluctantly joined the rest of us on the sidewalk.

It was a clear, cold, crisp winter night. I looked at the crowd around me and thought, *What a wonderful turnout for this little country church. It's too bad we can't be inside.*

Bright headlights from an oncoming vehicle illuminated the crowd awaiting the first hymn that signaled the beginning of the Christmas Eve service. The vehicle parked in front of the church garage/storage area across the street. A priest stepped out of the driver's door. With a huge grin on his face, he said, "Hi, I'm Father Dan. I understand there's a full house. Come help me set up for Mass."

We watched as he opened one of the overhead garage doors and flicked on the lights. Beckoning to the adults in the crowd, he said, "Many hands make light work. The chairs are stacked over there. Perhaps we could get a chain going. Is anyone here an altar server?"

A hand went up, and the volunteer was given tasks to help the priest set up a makeshift altar. Searching through a see-through plastic storage box, the priest found linens to use during the service. After producing a chalice, a carafe of wine, and a bowl containing the Eucharist, Father Dan was almost ready to begin.

The chair brigade was busy setting up rows of seating, and people were filing into each row. A strong baritone voice began singing "Silent Night," and one by one everyone joined in as the preparation for Mass continued. A lady of the parish found some candles complete with drip protectors and asked the children to distribute them. When the first hymn ended, strains of "Away in a Manger" began.

Two 100-watt light bulbs lit the interior of the unheated two-car garage as it was converted into a sanctuary. Warmth emanated from the number of bodies packed into the small space. A feeling of kinship fostered by the communal preparation for a very special Christmas Eve service warmed our hearts. Father Dan turned off the lights as candles were lit, softening the starkness of the garage bay.

The sermon was short, with the celebrant equating our improvisation that evening to the plight of Mary and Joseph having to find shelter in a barn where their baby boy was born. He couldn't have been more impactful, and he echoed what each person in the garage was feeling. But did my kids understand how incredible an experience this was?

Just then, eight-year-old Tim leaned over to me and whispered, "Mom, there was no room for us in the church tonight, just like there was no room at the inn for Joseph and Mary. They found space in a barn where Jesus was born, and we had Mass in a garage. This was neat! I'll always remember it!"

Tears of gratitude formed in my eyes as my son expressed exactly what I was thinking.

Tim is now forty-six and still remembers that night when there was "no room at the inn" for us on Christmas Eve.

—Nancy Emmick Panko—

27

To Iraq with Love

*So she poured out the liquid music of her voice
to quench the thirst of his spirit.*
~Nathaniel Hawthorne

I t was Christmas 2007, and I was busy with a visiting daughter, son-in-law and grandson as well as my daughter's best friend, her husband and two babies. Saying we had a houseful was putting it mildly. The best friend and her family had moved in with me a few weeks earlier when they were nearly homeless.

There were gifts, lights, decorations, and lots of noise and laughter. It should have been the happiest house in Smyrna, Tennessee, but someone was missing.

My fiancé, code-named Sgt. Sugarbear, was serving with the Army in Iraq. He'd been gone for about eight months and had four more to go. We were blessed to be able to talk frequently on the phone. I had sent him three boxes of gifts ranging from necessary (Remington gun oil from Walmart since the government's oil was not as good, according to him) to downright silly (a felt Christmas tree that played "Rockin' Around the Christmas Tree") figuring I would improve the odds that at least one box would reach him.

At any rate, a day or so before Christmas, I was shopping and came across a group of Girl Scouts caroling outside the store. They were so cute, bashful and sincere that I couldn't help but wish that Sugarbear could see them.

This is what America should look like, I thought. *Freedom to worship, freedom to sing, freedom to just be a kid singing Christmas carols because it's what you want to do!*

At that moment, my phone rang. It was Sugarbear calling from somewhere near Baghdad. We spoke for a few moments, and then I asked the girls to sing for him.

"There's a real American soldier fighting a real war on the other end of this call," I said. "He's fighting for all of us and our freedom to enjoy Christmas and every other day of the year. Please sing for him."

The girls sang "O Little Town of Bethlehem" and "We Wish You a Merry Christmas" as a dozen or so shoppers heard who was on the phone and joined in. The songs completed, people started yelling, "Thank you!" "Stay safe!" "We love you!" and "Come home soon!" Finally, I got back on the phone.

"That was the best present I could have gotten," Sugarbear said, sounding as near to tears as I could imagine. "Wow! Thank them for me!"

Not being able to resist, I sang the last line of "White Christmas" to him à la Dolores (Mrs. Bob) Hope to our soldiers in Vietnam a generation earlier: "May your days be merry and bright, and may all your Christmases be *home!*"

— Susan Stowell Bowmer —

28

The Red Suit

A little magic can take you a long way.
~Roald Dahl

I was spending the day with one of my grandchildren because he had a day off from school. We were going to run some errands and then go out for lunch. As I gathered what I needed for our errands, I opened the closet door and grabbed the red suit that needed to go to the cleaner.

As I turned around, my wide-eyed grandson stood staring at what I was holding.

"Poppy! What are you doing with Santa's suit?"

Oh no! Think fast! He's six years old!

"Umm, you know how Santa goes down all those chimneys on Christmas Eve? You know how dirty our fireplace is?"

He nodded with his eyes still wide.

"Well, Santa has to have clean suits. He can't work all night in dirty suits, can he?"

"But why do we have one? Does Santa get changed here?"

"Yes he does. He picks some special houses to keep his clean suits at. We were lucky to be picked to be one of those houses."

That explanation seemed to satisfy him. He has a very vivid imagination and I could see the wheels turning as he processed this new information.

We jumped into my pickup and off we went.

He accompanied me into the dry cleaner and proudly informed

the lady behind the counter that we were cleaning Santa's suit for him so he could change into clean clothes after going down all those chimneys. We were very special people helping Santa.

The lady smiled at his explanation and winked at me. And the magic was still alive for all of us.

— Gary S. Crawford —

Family Fun

29

The Ugly Elf Tradition

You will do foolish things,
but do them with enthusiasm.
~Colette

D ad never could resist an auction. The fast-talking auction-eer. Chattering bidders. A raised finger here and there. Excitement in the air. Best of all, mystery items. Who knew what kind of bargains one might get in a plain cardboard box?

Besides, it was almost Christmas, and Dad always put off his gift shopping until the last minute. This year, perhaps he could do his gift buying by bidding on those mystery boxes. And so he did.

The bidding moved fast and furious. Next thing we knew, Dad had snagged one of those promising, mysterious packages. It was a good-sized box, and we all felt excited when Dad cut it open.

What did we find? The most ugly Christmas ornament ever designed by a human being — a nasty little hard-plastic elf. It was red and green, traditional festive seasonal colors, but that elf frowned out at the world with pure hate. We'd never seen a belligerent Christmas ornament before.

Worst of all, the box held dozens and dozens of hateful, nasty little elves. Now what?

Determined to turn this disaster into a victory, Dad insisted on using those dreadful elves. Every gift we gave that year — to friends, neighbors, the milkman, letter carrier and trash collectors — included an elf tied cheerfully to the gift package, fastened firmly so nobody could pretend to lose theirs. To the best of my recollection, no one thanked us for the ugly elves. No one pretended to like them or called them cute.

And, of course, since there was an almost endless supply of nasty elves, we put a bunch on our own Christmas tree, too.

Those elves were sturdy. No matter how often I tried dropping them on hard floors, they never broke or even cracked. They were just about indestructible.

My very first Christmas tree in my own home had elves on it. Mom insisted, and Dad agreed. I'm sure my brother was forced to take his share, too.

And the ugly elf tradition persists. My daughter, in her own home with her own family, has to decorate her tree with an ugly elf or two or three. The things go on forever. Most likely, my kids' kids will be hanging nasty little ugly elves on their holiday trees some day.

By now, it's a solid family tradition, and we all have to do our part. Nobody gets a free pass. Nobody gets to skip the ugly elves. Being indestructible, the elves will be part of our Christmas celebration forever. Mine hang at the very back of the tree where I don't have to see them.

Did Dad learn his lesson about mystery auction items? Nope. Next, he bid on an English racing bike as a gift for me, and he won. The bike never did work right, but it looked great under the tree where it blocked our view of a couple of those ugly elves.

—Karen M. Leet—

A Traditional Norwegian Christmas

The bond that links your true family is not one of
blood, but of respect and joy in each other's life.
~Richard Bach

It was going to be my stepfather's first Christmas Eve without his kids, and he was in a funk. My little brother, David, and I didn't call him "Dad" yet. He was still just "my mom's boyfriend" or "Mr. Leiren," but we were hoping he'd soon be more than that.

Mr. Leiren had four daughters and, like most divorced dads, he had to figure out how to schedule his holiday season. Mom asked Mr. Leiren how we could help him have a happy Christmas. He explained that his tradition as a Canadian parent was to open presents Christmas morning and have a family dinner that night. But he was born and raised in a small town in Norway with a name that's pretty much impossible to pronounce unless you're Scandinavian. Mr. Leiren explained that in Norway they opened presents and had the festive feast on Christmas Eve. So Mom offered to create a traditional Norwegian Christmas Eve. Then, the next day, he'd get to see his kids after their presents were opened.

Like many North American Jewish kids, our Hanukkah wish was to celebrate Christmas. Instead, we had to settle for dreidels, latkes and eight days of candles. But my mom wanted to help Mr. Leiren enjoy his holiday, so she asked what one served for a traditional Norwegian Christmas meal.

The feast started with lutefisk — dried cod treated with lye. The main course was a rack of lamb accompanied by raspekake — huge grey potato balls, which were pretty much the anti-latke. This was served with lots of smør — my favorite Norwegian word: butter.

Dessert consisted of krumkakes — thin, crispy, pastry horns stuffed with whipped cream mixed with cloudberry jam. My mom had to search everywhere in the city and the suburbs to find a proper Norwegian "krumkake iron."

Mom made the lamb and the dessert. Mr. Leiren cooked the fish and potatoes. And our traditional Christmas feast was delicious — except for the lutefisk, which was an acquired taste one apparently needed to be born in Norway to acquire.

My mom completed the festivities by putting up a small tree, and that year Hanukkah presents became Christmas presents.

Mr. Leiren spent the night smiling, laughing and telling us how this was the perfect Norwegian Christmas. From that year on, he and Mom would prepare the traditional Norwegian delicacies every Christmas Eve (minus the lutefisk).

After my first year of university, my friend Bob and I went backpacking through Europe. One of our stops was Stamneshella, the village where Dad grew up. I met his relatives, and we swapped stories about Dad, Canada, Norway and the correct way to pronounce "Leiren" as everyone served us platters overflowing with Norwegian treats.

One afternoon, Dad's cousin arrived with a plate of krumkakes. She was delighted and shocked that I not only knew what these were, but pronounced the name — not quite correctly, but close enough to be recognizable as Norsk.

She wanted to know how I knew the word. I explained that I knew the names of all the foods that were part of a traditional Norwegian Christmas feast. She looked puzzled and asked me to tell her about the rest of the meal. The more I told her, the more confused she looked until, finally, she started to laugh. "That's not a traditional Norwegian Christmas dinner," she said. "Those are just your dad's favorite foods."

I thought about whether I should ask Dad about this, or at least mention it to my mom. But as I finished the last of the whipped cream from my krumkake, I realized something with perfect clarity: My dad's cousin didn't know anything about Norwegian Christmas traditions.

—Mark Leiren-Young—

31

The Turkey Thieves

*Siblings: children of the same parents, each of whom is
perfectly normal until they get together.*
~Sam Levenson

Thanksgiving was always hectic at our house. Being the last of seven children made it even more so. It seemed as though I was always last in line for everything, and my sister, Nancy, who was thirteen months older than me, didn't do any better. Every year, on Thanksgiving Day, she and I begged for the most sought-after part of the Thanksgiving turkey: the beloved turkey legs. And every year, they would end up with someone else.

That is, until the year Nancy and I decided we had had enough. We made a pact. Those turkey legs were going to be ours! We just had to figure out how.

We were quite young to take on such a big feat, but being the youngest sometimes had its advantages. We had watched our older brothers and sisters pulling off their own schemes many times. It didn't take long for us to come up with a plan.

When Thanksgiving Day finally came, we were ready. Watching and waiting for the right opportunity was the hardest part, but things seemed to work out perfectly. Mom had forgotten an ingredient for one of her dishes, so she headed out for a quick trip to town. All of the other kids were outside playing, and the turkey was sitting right there in the center of our kitchen table. Our perfect opportunity had arrived… time to carve the turkey!

Heading toward the kitchen, we were giggling so hard that we almost gave it away. "Shhh!" I whispered to Nancy. "The other kids will hear us."

Quietly, we scoured the kitchen in hopes of finding something to detach the drumsticks from the turkey. "Hey, this will work," Nancy spoke softly, trying hard to contain her excitement.

Quickly, I grabbed the knife she had found and, with a big grin, proceeded to carve the turkey. Giggling, Nancy reminded me to hurry.

"I'm trying," I replied, "but this knife isn't working."

By this time, I was starting to get pretty nervous. *What kind of knife is this anyway? It won't even cut!*

Desperate, we both grabbed a leg and pulled as hard as we could. We heard a loud snap, and both drumsticks came off simultaneously. We both hit the floor, a drumstick in hand. Success!

Looking at each other with wide-eyed excitement, we jumped to our feet, squealed with delight and began feasting on our yummy drumsticks. Oh, it was heavenly!

Then we heard a car door slam.

"Mom!" we both screamed at the same time.

"Run!" I yelled.

Nancy hit the stairs. I was right on her heels.

We quickly took refuge in our bedroom where we hopped into bed, carefully concealing our treasures under the blankets so no one would see them.

Now, all we had to do was close our eyes and convince everyone we were sound asleep.

Great plan! Or so we thought…

Being five and six years old, we didn't think about the fact that the Thanksgiving turkey no longer had legs. That was an afterthought. When we heard the front door open, Mom started yelling for all of our brothers.

The boys were always first to be blamed when something went wrong. After Mom finished questioning the boys, she started scouring the house for more suspects. She followed up with our older sister, Rene. Eventually, she made it into our room, only to find us snuggled up in bed, sleeping like little angels.

Things were going as planned, and we almost pulled it off, until Mom turned to leave the room. She caught a glimmer of something shiny on my face.

Mom slipped over for a closer look. My heart was pounding faster by now as I tried hard to keep still.

I felt Mom's hand slip beneath the covers and grasp my hidden turkey leg. My heart sank.

"Okay, girls, your little scheme is up," Mom said as she slipped the turkey leg out from under my covers.

Knowing we were busted, I slowly opened my eyes, trying to look as sad as possible in hopes of gaining some sympathy. We sat in silence and waited for the worst.

Mom was quiet for what seemed like forever. All the time, I was wondering what horrific punishment she was conjuring up for our bad deed.

Then, out of nowhere, she burst into laughter.

Bewildered, Nancy and I just looked at each other in silence.

"Couldn't wait for dinner?" Mom asked, still laughing uncontrollably. "I guess we won't have to argue over the turkey legs this Thanksgiving."

At that point, with great relief, Nancy and I joined in on the laughter. We laughed so hard that we were in tears.

Wondering what all of the laughter was about, the rest of the family came rushing in to investigate.

The sight of their two little sisters sitting on the bed, holding two large turkey legs, faces smeared with turkey juice, seemed to tickle their funny bone as well.

Within minutes, we were all laughing hysterically, cracking jokes about the two little turkey thieves.

Many years have passed since that Thanksgiving Day. Mom has passed away. But that Thanksgiving story has continued to bring smiles and laughter to our family over the years.

As we share it with each new generation, there is always an extra chuckle when we come to the part where we tried to carve the turkey with what I now realize was a butter knife. That didn't work out so well, but it made for a lot of fun memories.

—Irma A. Mason—

32

Fit to Be Tied

*I think the family is the place where the most ridiculous
and least respectable things in the world go on.*
~Ugo Betti

On Christmas night, the clan gathers at my house. It is a great clan in both quality and quantity — up to seventy strong — and there is much feasting and singing and toasting and putting on of skits. Friendly competition is a key component of these activities, but my brothers-in-law and I become quite serious when it comes to who has the finest Christmas tie of the season. The acknowledged champion has been known to break out the winning tie during Fourth of July celebrations to lord it over the lesser competitors of the previous year. Yup… it's that serious.

I have the finest group of brothers and brothers-in-law that I have ever seen, known or even heard about. We are best friends year 'round. Blood may be thicker than water, but our bond is thicker still. I love these guys with all of my heart. We're an incredible mix of diverse characters who live all over the northeast United States. When we gather (as at Christmastime), the bond is palpable. They are my best friends.

I have dozens of wonderful Yuletide-themed ties that I wear in ascending order of awesomeness, beginning immediately after Thanksgiving and reaching the pinnacle on Christmas night. My brothers-in-law also have fine collections, and it is a bone of contention as to whose is best. Ultimately, the kids proclaim a winner each Christmas night, but in our hearts we seven who wear ties know which one is most deserving. We are connoisseurs, and we know the unspoken nature of the "Christmas Tie Rivalry." It is very, very serious stuff.

Years ago, on the day after Christmas, I stumbled across the Holy Grail of Christmas Ties while cleaning up from the previous night's revelry. It was gorgeous in its silk construction, its background color a deep and delicious burgundy, a Dickensonian St. Nicholas joyous on winter white colored panels with hearty evergreen highlights and undertones throughout. It was breathtaking in its jaw-dropping ability to both start and stop conversations, and now it was all mine.

I love that tie dearly. I've never seen its like, and its beauty is unlikely to ever be matched. It speaks to me of the traditions and chaos of the Christmas season. The problem was that I was pretty sure the tie was a gift to my brother-in-law, Phil. And while I meant to return it to him, that somehow never happened. For years, I wore that wonderful necktie on Christmas Eve and to Midnight Mass… careful never to wear it during our annual Christmas Day festivities for fear of exposing my larceny to Phil. The guilt of my crime weighed heavy on me, for each Christmas I knew that Phil had the best Christmas tie of all time, yet he never knew it. That best ever Christmas tie lay dormant in my closet.

The fun was sucked out of the whole competition for me. It was time to come clean, admit my crime, beg for forgiveness, and hope that Phil would understand. Then we could move past the incident with our great friendship intact. But how?

Per usual, another brother-in-law, Bob, came to my rescue. Bob is as solid as they come: a wise man, a knowledgeable Wall Street attorney, and just the ticket to get me out of my holiday jam.

"Rence," said Bob, "go get the tie. I will talk to Phil in the meantime and smooth things over. This demonstration of loyalty combined with a genuine plea for forgiveness on Christmas night is sure to go over well. Handshakes will ensue with hearty slaps on the back; the past will recede into the past, and a good time will be had by all." A very wise man, that Bob.

And so I retrieved the finest Christmas tie I had ever known from its hiding place deep in the recesses of my closet. Downstairs, I ambled in a shamed gait to find Phil and Bob deep in a serious conversation. They both stared at me as I approached—Phil with a predictably puzzled look as if seeing me clearly for the first time, and Bob, ever the stone-faced councilor. He fixed me with a steady gaze, slapped me on the shoulder, and said stoically, "It's okay, Rence. It'll be fine."

Then I produced the best Christmas tie I had ever seen from behind my back and presented it to Phil, knowing terrible retribution was sure to come. "I'm so sorry, my brother," I said. "You left this at my house four Christmases ago. I meant to return it all these years, but it is the finest Christmas tie I've ever seen, and I loved it too much. I return it to you now. Please forgive me…"

Silence. Bob's jaw had gone slack, and the blood had drained from his face in what I assumed was anticipation of the Armageddon-like response that was sure to follow from Phil. However, Phil simply looked to me in blank, astonished bewilderment. It was as if antlers had suddenly sprouted full-grown from my ears, and he couldn't figure out why.

"Rence," said my good brother-in-law Phil calmly, "this is indeed the most spectacular example of Yuletide neckwear I've ever witnessed. I would certainly remember it had I ever seen it before, but in all honesty, I never have! It's awesome, but it was never mine."

Now it was my turn to be flummoxed. For the past four years, I had shielded the existence of this tie from Christmas night festivities for fear that my burglary would be exposed. My guilt was ill-founded! I was free… a true Christmas miracle!

"Well, no sense belaboring the issue," I said gleefully. "Merry Christmas, my brothers!" I shook hands with Phil, and we shared a laugh. I turned to Bob to thank him for his welcome yet ultimately unnecessary efforts when I noticed a perceptible drop in the temperature of the room. Bob was now the one looking at me as if I were sprouting antlers as he croaked out in a frigid voice, "My god, Rence! I've been searching for that tie for four years!"

—Rence Regan—

The Day We Launched Our Brother

*The best Christmas trees come very close
to exceeding nature.*
~Andy Rooney

I had the perfect tree in mind, I watched it grow all year
Up the snowy hill we climbed, I knew it must be near
I looked up and saw it, right before my eye
When, I do not know, the tree had grown so high
If we all climb up, I said, we can bend it down
Daddy can chop off the top, when it touches ground
We three went up, the tree bent down.
A plan that seemed so sound
This was the tree I had to have, I would choose no other
Two jumped off... that's when we launched our brother

— Debbie Sistare —

Author's note: We went into the woods to find a Christmas tree. Mary
(8), Deborah (7) and Thomas (5) all climbed to the top of a tall tree to
bend it down. Before their dad could cut off the top of the tree, Mary
and Deborah jumped off... That's when they launched their brother.

Plastic Santa!

*Christmas is a day of meaning and traditions, a special
day spent in the warm circle of family and friends.*
~Margaret Thatcher

lthough it was a cold December morning, the warmth of the Christmas season was everywhere. Wreaths hung from doors, welcoming the spirit of giving and hope. Homes were illuminated with lights streaming from rooftops, draped around trees and framing doorways. They created picturesque scenes as I drove my son Kris to preschool. In the car, we sang to my home-made Christmas CDs comprising an eclectic list of songs including, "Dominick the Donkey," "Run Rudolph Run" "I Saw Mommy Kissing Santa Claus," and "Silent Night."

Kris's school was about fifteen minutes from home, and I felt we needed a little more Christmas activity in the car. While stopped at a light, I looked to my left, and an idea came to me. The front lawn of this particular house was adorned with a plastic Santa. The Santa was about three feet high and made of hard plastic. It reminded me of one my family had when I was a child. I told Kris to look at the plastic Santa standing on the lawn. In the rearview mirror, I saw him smiling as he looked through his window. I then explained, "Every time you see a plastic Santa like this one, yell out 'Plastic Santa,' and I'll do the same. Whoever yells it first gets a point. Whoever has the most points before we get to preschool wins."

Kris observed every home's décor from his booster seat behind me, seeking out a plastic Santa. Soon, I heard an excited voice yell out, "Plastic Santa!" I told him he was winning with a score 1 to 0. I, too, was competitive, keeping a watchful eye and trying to score points. If we yelled at the same time, a tie was called, and we both received a point.

Kris played the game every time we rode in the car. One day, his grandparents were in the back seat with him, and he yelled out, "Plastic Santa!" They asked what he was doing. He explained the game to them, and they began to play. My husband was driving and joined in; with five players, the game came alive.

The Christmas season came and went. The following year, as we drove along in December, I heard Kris yell out, "Plastic Santa!" He hadn't forgotten about the game. After his brother was born and old enough to play, he was taught the rules and became a true competitor.

The game got so competitive that we added more rules. There would be a penalty whenever a false call was made, costing that player a point. That was to stop the boys from calling out "Plastic Santa" half a block away, when they were just guessing there would be one. The real genius was trying to remember exactly where each plastic Santa was spotted on the way to a destination, and then being the first to call it on the way back. My husband and sons excelled at this.

Years later, when we picked up Kris and his friends from college for Christmas break, he yelled out "Plastic Santa!" as we headed home. Surprised and curious, his friends asked why he did that. He explained the game to his friends, and they began to play. A game created while driving him to preschool was now in full swing with his college roommate and other friends. One of Kris's friends called "Plastic Santa," only to realize upon closer inspection that it was a snowman. Kris informed him quickly of the rules, and that it would cost his friend a point should it happen again.

My boys are now young men, and we still play "Plastic Santa" when driving together during Christmastime. Even when it's just my husband and me, we compete. It never occurred to me twenty-six years ago that "Plastic Santa" would be played for decades and become a family tradition.

—Valerie Testa Almquist—

35

A Second-String Santa and a Rookie Reindeer

The person who has a sense of humor is not just more relaxed in the face of a potentially stressful situation, but is more flexible in his approach.
~John Morreall

Three days before Christmas, my girlfriend called to ask for a favor. "The five-year-old girl who lives in the apartment above me has had a bad case of the flu and has been bedridden the past two weeks," she told me. "Her mom wasn't able to take her to the department store to see Santa Claus. Do you think you could ask your friend Red to come over?"

Red was probably as close to a professional Santa Claus as one could find. He had been the Santa Claus at the Monroeville Mall, just east of Pittsburgh. He had his own Santa Claus outfit and he even did professional gigs. Red was also 6'1", weighed 260 pounds, and needed no padding to play the part of Santa.

Unfortunately, when I called him and asked if he could visit the little girl and her single mom the next night, he said that he had previous plans.

"But, hey, I'll tell you what," he said. "How about if I lend you my outfit so you can be Santa Claus?"

When I called my girlfriend and told her the circumstances, she didn't seem overly enthused. She obviously preferred Red.

"Do you know how to be Santa Claus?" she asked.

"I think so," I answered. "I watched Red a couple of times when he was at the mall."

"Will you take it seriously?" she wanted to know. "You're not going to goof around, are you?"

I assured my girlfriend I would take it seriously.

The next evening, I donned the Santa Claus suit and went over to the little girl's apartment. I was told her name was Sarah.

The plan was for my girlfriend to go in first. I'd wait and go in five minutes later. And so I walked in and acted very jolly.

They sat the little girl on my lap. I asked her what she wanted for Christmas, and she told me what was on her wish list.

I tried to emulate some of the Santa Claus moves I'd seen Red perform when he was at the Monroeville Mall. At one point, I pretended I had fallen asleep.

"You better shake Santa, try to wake him up," said the little girl's mother and my girlfriend.

The little girl started patting my shoulder and said, "Santa, wake up, wake up. You've fallen asleep."

I woke up groggily.

"Oh, Santa's so tired. I've seen so many little girls and boys today," I said. "Now, where am I? I'm in Cleveland, right?"

"No," exclaimed the little girl. "This is Pittsburgh!"

"Oh, oh. You're right," I said. "Santa's getting so old and forgetful." The little girl and her mom were both smiling.

I glanced over at my girlfriend, and she had this look about her that said, "Wow, isn't my boyfriend wonderful?"

And, I admit, I was thinking to myself, *I am wonderful.* And I think I would have remained wonderful had it not been for the little girl's mother asking a question.

"Now, Santa, isn't it true that one of your reindeer is sick with the flu, just like Sarah?" she asked.

"Oh, yes," I said, playing along. "In fact, he's been ill the past two weeks, just like Sarah."

"Oh, I hope it's not Rudolph," the little girl blurted out, her eyes showing deep concern.

"No, no, Rudolph is fine," I said. "He drove me over here tonight. He's doing well."

"Which one of the reindeer is sick, Santa?" the little girl wanted to know.

"It's, um... it's ah... Chester," I said finally.

"Chester!" exclaimed the little girl. Her eyes turned from me to her mother.

"Mummy, I never heard of a reindeer named Chester."

My girlfriend elbowed me in the ribs. The little girl and her mother turned to me, seeking answers.

"Oh, Chester's new," I said. "This is his first year. We just brought him up."

I talked to the little girl for a few more minutes, and then it was time to leave, presumably to go up on the rooftop to gather Rudolph and the other reindeer and take off.

In actuality, I went downstairs and waited outside my girlfriend's apartment door so I could take off the Santa Claus outfit.

When my girlfriend showed up, the first words out of her mouth were: "Chester the Reindeer?"

I shrugged my shoulders.

"Why wouldn't you use the name of a regular reindeer?" she wanted to know.

When I told my girlfriend I don't know the names of "regular reindeer," she didn't believe me.

"Like Dancer or Prancer?" she insisted. "Why wouldn't you use one of those names? Didn't you ever listen to the song on the radio?"

My girlfriend may have thought I was "goofing around," but I honestly didn't know the names of the reindeer — especially when the little girl put me on the spot.

Eventually, I felt compelled to end the conversation. "Look, I'm Jewish," I reminded my girlfriend, who was Catholic. "We don't have reindeer."

***

Despite my poor performance as Santa, I ended up marrying the girlfriend. And some years later, we had children — a boy and a girl — which led to a complicated and busy holiday season.

During the eight days of Hanukkah, we'd light candles and spin dreidels. At Christmas time, we'd decorate a tree and put up stockings.

Red would come to the house and be Santa Claus. Presents were distributed during both holidays.

But I'm pretty sure my wife's favorite holiday custom came on Christmas Eve, just before we put the kids to bed.

She'd put out milk and cookies near the Christmas tree and tell the kids, "This is for Santa and the reindeer in case they're hungry from their long trip from the North Pole."

Then my wife would have the kids snuggle up next to me on the couch and hand me a deluxe illustrated book titled *The Night Before Christmas*. It was Clement Clarke Moore's classic poem.

Dutifully, I'd begin to read. And when I got to page 7, there it was: the mention of "eight tiny reindeer" — or the "regular reindeer" my wife had been blithering about some years before. Of course, I was forced to list all of them properly: Dasher, Dancer, Prancer, Vixen, Comet, Cupid, Donder and Blitzen!

My wife continued the family tradition of having me read *The Night Before Christmas* — even when the kids approached adulthood. My guess is she wanted to drive home the point that there never was a reindeer named Chester.

Except, of course, for that one year.

— Steve Hecht —

36

A Scottish Surprise

The best of all gifts around any Christmas tree:
the presence of a happy family
all wrapped up in each other.
~Burton Hillis

My brother Bill was unlucky enough to have his birthday fall on Christmas Day. Everyone sympathized with him, as he had to share his special day with our family's favourite holiday. He always felt shortchanged when it came to celebrations. Most of the time, his presents were labelled "Happy Birthday/Merry Christmas."

Therefore, a few years ago, my nephew decided to surprise his father on one of his milestone birthdays. Bill has lived in Southern Spain for the past fifteen years, and he normally gets to meet up with his brothers and sisters only occasionally. Our family is scattered throughout the world. As a result, it is difficult for us to come together on a regular basis. My nephew, who lives in Madrid, contacted Bill's five siblings saying he was organizing a surprise celebration for his father's sixtieth birthday. We all made plans to attend. Two of Bill's sons still live in Scotland, so that was where the event was to take place.

My nephew booked a castle hotel overlooking a scenic highland loch. It would easily accommodate our large group of thirty. We made our way to the highland location from places as far as the United States, Canada, Belgium, Spain and Turkey.

After a very scenic drive through the Scottish countryside, we arrived in front of two enormous iron gates decorated with the castle's coat of arms. The gates were flanked by two small, stone gatehouses that housed estate workers. They were beautifully decorated with festive wreaths on the doors and Christmas trees in the windows. Thin wisps of smoke curled from the chimneys up into the blue sky, making a picture-postcard scene — an introduction to what was to come. We drove through the gates and up the long, winding, tree-lined driveway. Every hundred yards or so, the many huge, ancient trees were decorated with large tartan bows over golden bells.

The first glimpse of the castle took away my breath. It was everything I had come to think of as a Scottish castle. It consisted of a central stone tower that had been built in the 16th century, plus two wings that had been added on a century later. It was still owned and operated by descendants of the original owners. A crushed gravel driveway led up to the castle and the covered stone portico. Willing hands appeared and helped us unload our luggage. Normally, the castle was closed over Christmas so we were to be the only guests. My nephew had agreed to a reduction in staff to allow some of them to spend time with their own families. We were to share our festivities with the owners, their family and some staff who were happy to volunteer to work through the holiday.

As I entered the castle, I was impressed by the magnificent hallway. A large, carved oak table located in the middle of the hall supported a huge, cut-glass vase overflowing with fresh flowers. Along one wall was a beautiful, fresh-cut decorated tree. All around the grand hall, I could see portraits of the owners' ancestors hanging on the dark wood panelling alongside Christmas wreaths.

The owner led us up a grand, sweeping staircase to the upper floor where the bedrooms were located. Our room was beautifully appointed. As he showed us into the room, our host told us conspiratorially, "Mary, Queen of Scots once slept in this very bed." Judging by the number of times I have heard a similar tale, I have to assume that she travelled a lot. My skepticism faded when I looked around the room and its ancient fixtures. I began to feel that this perhaps was her bed.

The room certainly had a royal feel to it. The exquisitely carved wood of the four-poster bed projected a sense of solidity and permanence. It would not be difficult to imagine a royal person lying on the bed, propped up by huge, soft pillows and ordering around the servants. Intricately carved wooden furniture was arranged tastefully around the room. I had to stifle an urge to search the panelled walls for secret passages. Huge bay windows outlined in colourful plaids framed a comfortable, cushioned window seat. There was a wonderful view over the extensive grounds. Huge, ancient trees spread down to the still waters of the loch. After we had settled in, everyone made their way down to the dining room. We met and made plans for the following day when my brother and his family were due to arrive.

The next morning, after a full Scottish breakfast in a dining room warmed by a wood-burning fireplace, we finalized the preparations to greet the guest of honour. We blew up balloons, food and bubbly wine were laid out, and party favours and decorations were organized. The nephews and nieces arrived late in the morning. They came laden with extravagantly wrapped presents. Earlier in the month, my sister had sent out requests for photos of my brother throughout the years. She had arranged them in a huge, colourful collage. We decorated the hallway with festive hangings, and bunches of balloons all welcoming the birthday boy. A local man was engaged to play the bagpipes as part of the welcoming committee.

When my brother and his wife stepped out of their car, they looked relieved to finally be at their destination. As they had expected to share the holiday with immediate family only, they were stunned when we all emerged from the hotel led by the piper and called out birthday wishes. His face crumpled and he burst into tears. For the next ten minutes, he went from person to person, hugging tightly and sharing tears with his daughter and his three sisters. The rest of us boys were each given long, tight hugs — probably just as well as I suspect he was still speechless. The piped welcome also kept the need for conversation to a minimum.

We had a wonderful holiday. As the weekend progressed, the hotel owners and their staff joined enthusiastically in our celebrations. In the end, I am sure they felt they had gained some new relatives. I know that we did. We will never get a chance to spend such quality time together as a family again. I know that this event finally made up for all those combination Christmas and birthday celebrations my brother had endured for the first fifty-nine years of his life.

—James A. Gemmell—

37

Chicken Soup for the Soul

There's Always Room at the Inn

Fiction reveals truths that reality obscures.
~Jessamyn West

I love all the Christmas traditions that my friends have. Some send Christmas letters. Every year, I look forward to receiving those notes that laud their children's achievements, even when the youngest is thirty-five and makes fifty dollars a month as a street musician in San Francisco. I have friends who build a gingerbread house every holiday season. The finished product may look like it was struck by Hurricane Katrina, but they still treasure the tradition. Then there's a gag-gift group that raffles off inappropriate gifts to family members every Christmas. My friend yearns to possess the Barbie doll with the knitted skirt that is made to disguise a roll of toilet paper.

My own family has had a unique Christmas tradition for more than four decades. We put on a play called "No Room at the Inn," a family drama that has had a longer run than *Phantom of the Opera*. When we started this tradition, we were involved in various civil-rights activities, and we felt it was important to teach our kids to be open-minded and accept other people's differences. Because humor is an important part of our family communication system, we also had to incorporate a few laughs into the lesson.

I have always been the creative director and author, and I write the play fresh each season and I keep it topical. We assign parts, with some people playing against type. My father, who was not as "evolved" as we would have liked, once played the part of an African American looking for housing. When the actor playing the landlord refused him shelter by saying, "There's no room at the inn for non-white people," we all booed. When our lone Republican, Dirk, joined the family, he was usually assigned the part of some liberal political figure, while I played the role of a conservative. One time, I did a Rush Limbaugh imitation when I stated: "There's no room at the inn for feminazis."

Most responses were more positive. We often cheered as the "no room" theme carried through each act of the play in an affirming way. Although we sometimes tease family members about their various lifestyles or professions, we've made "room at the inn" over the years for recovering alcoholics, bullied teenagers, animal-rights people, senior citizens, former prisoners, and people who feel like outsiders.

The end of the play is always the same, even though the actors have changed many times. In the old days, the three youngest, who are now in their fifties, would alternate playing Mary, Joseph, and an angel. They would knock on several doors, pleading to be let in. Various family members would shout: "There's no room at the inn." Finally, a kindly landlord (oftentimes, my dad) would welcome the little family. When the grandchildren were old enough to understand, they assumed their parents' roles and still do to this day, even though they range in age from sixteen to twenty.

Friends love to be in the play. Sometimes, we've had as many as twenty people take part. Anyone who's home alone on Christmas Eve is welcome to stop by. They show up, and I'll write them a part, because there's always room at the inn!

— Ellie Spence —

Chapter 5

Best Gift Ever

A Little Girl's Gift of Love

The excellence of a gift lies in its appropriateness
rather than in its value.
~Charles Dudley Warner

Our four children usually did their Christmas shopping at the elementary school's Secret Santa Shop. Items were donated by community members throughout the year. Just before Christmas, children could pick out items to purchase at very low prices. Since my wife and I and our four children survived on my rather meager teacher's salary, the Secret Santa Shop was an ideal place for our children to buy their Christmas gifts.

We gave each child enough money to buy small items for family members, and it was up to them to budget their money so they would be able to get something for each person. We thought this was a good way for them to learn to manage their money, but also to experience the joy of giving to others. We were always amazed at how well they did and how personal their gifts were.

Our six-year-old daughter Claudia secretly told my wife that the gift she wanted to purchase for me—a handkerchief—was not in the Secret Santa Shop. She had noticed that the handkerchief I always wore in my coat pocket on Sunday morning for church was getting rather worn, and she wanted to buy me a new one. She had seen on television that men's monogrammed handkerchiefs were on sale at the mall, and she had her heart set on getting one with the letter C on it for me.

After daily reminders by Claudia, my wife finally worked out a time to take her to the mall to buy the handkerchief. It was just two days before Christmas.

At the mall, my wife took Claudia to the department store that advertised the handkerchiefs. They found the counter that displayed the handkerchiefs, and Claudia told my wife to please stand a few feet away because she wanted to do the entire transaction on her own. My wife complied but was close enough to hear Claudia's conversation with the sales clerk.

"May I help you?" the clerk asked.

"Yes, you can," Claudia said. "I want to buy one of your men's handkerchiefs that comes with a letter on it."

"Good choice," the clerk said. "These handkerchiefs make wonderful gifts. We've sold a lot of them. And what letter are you looking for?"

"I would like one with a C on it," Claudia said. "My dad's name is Charles."

"Well, let me look," the clerk said. She sorted through the box of handkerchiefs once and then sorted a second time. "Oh, dear," she said. "We don't have any C's left. I'm so sorry."

"Are you sure?" Claudia asked. "There must be at least one C in there. Would you please look again?"

The clerk looked again. "No, honey," she said. "There are simply no C's in the box. These handkerchiefs have been very popular this year. Is there perhaps another letter that would work?"

Claudia was silent for a moment and then said, "His last name is Lee. Do you have an L?"

"I sure hope so," the clerk said. She took her time and sorted through the box. She stopped and then sorted a second time. "Oh, dear," she said. "I can't seem to find an L. I just can't believe it. I'm sure I saw one in the box earlier today."

"What am I going to do?" Claudia asked. "I want to get a handkerchief for my daddy. It's very important."

"Honey, I don't know what to say," the clerk said. "Would you like me to show you some other possibilities?"

"No, ma'am," Claudia said. "I really want a handkerchief. My daddy needs a new one."

"I see," the clerk said. "Well, how about a plain handkerchief, one without any letters on it?"

"Oh, no," Claudia said. "I want it to be really special. With a letter on it."

"You certainly are a very determined little girl," the clerk said, "and I wish I could help you, but I simply don't have anything else to offer."

Claudia was quiet for a moment and then said, "Ma'am, just what letters do you have in that box?"

The surprised clerk said, "Well, let me see. I have some Z's and X's. Here are some U's and V's, and here are a few Q's. Oh, and here are a few Y's, O's, and M's...."

Claudia interrupted. "Wait. I'll take the M. My daddy's middle name is Milton. That's perfect." She smiled and handed the clerk her money.

"That's a very creative solution," the clerk said. "You're one special little girl."

The clerk placed the handkerchief in a box and handed it to Claudia. Then she gave back her money.

"Honey, you can keep your money," the clerk said. "That's my gift to you. I hope your daddy likes his gift. Merry Christmas."

On Christmas morning, our house was filled with excitement as everyone opened their gifts. Claudia watched me closely as I opened her gift to me.

"Would you look at this," I said. "What a nice handkerchief, and it's even monogrammed. Wow. And it's got an M on it for... let me guess... for Mister?"

Claudia laughed and shook her head.

"Let me guess again," I said. "An M for... Magnificent?"

Everyone laughed, and Claudia shook her head again.

"Aha," I said. "I've got it. An M for... Milton, my middle name. How thoughtful. I've never had a handkerchief for my middle name before. I bet no one in the whole wide world has ever had a handkerchief for their middle name. That makes it extra special. Thank you,

Claudia. I love it."

I'm now eighty years old, and I still have that handkerchief. I proudly wore it in my coat pocket for many years, but it's now in a drawer for safekeeping. I get it out and look at it once in a while. And when I do, tears come to my eyes because I know the tremendous love a little girl had for her daddy when she purchased it. It's amazing how one small gift, given with love, can mean so much over all these years.

Claudia now lives in New Zealand, and I asked her recently if she remembered purchasing the handkerchief. "I remember it clear as a bell," she said. "I'll never forget it."

Someday, the handkerchief will be passed on to Claudia. I have a note in the box that says, "This handkerchief has always been one of my most cherished gifts. There's no gift greater than the one given with love."

— Charles Milton Lee —

39

He Came Upon a Midnight Clear

Good news from heaven the angels bring, Glad tidings
to the earth they sing: To us this day a child is given,
to crown us with the joy of heaven.
~Martin Luther

It was the twelfth of December, and I was running around town with my mother and daughter, doing some last-minute shopping, teaching my final voice lessons before the Christmas break, attending my weekly prenatal exam, and singing at a Christmas party. It was a busy day, but I was happy with everything I had accomplished at thirty-nine weeks pregnant. We even picked up the Christmas tree… our last stop before home.

As we left the city lights behind, I realized I had forgotten to fill up the gas tank. I was very tired and decided it could wait until morning. We got home late, and I went straight to bed.

We were in the middle of restoring the larger of two houses on our isolated property in the California Mojave Desert. My husband Chris and I, and our two-year-old daughter Bella were living in the small, unfinished brick cottage, and my mum was sleeping in the large, unfinished house at the other end of the acreage.

Around 3:30 in the morning I woke up with some uncomfortable stomach cramps. My whole life, I have suffered with food sensitivities, and the resulting pain is often accompanied by cold sweats and hot flashes. Having broken my regular diet restrictions so I could enjoy some of the richer treats at the Christmas party, I knew I was now paying for my transgressions. It seemed unusual that each cramp consistently lasted thirty seconds, and then it hit me: *This might be it... maybe I'm in labor!*

A jolt of panic gripped me; I wasn't ready! I still had shopping to do and gifts to make. I had to wrap everything, make Christmas cards, write Christmas cards, and send everything out. We had to set up the tree and decorate... We had to finish restoring the house!

But I quickly realized the timing was all over the board. Eleven minutes between pains, then five, then ten... There was no rhythm to it, so it had to be the food. I relaxed a little, content that I still had time to make Christmas happen.

I tossed and turned in bed for another forty-five minutes before giving in to the inevitable; I got up to go to the bathroom. It was just like every other time, with cold sweats and hot flashes. I was playing solitaire on my phone to try and take my mind off the discomfort. At one point, the pain overtook me, and I had to put down the phone. Then my water broke, and I felt the irrepressible urge to push. That was a feeling I remembered, and it wasn't from eating rich food.

I called out Chris's name. I knew the baby was coming, and it was coming fast. I grabbed the two towels hanging on the back of the door and threw them on the raw concrete floor, and then I lay down in the small bathroom. I just fit with my knees bent, feet against the wall. My head was under the sink, and my right arm was squished up against the shower. Like I said, it was a small cottage!

Chris didn't wake up to me calling his name, but he certainly woke up to the primal screams that started emanating from the tiny bathroom.

The contractions were just seconds apart.

Bella woke up, too, and started crying in alarm. Chris came running in, fearing every worst-case scenario. I told him (or screamed at him, I don't remember) that the baby was coming, and to get my phone; I had to call the midwife. He asked if he could get me to the car so we could drive to the birth center, but, being the epitome of composure, I said, "No, the baby's head is already out."

I only had about five minutes from the time my water broke to the time the baby arrived. I managed to call the midwife, and she listened to me as I gave birth on the bathroom floor. Luckily, Chris caught the baby before it touched the cold concrete. The midwife directed my stunned husband on what to do next.

"Here," he said to me, "you have to hold her, skin to skin, on your chest."

Teary-eyed, I said, "It's a girl?"

"I don't know!" he replied, still in shock.

It was so cold, and we had to keep the baby warm, so Chris did his best to get me, clutching the tiny slippery baby, off the floor and into the bedroom. Bella was sitting in the middle of the bed, bawling. As we lay down beside her, she calmed down immediately, crawled over to us, and said, "Baby?" Ever so gently, she ran her hand across the new baby's forehead. My heart melted; I pray I never forget that tender moment.

Chris had my phone, which was almost out of power, in one hand, and his phone, with even less power, in the other. He just managed to call 911 and report what happened before his phone died; at least we knew the ambulance was on its way. Then he ran down the street to get my mum. She didn't quite know what to make of it when he said, "You have to come. The baby is here!"

The EMTs arrived about twenty minutes later. They checked me and the baby; it wasn't until then that we found out he was a boy! We named him Turner.

I had to get in the ambulance, but there was just one problem: They couldn't get the gurney into the house because the doorway was so small. I was completely naked under an open robe, with Turner still clutched in my arms and attached to me by the umbilical cord. They threw a couple of towels over us for warmth, and I walked out into the cold desert under myriad twinkling stars that lit up the heavens.

My mum sat in the front of the ambulance, and Turner and I were in the back. The heat was cranked up to keep my precious infant from getting too cold. The one-hour ride to the hospital was uneventful.

My husband's ride to the hospital did not go as smoothly.

He quickly grabbed our daughter and ran out to follow the ambulance, only to find it had already gone. He was left with a toddler, in a car with almost no gas, and two phones with dead batteries in the middle of the desert. Luckily, he made it to the nearest gas station and found the hospital without a hitch.

We were so fortunate; so many things could have gone terribly wrong. We will always be eternally grateful that nothing did.

And despite not being prepared for Christmas — never getting the cards or presents finished, wrapped, or sent — we were wholly blessed to receive the greatest gift of all: a healthy baby, just in time for Christmas.

— Michelle DelaPlace —

40

Santa's Magic

*Our hearts grow tender with childhood memories and
love of kindred, and we are better throughout the year
for having, in spirit, become a child again
at Christmas-time.*
~Laura Ingalls Wilder

Santa always delivered our gifts on Christmas Eve, as he knew we participated in the evening pageant at church and returned home ready to celebrate. We were always filled with anticipation while at church, but this Christmas Eve felt different, layered deeper in tension and excitement. I would play the part of Mary in the Christmas story, which terrified me because it included singing a soprano solo.

My breathing picked up as I saw people in the congregation scrambling for the remaining seats. I would be singing to a full house. As instructed, I hunkered down behind the pulpit until it was time for my performance. Going over the song lyrics in my head, each line made my heart beat faster. *What if I opened my mouth to sing and forgot the words?* I tucked back the long white sleeves on my flowing gown, pushed the headscarf away from my eyes, and risked peeking around the corner of the lectern. I saw my entire family waiting, supporting me.

On my cue to appear, I stepped out onto the stage. As I stood and sang "My Soul Magnifies the Lord," the meaning of the song itself gave me confidence. For those few minutes, I became Mary singing her love. My fear fell away, and I remembered every word.

Later, after the last verse of "Silent Night" filled the sanctuary and the candles were snuffed out, my brother, sisters and I shed our costumes, excited to be going home. We darted around the church folks, made a beeline to our Ford station wagon and jumped into the back seat. Like every year before, we craned our necks, peering out the windows to catch a view of Santa and his sleigh. We were sure we caught a glimpse of red in the blue-black sky, certain it was Rudolph and his red nose.

As always, we sang Christmas carols all the way home. My older sister took some of the sincere, respectful words and added to them to make my little brother and me giggle even louder. We belted out off-key, "God rest ye merry gentleman, let nothing you dismay," followed with the word "hey," feet stomping, fists pumping up and down. Still gulping for air in between lyrics and laughs, we warbled through the next song, making sure to increase the volume with each repetition of "Oh tidings of comfort and joy, comfort and joy."

Our father must have had nerves of steel. He responded to the din by deliberately slowing the car to a crawl on the last excruciating leg of the ride home.

"Dad, no, drive faster," we roared. It seemed the louder we yelled, the slower he drove.

When we finally pulled into our driveway, we flung open the car doors. It was almost impossible to obey Mom and Dad's requirement for everybody to step out of the car before anyone could make a move toward the house. Only then was it okay to race across the lawn.

This year I had a secret. I had told only Santa, and no one else, about the gift I wanted the most. I wanted to see if Santa would come through, if he were as magical as everyone said. After all, I was nine years old and starting to get a little old for such things.

I made it to the front door first, yanked it open and stepped inside, only to freeze in amazement. All noise and bedlam stopped. Or maybe I just couldn't hear anything through my astonishment. As if they were in suspended animation, the family turned to watch my reaction. With no ability left to speak, I screamed in delight. For there it was, the gift I had so longed for, the one thing only Santa knew about: a full-length rowboat right smack in the middle of our living room.

Ecstatic, blinking back tears of joy I circled the boat, inspecting every inch. Then I stepped in, sat on the wooden seat, and raised one of the oars to paddle through the air. Eventually, I let my brother and sisters get in and have their turns. The night was a blur of us all ripping wrapping paper off gifts, laughing, hugging, and enjoying the evergreen smell of our hand-picked tree and the aroma of Mom's Christmas chili simmering on the stove. I can't even recall any other presents that night, just my shiny green rowboat with two beautiful wooden oars.

After practicing for only one day, I learned how to handle those oars. My parents made me promise to sit on the flotation cushion for safety, and then I was free. Out on the water without anybody nearby, I rowed in joyful liberty, traveling across our little lake, navigating the serpentine canals.

I explored it all, rowing after birds and turtles until they escaped my view, stopping often to step onto the shoreline to identify tracks in the damp sand from birds and small animals. The largemouth bass made beds in the lake bottom to lay eggs, usually at the spot just before the lake deepened into dark murkiness. I tried to picture what creatures and discoveries would remain on the lake's floor if all the water disappeared.

Sometimes, I would stop exploring, lie on the bottom of the boat and look up at the clouds, never knowing exactly where I would end up. Once, I dozed off until darts of cool drops peppered me from head to toe. The pungent air, laden with the heavy earthy mustiness of promised rain, made me scramble to my seat and head home, pulling hard on the oars to escape the ominous thunder growling close behind me.

In my amazing rowboat, I logged many miles on Little Lake Jackson. Over the years, I took family, friends and, eventually, an occasional boyfriend out on the lake to share the beauty of sunsets on the water.

That rowboat was the perfect combination for me: a newfound independence combined with a healthy dose of childlike amazement that Santa had provided the gift of my dreams. I never did find out how it got into the living room while we were at church. It doesn't really matter. Over the years, when I remember the rowboat in the living room, I choose to call it, simply, Santa's magic.

—Wendy Keppley—

41

Our Silly Gift

You can be childlike without being childish. A child
always wants to have fun. Ask yourself,
"Am I having fun?"
~Christopher Meloni

With all the dazzling, technology-based toys coming out every year, the pressure to get the latest — and most expensive — is never more evident than at Christmastime. Alas, our desire to give such gifts is rarely in line with our holiday budget, especially when our gift recipient list includes numerous nephews and nieces. I had to resist going into debt each year when I shopped as I imagined the happy faces on the kids as they unwrapped flying drones, iPhones or virtual-reality headsets.

My merry feeling always dimmed when I had to pass on these tempting choices to look for more affordable options. One year, my husband joined in the hunt. True to his fun-loving nature, he found these silly, screaming monkeys with stretchy bands in them. You could pull back on the tail and release the monkey to fly through the air as it let out a horrible screeching sound. He laughed as he shot one across the toy store toward our son.

"You can't be serious," I told him. "The kids are not going to want these. They're *older* now." It was a useless gift as far as I was concerned, and one that my sisters would hate me for giving their not-so-young kids. But my husband has a knack for knowing fun, so I relented.

Anyway, we could afford them. And if it seemed too cheap a gift, I would blame it on my famously cheap husband.

Our traditional Christmas morning brunch arrived, and after all the gifts had been opened, I sheepishly and non-ceremoniously handed out "Uncle Scott's silly gift." There was a brief moment of silence — and then suddenly all the kids began to laugh as they sent flying monkeys screeching across the room. True to my prediction, my sisters were not happy with the horrid racket.

"Are you kidding me, Lori? You're taking them back!"

My aged mother rolled her eyes and clamped both hands on her ears, saying, "Who got THOSE RIDICULOUS THINGS?"

But the kids. Oh, the kids. No matter their age, they scrambled around the room, ducking around corners, hiding behind the sofa, and then rising to attack each other with a floppy, stuffed mini-primate. The dads couldn't resist and they joined in, too.

Finally, even my mother and sisters couldn't help but laugh at the gleeful pandemonium. I looked at my husband and had to concede. "I can't believe it," I said. "Your choice is a hit."

He grinned. "I know fun."

To this day, the kids, who have kids of their own now, remember that screaming monkey blitz on Christmas.

When one of our nieces remarked that it was her favorite present at Christmas and declared it "Uncle Scott's silly gift," we realized we had begun a new tradition. So each year, the pressure is on to find a fun, whimsical, yet small and inexpensive gift. One year, they all got to have mock battles with mini "bugs." Another year, it was gooey "eggs" that splotched when thrown on the wall or table.

Last year, each one got a small, wind-up toy to race. I found a fun way to wrap them by winding colorful yarn around and around them. To unwrap, the kids had to unwind yards of yarn to get to the silly prize, and yarn balls rolled all over the place with each one trying to follow theirs. They're all adults now, but they look forward to their silly gift each year like eager little children. Even if it's just for a few precious moments, their inner child comes out to play.

And giving surely is a gift that returns to the giver because we look forward to finding a new and silly, little gift each year. Once upon a time, choosing pretty sweaters, comparing the pros and cons of electronic products, or resorting to gift cards made holiday shopping so perfunctory. But now Christmas gift shopping — thanks to my creative, fun-loving husband — is, well... fun again. As our budget grew, we added gift cards to the mix to help cover needs and wants, but the silly gift is still the foundation.

It is never more evident than at Christmas time that it truly is the thought that counts, and the best thoughts during the holidays bring child-like joy that lives on in fond memories. I try to remember that because as much as we need our inner child to come out to play, we also need our inner child to remind us that love and joy really don't cost much at all.

— Lori Phillips —

42

A Tiny Bit of the Desert

*We must find time to stop and thank the people
who make a difference in our lives.*
~John F. Kennedy

Our twenty-one-year-old son Darren was serving with the Army's 82nd Airborne Division when it was deployed to Saudi Arabia for Operation Desert Shield in August 1990. We learned through his letters that fighting was imminent, and the 82nd was prepared to go into Iraq sometime during the Christmas season

I had been sending Darren lots of letters, photos, and care packages since his deployment. As the holidays approached, his brothers and sister (and their spouses) also took part in the joy of giving — not only for their brother but for his fellow soldiers, as well.

We sent clothing that would be comfortable during the hot desert days, and attire that would also keep them warm during the surprisingly cool nights. The clothing gifts ranged from T-shirts and shorts to thermal underwear and hooded sweatshirts.

While the guys in the family picked out music tapes, paperback books, playing cards, a basketball, and other gifts to help the soldiers pass the time in the desert, we women spent hours in the kitchen several days a week baking cookies and a variety of delicious pastries. We also made holiday candies like divinity, caramels and fudge.

The younger children were not about to be left out. They wrote letters and drew pictures for Uncle Darren and his buddies. Their parents also let them pick out small gifts to include in our packages. It was an excellent way for them to share in the joy of giving, while it also helped to ease the pain of missing their uncle during the holidays.

Although we prayed that Desert Shield would not escalate into a ground war, we knew there was a strong probability it would. We began sending our Christmas care packages well before Thanksgiving to ensure that the troops could savor a touch of home throughout the holiday season.

Taking turns, we managed to send a parcel every couple of days, and the troops were tremendously appreciative. But I think we took as much (if not more) pleasure in preparing the packages as they did in receiving them.

Most gratifying were the times in which we gathered at the house to put together a parcel. With the aroma of freshly baked cookies lingering in the air, glowing flames leaping in the fireplace, and Christmas music playing in the background, we basked in the true spirit of the season as we joyfully wrapped each gift in vibrant holiday paper.

Working together as a family to support the soldiers warmed our hearts and eased our worry. What could have been a very sad and lonely holiday season became a special time of sharing.

Darren even managed to send us a gift, too — a miniature Tabasco sauce bottle saved from his MREs (meals ready to eat), washed and refilled with grains of sand from the Arabian Desert. He sent it with the following note:

Mom, as you can imagine, we have a very limited selection of gifts out here, so I'm hoping that this tiny bit of the desert will help you feel closer to my friends and me during the holidays. I love you all very much, Darren.

That small gift did make us feel closer to the troops and meant more to me than anything that could have been purchased at one of the world's finest malls. To this day, it serves as an ideal reminder that together we can get through the worst of times — especially during the holidays.

— Connie Kaseweter Pullen —

A Timeless Gift

We can only be said to be alive in those moments when our hearts are conscious of our treasures.
~Thornton Wilder

My sister and I each received a new calendar every Christmas. And even though we shared a bedroom and could have shared a calendar, too, we always got our own.

My sister is three years younger than me, and for many years she requested teddy bear calendars. One year, she made the jump to a *Beverly Hills, 90210* cast calendar. Another year, the cast of *Saved by the Bell* hung in our bedroom for a year.

My calendars always contained photos of beauty. Seashells. Sunsets. Flowers.

After I completed a school project about Paris, I requested a Paris calendar. For twelve months, I saw idyllic Paris — the majestic Eiffel Tower, the distinctive pyramid of the Louvre, the impressive Arc de Triomphe.

Fast-forward to the present. My husband of twenty years, Paul, and our eleven-year-old son, Ryan, have continued the calendar tradition. Unlike when I was a kid, I know exactly what the theme of my calendar will be — our family. Each year, the calendar's cover sports a photo of the three of us and the title "The Kennar Family."

We started this tradition back in 2008, the year our son was born.

I told my husband there was only one Christmas present I'd want every year for the next eighteen years — a family photo calendar.

And each year, he's delivered.

Each month of my calendar features a few photos taken in the same month of the year that just passed. (So the January 2019 page shows photos from January 2018.) These photos are a way for our family to revisit fun events (attending our first Los Angeles Sparks game, our yearly visit to the Aquarium of the Pacific, Crazy Hair Day at school) or to acknowledge just how much Ryan has grown in one year's time.

Christmas morning, Ryan sits close to the tree while still wearing his Super Mario pajamas, looks under the tree, and "delivers" the gifts. "This is Mommy's," he says as he hands me what we all know is the calendar.

In a sense, it is my calendar because I'll hang it in the kitchen and update the calendar as the year goes on, recording doctors' appointments, school events, and other special activities.

At the end of the year, the completed calendar will go on the bookshelf with every other photo calendar that's come before it. Our yearly photo calendar serves as a time capsule, in a way, of what our family was like then — what we looked like the year before and how we filled our days in the new year.

When I was a kid, unwrapping each new calendar gave me a sense of hope and promise for the year to come. The younger I was, the less there was to record in each date's box. "Social studies test," "half day," and "birthday party" were the extent of my obligations "back then," as my son would say, in the days when photo calendars didn't exist because digital photos didn't exist.

Times have changed. Now, unwrapping the new calendar brings me mixed emotions. I feel a sense of pride and joy when I look at our family and revisit our good times. But there is also a sense of sadness and nostalgia when I realize how big Ryan has gotten. Where did our little boy go?

As I flip through the pages, I don't know exactly what the year ahead will hold for us, except that they will be all about our family.

The photos from the prior year connect us to our treasured past, while those empty boxes hold the promise of new treasures — adventures to be pursued and memories to be created.

And that is the true gift.

— Wendy Kennar —

A Kitty, a Puppy, and a Pony

A person often meets his destiny
on the road he took to avoid it.
~Jean de La Fontaine

The Christmas season arrived, and as always, my mother asked, "What would you like for Christmas?"

"A kitty, a puppy, and a pony," I responded without hesitation. One could say I "placed my order."

My mom explained we didn't need another dog, as we already had one. Of course, I responded, "We do not have a puppy." She had no protest against the kitty, although she may have said something about the cost of vaccinations. As for the pony, it was a downright "no."

"Ponies are a lot of work," she said. "Not to mention they cost a small fortune."

A few days later, on a particularly cold December day, our friends called, begging us to take a kitten. Apparently, the mother had been killed. Once the kitten was in my mother's arms, she instantly gave in to those darling, green eyes hidden among black fur. He was cold and wet, and my mother's heart went out to him. She hand-fed him and tucked him inside her sweater until he was warm. Our friends named him Nicodemus, and there was no going back. I got my kitty.

A few weeks passed. Mom was coming home one evening when she spotted a stray mother dog and two puppies running in the road.

She got out and tried to catch them, but only managed to catch one puppy. When she got the puppy in the back of the van, it snarled and snapped. I think the puppy thought it was much larger than it was. At last, Mom came home and brought the puppy in the house. The puppy was very scared, shaking and barking aggressively. It was rather snappish, so after lots of consideration, we named it Gingersnap. And there was my puppy.

At this point, I suppose my mom became a little afraid of a pony showing up. As a precaution, she bought a small pony figurine to give me on Christmas morning.

It seemed like forever until Christmas arrived. Finally, it did. I raced downstairs alongside my siblings and peered out the window. To my dismay, there was no pony. When I opened my stocking, I found the small pony figurine. Filled with disappointment, I looked into my mother's eyes. "I wanted a real pony," I said. It seemed as though my mother didn't understand.

"I would get one if I could, but ponies are expensive and require a lot of work," my mother responded sensibly. My heart sank.

A few days after Christmas, Mom was talking to the insurance man. I bet they had a normal conversation discussing each other's Christmases. However, seemingly out of nowhere, the man said, "I had the strangest thing happen to me! This pony showed up in my back yard and won't leave. Do you want it?" My mother about died laughing. Then she firmly said "no" and immediately hung up the phone.

— Rachel Katherine —

45

Home for Christmas

I would maintain that thanks are the highest form
of thought, and that gratitude is happiness
doubled by wonder.
~Gilbert K. Chesterton

My husband and I were waiting for good news from the adoption agency. In November, we received an e-mail from our caseworker. A birth mom was interested in us. Could we meet with her? Oh, by the way, she was having twins.

Twins? Well, that was interesting — and terrifying, wonderful, and amazing. One was scary enough, but two? My husband barely needed to think about it — he was in. I was more apprehensive.

We arranged to meet with the birth mom the week of Thanksgiving at a local mall play area. She had a three-year-old son and needed him to be occupied so we could chat. In nervous excitement, my husband and I circled the play area, scoping out people we thought might fit the description. But at twenty minutes past our meeting time, no one was there. Had she taken one look at us and changed her mind?

She hadn't. She was just running late.

I remember seeing her for the first time and was struck by her hair. It was long and a beautiful strawberry blonde. She was hugely pregnant and had "the waddle." Exhausted didn't even cover how she looked. I imagine the combination of life circumstances, thirty-two weeks of pregnancy, a toddler and a weighty decision eventually took its toll.

Meeting a birth parent is a surreal experience. I wanted to make the best impression possible, but not come off too snobby. Be warm and funny, but not corny. Show her I'm not judging her, but she's more than welcome to judge me. Being an adoptive parent means laying it all out there.

Most of all, I wanted her to feel my respect and love. I didn't know this woman, but here she was with notebook pages of questions for us because she saw something special in us. She saw something that made it possible for her to choose me — for her to give her children that she carried under her heart to me.

Less than a week after that meeting, we got word that she did, in fact, choose us. The babies were due in mid-January, so we had time to get ready. I had planned to ransack after-Christmas sales for clothes, toys and the other things that babies need.

But it was twins, so what was I thinking? Just two weeks after our meeting, my husband and I were having a typical evening at home. We had both gotten in our treadmill time, had dinner and cleaned up. I was in the living room, reading in front of the tree, while my husband was in his office working on his doctoral dissertation. Suddenly, my cell phone rang. It was the birth mom.

She explained how she hadn't been feeling well, and her doctor sent her to the emergency room. The babies were coming tonight. Could we please come to the hospital so we could be there when they were born?

Explaining that moment to people never quite drives home the point. My heart raced and stopped at the same time. I was shaking. And I had to go tell my husband.

I walked down the stairs and into his office. "You're going to be a daddy tonight," I told him. That sentence didn't sink in right away. "C'mon! We have to go to the hospital now!"

I wasn't prepared. I had planned to pack a bag for this: my camera, a gift for the birth mom, something for the twins, snacks. That never happened. Instead, we jumped in the car and drove as fast as we could without being pulled over. I remember as I held the steering wheel, my hands went cold from nerves. A funny thought struck me then, and looking back, I think it was my first experience with mom guilt. Just that day, I had dropped our Christmas cards in the mail, signed from my husband and me. If only hindsight was 20/20.

Once we got there, things happened very quickly. We were given special suits to wear in the operating room and told to wait in the hallway. Standing there staring at the OR sign, reality began to sink in. Also, we didn't have a name for one of the kids. Going into it, we knew that we were going to be parents to a boy and a girl. Our girl had a name. Our boy did not. We had it narrowed to two names, but we were still in negotiations. The only thing our birth mom had asked of us was that the twins have names. No "Baby A" and "Baby B."

The pressure was on.

In the moment, my husband said I could choose, and either name we had was fine with him. Crisis averted.

The OR was a blur for the C-section. Everyone was excited and happy, but I was in disbelief. This wasn't really happening.

Then, suddenly, they were there.

We spent the next week bouncing between our birth mom's room and the special-care nursery. She talked, and I listened. I think she really wanted us to know as much about her as possible, sharing stories about her family and her upbringing.

But then the time came for her to go home.

I'd never felt more torn in my life. On one hand, there was a mother leaving her babies in my care. Trusting me with their lives. Then there was the reality that when she left, it really was all me. I was the mom.

The single strongest, most impressive thing I've ever seen was her walking out the door and getting in the car. She hugged my husband and me and told us how proud she was of us. If she cried, she held off until she was in the car. Fortitude, courage and confidence sum her up. She wasn't relieved to be leaving her children behind, but rather confident in her choice.

Shell-shocked, we went back to the nursery to hold the kids.

They stayed in the hospital for a week, but we got to take them home on December 20th — our little Christmas gifts that made our family complete.

— Rebecca Calappi —

46

My Best Ever Christmas Present

Each day of our lives we make deposits
in the memory banks of our children.
~Charles R. Swindoll

H e was a poor farmer who had joined the Royal Canadian Air Force to fight in World War I. I was only one when he left to go overseas. He was like a stranger to us upon his return and seemed to favour our sister, who was born just after he reached England.

Although his release from the RCAF provided enough money to pay for his small farm, Dad had to work to keep us fed and clothed. He became a block-man mechanic for the Canadian Co-operative Implements Limited and had to drive twenty-five miles to work each weekday. That meant leaving at seven in the morning and getting home around seven at night. He was so tired that he went to bed a couple of hours after supper. On his days off, he often repaired machinery for nearby farmers, so we didn't get to see him for very long.

Our father-son relationship was hindered by our mother's method of discipline. She would scold us and say, "Your father will deal with you when he gets home." Poor Dad became "the strap man," and we were afraid of him. It was difficult for us to feel that he cared for us boys at all.

That ended for me one Christmas when I received a gift from him. It was not some expensive toy, but was more precious to me than gold. It was paid for by something money couldn't buy — Dad's time! The gift was a big, homemade sled. He must have spent hours and hours making it. He used hardwood boards from the heavy boxes that contained the parts for the machinery that he assembled. He used the power tools at his workplace to cut out the runners and other parts piece by piece. Store-bought sleds usually had narrow metal strips on the bottom of the runners to help them slide through the snow. Dad used the metal bands that held the hardwood boxes together. He then sanded the complete sled and painted it machinery red.

When Dad gave me that sled, I cried. He thought I was disappointed until I told him how proud I was that he had made it just for me. I thanked him for the gift and all the hours he had put into making it. I told him that my tears were of joy.

Within a few days, the real test came for my Christmas sleigh. A bunch of us guys went out to Bulldog Hill to go sledding. The ones with their fancy toboggans and sleighs with steel runners looked at my sled and laughed. They made fun of Dad's work. That made me so mad that I bet them I would go farther than any of them.

I was tired from dragging my heavy Christmas gift the two miles to the hill, but I found enough energy to take a good run, pushing the sleigh before jumping on. To my great joy and the amazement of all the others, my homemade missile streaked down the hill and into the bushes well past the end of the hill. Not one of the others came even close to the point where I had ended my slide. I made a number of other runs with the same result before freezing feet forced us to return home.

I told Dad how well his sled preformed and how proud I was of him for making it. A special bond occurred between us because of that Christmas gift. It became my working partner, carrying milk home when I skied to a farm out of town, carrying groceries from the store, and bringing loads of wood to the house from the woodpile.

When I left home, I gave my special Christmas gift, along with many stories about it, to my younger brother. To this very day, it remains in my memory as my best ever Christmas present!

—Jim Jenkins—

Chapter 6

Getting Creative

47

Chicken Soup for the Soul

A Circus Christmas

*Memories of childhood were the dreams
that stayed with you after you woke.*
~Julian Barnes, England, England

One Christmas Eve, when I was ten years old, my family and I were riding on a train through the open stretches of Colorado. Pressing my face to the window, I watched as the train carried us past miles of farmland and rocky, wide-open spaces. The snow outside, deep in shadow from the setting sun, blanketed the scenery.

Some children might have been bored after a day-and-a-half on a train with nothing to see out the window but the occasional small town. However, I wasn't on an ordinary train. I was on a train belonging to The Greatest Show on Earth: the Ringling Bros. and Barnum & Bailey Circus.

My mother and father were performers in the show. Mom was an aerialist, and Dad was a clown. Occasionally, I helped out by doing small jobs like selling peanuts or cleaning props. And although the train was filled with people from many different countries, we were a close-knit family of travelers that cold Christmas Eve. Among those on the train were trapeze artists, sword swallowers, tightrope walkers, clowns, acrobats, musicians, and even the people who got shot out of a cannon!

As the train gently rocked from side to side and the click-clack of the wheels hummed throughout the cars, I got up and explored.

Even at my age, I couldn't help but notice that many of the performers were quiet and a bit glum—not as lively as they usually were. They were talking about how we would be on the train for another day, and how no one wanted to let Christmas go by without observing the holiday. Then, as they began to talk about what they could do to celebrate Christmas, their spirits began to pick up. As the idea of finding a way to have Christmas on the train spread, the performers got more animated. There were a dozen or so of us kids on the train, and the adults were especially intent on giving us a fun Christmas.

The train would stop occasionally at a small town to take on a few supplies and such. At one of the stops, someone got off and found a small tree. Some of the grownups got candy, comic books, and other small gifts at the station gift shop.

The tree, which was about five feet tall, was set up in a large pot that was packed with dirt and held in place with guidelines that the tightrope walker used to secure the wire he walked on. Once the tree was up, everyone began thinking about how it could be decorated. No one had traditional tree ornaments, so everyone came up with creative ideas. They used whatever they could find. Someone took the silver paper from their gum wrappers and made little silver bells; jawbreakers were used for bulbs and tied to the tree with loose threads from the costumes; and ribbons took the place of tinsel. There was excitement in the air.

Someone found a few small candles and, making sure they were not too close to the tree, we placed them around the base.

One of the trapeze artists found enough tin foil to make a small silver star for the top of the tree. Meanwhile, a portly clown borrowed a red jumper with a hood and donned it while somebody else raided the first-aid kit and got a handful of cotton to make a beard. Together, they created a circus Santa Claus to pass out the gifts to the kids.

A juggler gave me a set of three rubber balls and a card that was good for juggling lessons. I also received a few candy bars which, to tell the truth, excited me more than the possibility of learning to juggle.

Several of the musicians went to the baggage car and got their instruments, and we sang "Silent Night" and "O Come, All Ye Faithful."

Then people from other countries sang carols in different languages: Polish, German, Spanish, and so on. Outside, the dark landscape no longer seemed cold and bleak, but rather like we were wrapped in a secure blanket of freshly fallen snow.

We kids ate our candy and curled up in the seats, enveloped in the feelings of good cheer and friendship that filled the train. It was a beautiful coming together of diverse people. And as the circus Christmas train wound its way through the snowy plains and mountains, we kids were gently rocked to sleep.

A year later, my family left the circus, settled in Los Angeles and became more traditional in our Christmas celebrations. But we would always hand-make one ornament for the tree to remind us of that Christmas on the train.

To this day, whenever I have a tree of my own or go to someone's house during the season, I continue that tradition and create an ornament from whatever I have on hand. (Last year, I made miniature Christmas cards that could be hung on a tree.) In this way, I keep that long-ago memory alive — how people from many different lands and cultures all came together to celebrate the true spirit of Christmas.

P.S. I did eventually take those juggling lessons and can still juggle to this day.

— Michael D. Nye —

48

Flyby Christmas

Time spent with family is worth every second.
~Author Unknown

My husband and I were empty nesters living in Sioux Falls, South Dakota. Two of our children were in Minnesota. Our youngest, Shana, was going to graduate school in St. Paul, and our oldest, Ryan, was living with his young family in a Minneapolis suburb. Our middle child, Michael, was teaching in Las Vegas. Everyone had to come from far away to gather in our hometown for Christmas.

When you have grown children who lead separate lives you learn to graciously accept whatever quality time you get with them. One particular Christmas, we had only a two-day window in which to revel. Holiday cheer needed to start Saturday afternoon and end forty-eight hours later. Shana was leaving on a trip, and Ryan's trio was getting together with his wife's family. Only Michael had the luxury of staying with us for a full week.

Everyone made it at the appointed hour except for Michael, who was grounded by a snowstorm at the Denver International Airport.

"It's pretty bad here," Michael reported over the phone. "I'm stuck overnight at least."

"We'll save your king crab legs so you can eat them when you get here," I said. "Dad and I will make sure your gifts stay under the tree until you arrive. Keep us posted."

Saturday night came and went. On Sunday, after a brunch of egg bake and cinnamon rolls, we filled the day playing newly opened board games and watching Christmas movies. That evening, Michael called to tell us he would be spending one more night in Denver, and then arrive at Sioux Falls Regional Airport at noon the next day.

"It will be great when you finally get here," I told him, keeping the trepidation out of my voice. My mind was doing mental math about how much of the forty-eight hours we would have left if the plane arrived on time. Not many! By my calculations, we would only be together for one hour. I decided then and there we would have Christmas at the airport.

The next morning, I announced my decision. There was grumbling and comments like, "You've got to be kidding!" I muddied the waters by dictating that I was bringing a Christmas CD and decorated sugar cookies — and I was going to wear a Santa hat!

Shana and Ryan packed their cars since they would be driving to their homes straight from the airport. I put the CD player and food along with the Christmas gifts in our car, and we caravanned to the terminal.

Michael's plane was on time. We hurried to find an empty booth in the airport restaurant. I turned on the CD player and holiday tunes quickly filled our little corner of the world. We ate our food and opened our gifts. We posed in front of a decorated Christmas tree in the airport lobby, with me standing in the middle and still wearing the Santa hat. A traveler lugging suitcases walked by, and we asked him to take our picture. Then Shana and Ryan's group started their journey home, all festivities over.

When I finally got the photo developed, it revealed four people anxious to get on their way; one harried traveler in shorts and flip-flops; one dad who had graciously supported his wife's wishes; and, because her family was finally all together, one beaming momma! I realized what thousands of mothers over centuries past have kept in their hearts: grab every precious family minute you can.

— Jeanne Green —

Double the Gift

How beautiful a day can be when kindness touches it!
~George Elliston

I always try to find something different and unusual when giving a gift, but it's often a real challenge to do that for extended family members. But one year, the decision was made for me.

"I want *Chicken Soup for the Soul: Random Acts of Kindness*," my niece Linda declared. I hadn't even asked what she or my other niece, Valerie, wanted. I shouldn't have been surprised because my family loves the *Chicken Soup for the Soul* books, especially when one of my stories is included, and Val had already asked me earlier about getting a copy.

With that decided, I purchased decorative, battery-operated micro-lights to make their gifts a bit more unusual. And then the ultimate gift idea hit me like a bolt of lightning — add a small gift card for each of them to perform a random act of kindness of their own! I knew it was the perfect complement to the book, and they would love the opportunity to do something special.

About a week after receiving their gifts, I heard from them both. Val had known immediately what she would do with her gift card, something she had done many times.

People in need are often standing by a highway off-ramp that she passes on her way to work. This time, a poor man was holding a sign that said, "Please help." She quickly pulled to the side of the road and rolled down the window. "I'm afraid I can't give you cash, but here is a Walmart gift card. Maybe you can find something there to help you." After a quick thanks from the man, she drove off with a smile on her face — just like the one she created on her grateful recipient.

The next day, I heard Linda's excited voice on the phone. "You won't believe this, Vicki, but I just had the greatest experience! I was at Walmart, and I heard an elderly woman on the other side of the aisle speaking to a clerk. She asked if there was anything cheaper because she was short four dollars. When I heard the clerk say, 'I'm sorry, no,' I popped around the corner and offered the gift card. The woman was so excited and surprised that she kept thanking me over and over!"

After relating the story, Linda said, "It was so much fun, and it just made my heart feel good. I loved it so much that I want to buy more gift cards to keep just for such moments."

I wasn't at all surprised that both Linda and Val enjoyed performing their random acts of kindness, or that they wanted to continue giving gift cards in the future. What was surprising, though, was that a simple five-dollar gift card could bring such happiness to both the giver and the receiver.

And I was happy, too. A *Chicken Soup for the Soul* book, a microlight, and a gift card to give away — it was double the gift!

— Vicki L. Julian —

Christmas Racing

*Christmas is the season of joy, of holiday greetings
exchanged, of gift-giving, and of families united.*
~Norman Vincent Peale

"Oh, ho, ho! I got a racecar! Y'all don't stand a chance!" I exclaimed. I nudged my husband. "What did you get?"

"That's not a racecar; it's a bumper car," my sister pointed out. "They are notoriously bad at moving around."

"I got a pink robot," my husband showed me, "so I'm pretty sure I'm going to win."

"You can't win your first race. You have to work your way up to that," my dad said.

"Otherwise, they'll all hold it against you," my brother-in-law added. He had won the race his first Christmas with the family and was still getting grief for that.

We waited for everyone else to find out what Santa had brought. My sister received an orange alligator with light blue scales on its back. We had a brief family argument about whether it was an alligator or a crocodile, but relied on the snout to figure it out. My mom pulled a blue hedgehog out of her stocking. My dad showed off his yellow hedgehog, which was exactly like Mom's except for the color. Finally, my brother-in-law pulled the silliest wind-up toy from his stocking.

"It's a..." He tilted his head and laughed.

"Is it a flower?" I asked.

His toy had two green feet, a round brown head and two ridiculous white ears emerging from the top.

"I think it's a bug," my mom answered. We shrugged and moved toward the kitchen. My dad started a new pot of coffee so that we could all get refills.

"How are we going to do the race this year?" I asked. Our family had grown, and I didn't think six adults could quite fit into the opening where our living room met the kitchen.

"We could work in heats," my husband suggested.

"Why don't we just start somewhere else?" my sister said, moving into the kitchen. "We would all fit over here!"

For as long as I could remember, we'd received two items in our stockings along with various other gifts from Santa. One was an orange, and the second was a wind-up toy. Once we had finished exploring the gifts Santa brought, we'd take our wind-up toys to the kitchen and start The Christmas Race.

That day we lined up, and wound our toys as far as they would go. "Everyone ready?" my mom asked. We set the toys down on the starting line and waited.

"Go!" she said, and the room filled with the scratchy buzz of wind-up toys moving along the tile floor. My bumper car and my husband's robot headed in the same direction until my bumper car bumped the robot off course.

My parents laughed at their hedgehogs, which both looked promising until they began turning in circles.

My bumper car was ahead of the pack with only my sister's alligator behind it. However, while my bumper car was wheeling along, the alligator was moving at a slow crawl. I cheered on the bumper car as we heard the wind-up toys slowly lose steam. They began to slow down and creep to a stop.

"Yes!" I shouted. "I won!"

"Your bumper car knocked mine into the island!" My husband laughed. "I could have won!"

"It was just doing what it does best. Your robot should have known better than to get into a bumping fight with a bumper car!" I picked up my wind-up car and set it on the counter to take a picture with my phone. The race was over, but we continued talking about the way it progressed. We took some time to laugh over my brother-in-law's jumping bug, which never made it past the starting line. Mom and Dad gave each other a kiss, talking about how their hedgehogs just wanted to be together. We all reminisced about the time that Dad had a robot whose arm fell off in the middle of the race. The toys were put in a basket with all the old wind-up toys, and my sister and I regaled our husbands with stories of past races.

Christmas mornings were always more magical because of those wind-up toys. We all became kids again. There were always plenty more gifts to be shared after our breakfast of ham and grits, but my wind-up toy was always my favorite.

—Savannah Flowers—

Welcome to Whoville

Do what you can, with what you have, where you are.
~Theodore Roosevelt

"I t's beginning to look a lot like Christmas…" Every year during the Christmas season at the Federal Correctional Institution in Seagoville, Texas, the compound is changed into a Christmas spectacular, with an array of decorations among the seven different units. Each unit is entered into a decorating contest to compete for the prize of a new-release movie and popcorn in the auditorium. Watching a new-release movie and receiving "free" popcorn is a very big deal in prison, so most units go all out in trying to win the award.

This year, my unit decided to do the theme from the movie *How the Grinch Stole Christmas!* My unit has 150 two-man rooms, a number of six-to-twelve-man rooms, two levels, two sides, and sleeps 375 inmates. It is the largest unit on the compound. In other words, a lot of space needs to be filled with decorations. But we also have many more inmates to help out with decorating. The rules stipulate that any material found on the compound can be used for decorating, except wood, plastic, and any other dangerous or hazardous material. Basically, the only materials we are allowed to use are paper, cardboard, soda cans, and paint (which the unit counselor can buy, if asked).

With the artistry and creative minds that are on this compound, just a few supplies and materials are all one needs to make a Christmas spectacular. And let me tell you, it was more than just a Christmas spectacular in my unit—it was a Christmas production! Here is a list of some of the decorations and events that happened in my unit:

- Each room was turned into a Whoville home, with both a cardboard mailbox and a porch light that could light up, using a handheld commissary reading light.
- Street signs and "Welcome to Whoville" entryways
- Multiple Christmas murals painted on the walls
- A twenty-foot-tall Christmas tree made out of 2,000 soda cans, with shredded paper and presents underneath it
- A cardboard fireplace protruding from the wall
- A sixteen-person choir
- Shredded paper falling from the second floor to make it look like it was snowing
- Giant 3D snowflakes hung across the balcony
- A Grinch lair
- An inmate emulating Cindy Lou Who's great-grandson, giving a tour while telling a story to the judges
- Colored paper covering the walls
- A twenty-foot-tall, blow-up snowman made out of paper (I'm still not sure how they were able to blow it up)

After a month of planning, organizing and decorating, my unit was ready for the show-and-tell and to be judged by the "bigwigs" of the compound. With snow gently falling from our balcony, Cindy Lou Who's great grandson gave the tour and told a story while the choir sang in the background. It was well rehearsed. It took about fifteen minutes from start to finish with a lot of *oohing* and *aahing* from the judges. Needless to say, they were all very impressed and said it was the best overall showing in all the years of the decorating contest. It was quite the scene to see.

We earned first-place honors this year. And, yes, this was the highlight of my Christmas. No presents or visits from any family and friends, but still a good time with inmates who have become friends and family. Together, we made this Christmas a positive experience.

—Craig Perino—

52

Dollhouse

If you carry your childhood with you,
you never become older.
~Tom Stoppard

I grew up in a family of modest means. My mom worked as a secretary, and my dad worked in a factory. I stayed with my grandma while they worked. I loved spending the days with Grandma. She made everything fun. She was on an even tighter budget than my family, so she didn't spend much money on toys. She made them instead. Grandma was incredibly creative and spent hours making my toys.

I had a passion for dollhouses. Grandma made dollhouses for me from cardboard boxes. She used shoeboxes, laundry-soap boxes, cereal boxes, and canning jar boxes. The canning jar boxes were the best. They had dividers, which provided many rooms. One average-size canning jar box became a twelve-room mansion for me. Grandma decorated my cardboard dollhouses with aluminum foil, wrapping paper, magazine pages, and whatever she had lying around the house.

I played for countless hours with my cardboard homes. A tiny, rubber, posable doll and plastic baby from the dollar store usually lived in my temporary homes. Sometimes, Grandma made paper dolls and paper clothes for them. They were the perfect size to live in my cardboard mansions, and very special because Grandma drew happy faces on them for me. I didn't realize that other little girls had Barbie Dream Houses. I thought everyone had cardboard dollhouses.

One day, my uncle came to visit while I was at Grandma's. He saw me playing with my cardboard dollhouse and asked, "What are you doing with that box?"

"It's a dollhouse. See the windows?" I said, pointing to the aluminum-foil windows Grandma had taped to the side of the box.

"I see. Do you play with this dollhouse a lot?" he asked.

"Yes. When it wears out, Grandma will make me another one," I answered proudly.

My uncle turned to my grandma and asked, "Why doesn't she have a real dollhouse?"

Grandma replied, "The boxes don't cost anything. Dollhouses are expensive. Have you ever looked at them in the store? Besides, she doesn't need one. She has a great imagination. She's just as happy with a box."

They moved on to other topics of conversation that didn't interest me as a four-year-old, so I went back to playing. My uncle didn't stay very long, and I forgot about the entire conversation.

The days rolled into months, and it was soon Christmas. My family happily gathered at Grandma's house to feast and open presents. Everyone was all decked out in their Sunday best. I was wearing my red-velvet dress with the tiny, silk rose on the front and my shiny, black patent-leather shoes. I was only allowed to wear those things for special occasions. My mom tied a dishtowel around my neck to make sure I didn't spill anything on it.

We opened presents once our Christmas dinner was eaten and the kitchen cleaned. I opened presents from Grandma and my cousins, but noticed that my aunt and uncle hadn't given me a package. My mom always told me not to bring attention to those types of things, so I kept quiet. Toward the end of our celebration, my uncle announced there was one more gift.

He went into Grandma's spare bedroom and brought out an enormous box. It was big enough for Grandma to make into a dollhouse, racecar, or pirate ship. I was hoping that whoever got the present would give us the box when he gently set it down in front of me.

"I made this for you," he said as he stood back to watch me open it.

I tore into the package like a wild animal. He had to help me with the tape on the box, but then I was all over it. I opened the flaps to reveal a wooden dollhouse! The outside of the house was painted white, and the roof was forest green. It even had wood paneling on the walls. The house was two stories and had four rooms. The bottom story featured orange floral flooring, and the top featured pink floral flooring. Two white doors made up the front of the house and opened to reveal all of the rooms. I was beside myself looking for my little, rubber doll and plastic baby, so I could play with my new house right away.

"Wait," my aunt said, "I think you missed something."

In the bottom of the giant box was a shoebox filled with plastic doll furniture. There were little yellow beds, a lamp, a kitchen table with chairs, a pink couch, and a TV. There was even a complete rubber family with a mom, dad, and little girl. I had the best time with that dollhouse.

I took the dollhouse home with me, so I still played with cardboard dollhouses at Grandma's. The giant box didn't go to waste. Grandma used it to make a fire truck for me. She covered the sides with red wrapping paper, glued on paper plates colored black for tires, and gave me a red plastic fire chief's hat. My fire truck saw lots of action before the sides collapsed.

It has been over forty years since that Christmas. Grandma has been gone for over thirty-five years, and we long ago stopped celebrating Christmas with my aunt, uncle, and cousins. I've grown up and have grandchildren of my own now.

That old dollhouse has been through a lot. The doors are missing. The paint is chipped. The roof needs to be glued at the peak. The furniture was lost years ago. However, I keep my dollhouse in a place of honor in my study where I create my best art. The four spacious rooms that once housed my little, rubber family now hold other treasures that I have picked up along the journey of my life.

Starting out life by using my imagination taught me the importance of creativity. I've always been able to entertain myself due to Grandma teaching me how to pretend and make up my own stories. She taught me to be happy with what I have, and not spend my time wishing for other things. Someday, I will teach my granddaughter how to create a happy, little home with nothing but a cardboard box and her imagination. I may even make her some paper dolls with happy faces.

—Margarite R. Stever—

53

ThanksChristGivingMas

I don't think quantity time is as special
as quality time with your family.
~Reba McEntire

Ted and I watched our daughter Elizabeth get married in Ogunquit, Maine over Memorial Day weekend, and then we flew back to Ohio while the young marrieds went home to New York City. When the winter holidays rolled around that year, Vince and Elizabeth decided to spend Thanksgiving with Vince's family in Massachusetts and Christmas at our home in Ohio. It was a beautiful Christmas, and we had quite a bit of fun. Vince got to experience our family traditions, including playing board games on Christmas Eve attired in new Christmas pajamas.

We laughed, baked, ate and ate some more. We also bundled up to take a walk through the neighborhood and look at the Christmas lights. Christmas morning brought an array of gifts under the tree while an egg casserole cooked in the Crock-Pot over the wee hours, leaving a wonderful aroma throughout the house. When I talked to Elizabeth after they returned to New York, she told me how thankful Vince was for being with us. Ours had been the first Christmas spent away from his family, and he so much appreciated the warmth and traditions that were shared. After all, Vince is now part of both families, as is Elizabeth.

The next year, the tables were flipped, and Vince and Elizabeth were going to spend Christmas in Massachusetts and Thanksgiving in

Ohio. In October, I was chatting with Elizabeth on our usual weekend call. Elizabeth said, "Wouldn't it be fun to celebrate both Thanksgiving and Christmas while we are home?" I'm not sure if she actually heard the thoughts flying around in my head... *I have less than a month to plan, bake, cook, decorate, shop, wrap and clean!* I wasn't quite sure how we were going to do both holidays in one chaotic week, but my reply was, "Sure! Why not?" The newly dubbed ThanksChristGivingMas holiday was born.

Immediately, I began online shopping from wish lists that I asked Elizabeth and Vince to prepare. Packages were arriving nearly daily, and I tried to wrap the gifts as they came in so as not to get behind. I wrote a grocery list for the feast, and we picked up any nonperishable items with our typical grocery shopping. Ted did much of the cleaning while I was at work. After a couple of weeks, I found I was enjoying the preparations for the ThanksChristGivingMas season!

Vince and Elizabeth were scheduled to arrive the Sunday before Thanksgiving. Ted and I put up the Christmas tree in the living room with lights and beads as usual, but this year the angel on top was replaced with a large and incredibly ugly papier-mâché turkey. Ted had purchased the decoration years prior, and it had become a Thanksgiving tradition. Small pilgrim decorations were also hung on the tree. We had our typical Thanksgiving dinner on — well, Thanksgiving.

On Friday, the next day of ThanksChristGivingMas, we did the rest of the decorating. I gave Vince a Disney Christmas tree hat, Elizabeth wore a Santa hat, Ted wore a Grinch hat, and I wore a reindeer mask made by Elizabeth when she was quite young. The Christmas Village went up in the family room, and the actual ornaments and angel replaced the turkey and pilgrims on the tree. Vince and Elizabeth arranged our nativity and our decorative scene of the entire cast of Rudolph the Red-Nosed Reindeer characters. As we decorated outdoors, we said "Merry Christmas" to our neighbors!

That evening became Christmas Eve, and outfitted in new Christmas pajamas, we played *Life*. I could not believe that Vince had never experienced this game, and we laughed continuously. Vince ended up being the big winner to boot!

Saturday morning, the house was filled with the breakfast casserole aroma as we woke to see what Santa had brought. It was so nice that he delivered early for our special ThanksChristGivingMas holiday! The gifts were opened and hugs given all around. Vince, Elizabeth and I all have December birthdays, so we went ahead and threw in those as part of the celebration.

I must admit, I wasn't sure how we would possibly pull off our combination holiday, but it could not have gone better. Everyone had so much fun, and we were immediately filled with the warmth and spirit of the season. Now I look forward to celebrating our new combination holiday in November — every other year.

— Lil Blosfield —

The Smorgasbord

Your children get only one childhood.
Make it memorable.
~Regina Brett

I grew up in a home with very few holiday traditions. I can vaguely recall the smell of corned beef and cabbage wafting through my grandmother's home on St. Patrick's Day. Thanksgiving and Christmas dinners were a more formal affair during my grandmother's reign as the matriarch of our family.

When I started my own family, I really didn't know where to begin with establishing holiday traditions. My husband's family didn't have many traditions either. We attempted to come up with some ideas, but they were always thwarted by the various family commitments that filled our holiday calendars.

Finally, inspiration struck. We realized that the only holiday that was unclaimed by either of our families was New Year's Eve. My husband and I were never ones for going out to parties, even before we had children. We decided that New Year's Eve would be ours. We would always stay home and have a big celebration. This would be our children's tradition.

Throughout the year, we are pretty healthy eaters. Dessert is a special treat, as is eating take-out. We decided that on New Year's Eve, all rules would go out the window. This would be a night of junk food, sweet treats, favorite appetizers, soda, and whatever our hearts desired.

Seventeen years later, we have yet to miss a single year of this tradition. The menu has evolved as our daughters have begun to make requests.

Thanks to Facebook, we have even begun documenting our annual spread. It is our most commented-on post each year, with friends writing that they look forward to our annual New Year's Eve smorgasbord post. They are curious to see what is on the menu and to live vicariously through us.

This made us realize that we were being selfish keeping this bounty of goodness all to ourselves. We began extending invitations to our friends and family to join us if they were looking for a New Year's Eve alternative. Besides the food, we play board games and watch silly movies. One year, we ordered colored powder (used for Color Run races) for a color-bomb war in the front yard. We invited the neighborhood kids to join us. We've also shared our food with our neighbors while shooting off fireworks.

It's funny to us now that something we struggled to create for our family would be of such interest to others. I love to look back at our photos and read through the various comments. We also started posting before-and-after photos, which are now called The Smorgasbord and The Aftermath. It allows me to bring out some of my favorite appetizer recipes and indulge in my own childhood favorites.

Our New Year's Eve has grown into an honored community tradition—although, occasionally, one of my kids will ask, "Can we also have a salad this year?"

—Gena B. McCown—

The Repair Shop

*It is not the magnitude of our actions but the amount
of love that is put into them that matters.*

~Mother Teresa

othing compares to Christmas. It is the best holiday ever. As
a young child, I loved the stories about flying reindeer, Jack
Frost nipping at your nose, and the baby Jesus wrapped
in swaddling clothes. I didn't understand how all these
holiday images fit together. Still, one thing seemed clear — a special
feeling or spirit prevailed during Christmas. My parents would sit
closer together on the sofa, whispering secrets and laughing. Nita and
I would put aside our sibling rivalry for a few weeks. Even our dog,
normally quiet and reserved, would prance around the yard, barking
and offering a playful growl or two.

Giving and receiving Christmas gifts were the main events. I guess
it's that way with most families. Both practices had their advantages
and intrigue. For me, the receiving aspect held a higher priority. Santa
dropped off one present per child at our home, occasionally two. All
other gifts had to come from our parents, family, or friends. I think
Santa also filled the stockings we hung from the fireplace mantel. In
the morning, our socks contained chocolate bars, oranges, assorted
nuts, and other handy items we needed for school.

On Christmas Eve, we put out a plate of homemade cookies for
Santa on the fireplace mantel, usually chocolate-chip or gingerbread
ones that Mom helped us bake, and a glass of skim milk. He never

ate the whole cookie, just took a bite of each one and a sip or two of milk. With a ton of deliveries to finish before morning, he must have been in a hurry. One year, I put out a few carrot slices and some peanut butter on celery, but those were left untouched. I got the point; next year, we went back to cookies.

Santa's gifts were always nice, but not really a surprise. My sister and I had already talked to him or one of his helpers at the Montrose Mall or written him a letter a few weeks earlier. Sometimes, we did both, so Santa knew about our wish list. And he was pretty good at remembering what we talked about because we usually received at least one of the things we mentioned. Even so, I liked the gifts my parents gave better. They seemed more personal. Parental presents were joint gifts, addressed from both of them, but I knew the difference. Moms usually gave socks, underwear, and knitted slippers. Dads, on the other hand, understood what little boys wanted most. Therefore, if I received a baseball glove, ten-speed bicycle, or Radio Flyer wagon, it probably came from Dad.

The only thing I disliked about the holiday was my father's disappearance on Christmas Eve. He always left right after dinner and stayed out most of the evening. Of course, being a child, I went to bed early, so that may have affected my perception of time. Nevertheless, I would not see him again until Christmas Day. In the morning, he had difficulty waking up. He kept yawning, too. His eyes looked tired and bloodshot. If I glanced into my parents' bedroom, I could see that Dad had not slept on his side of the bed. He must have been out all night doing something. But what?

Then one Christmas Eve, out of concern, I asked Mom the dreaded question, "Why does Dad leave every Christmas Eve, and where does he go that's so important?"

I realized my father, a Los Angeles County firefighter, might leave unexpectedly if the firehouse captain asked him to cover a shift or help with an emergency. However, if that were the case, Dad would be wearing his uniform, not his regular clothing. Mom only shrugged her shoulders and smiled at my concerns. She never seemed to worry about his untimely departures; she just kissed him goodbye as if everything were fine.

Years later, after cancer took Dad's life prematurely, Mom explained the reason for his mysterious absences. "Your father would drive downtown to Montrose for some last-minute Christmas shopping. He would walk through the stores looking for broken items — things he could repaint, repair, or refurbish. Before the days of full refunds and instant in-store credits, most shop owners wanted to offset their losses by selling worn-out demos, dismembered toys, and other defective products. Your dad, always a good negotiator, whittled the prices down to almost nothing. Money was tight in those days, so buying expensive new gifts was not an option for us.

"When he got back home, he'd sneak past your bedroom and head for his workshop in the garage with an armload of bargains. If necessary, your father would stay up all night to repair the damage and restore them. The Christmas presents from us — your new bicycle, wagon, train, baseball glove, and most everything else — were broken items your dad had fixed."

Every Christmas Eve, I follow my father's example and shop the stores for damaged products to refurbish as gifts. It makes Christmas more meaningful. In fact, it reminds me of the baby born in Bethlehem on that very first Christmas. He grew up to be a repairer too, just like my dad. The only difference — He fixes broken lives and repairs wounded souls. No doubt, those gifts are the best ones of all.

— Charles Earl Harrel —

Chapter 7

Through the Eyes of a Child

Double Boiler Bliss

No matter our age, everyone in our household knows
that cooking and eating together is where the fun is.
~Corky Pollan

W hen I was a child, the first hint of the holiday season was not frost on the pumpkin or ice on the driveway — because we lived in Anaheim, California. And it wasn't the rolls of wrapping paper tucked furtively behind the laundry room door or the mysterious stapled bags stashed in the back of the linen closet.

The first sign of the Christmas season was the clanking of a double boiler. I remember walking through the door after school with my sister Mari and stopping abruptly, recognizing the unmistakable knocking of a pot in boiling water. And then — Eureka! — the faint, sweet smell of dark chocolate drifting through the air. This could only mean one thing — our grandmother Nana's chocolate coconut cookies. They only made an appearance during the holidays, their rarity compounding their sheer deliciousness.

My sister and I would drop our book bags and race into the kitchen. We hopped up and down with excitement when we saw the large double boiler melting big square blocks of unsweetened chocolate — creating a beautiful brown swirl in a soup of sweetened condensed milk. On the counter was one of the treasures of our modest household — our large yellow ceramic mixing bowl. My sister and I clambered onto barstools to peer at the huge mounds of fluffy coconut that filled the bowl. I reached out to test the coconut as Mari stood on her tiptoes to inspect the simmering chocolate. Our mother stood by the stove, humming softly to herself, gently stirring the liquid, fudgy heaven.

"Leave the coconut for the cookies, please," my mother said.

How she did this with her back to me, I'll never know. Maybe my brother Kevin was right, and she really did have eyes in the back of her head. I stuffed the pilfered shreds of coconut into my mouth.

"Can we help?" we squeaked in unison.

"Go change your clothes," my mom said, smiling. "And take your book bags with you."

My sister and I raced down the hallway, swapped our red plaid uniforms for play clothes, and sprinted back to the kitchen. The double boiler pot continued to bump softly in the water, its slow rocking tuned to a perfect simmer.

"Is the chocolate almost melted?" I asked, eager to mix and taste.

"You can't rush the chocolate," my mom said. "It gets angry if you do. The chocolate will separate, and the cookies won't be glossy or as tasty."

After an eternity, the chocolate and sweetened milk were well blended. And my mother was right — it was worth the wait. The mixture was now satiny smooth — and a beautiful shade of mahogany brown.

"Ready?" she asked, as she lifted the dripping pot from the water.

The chocolate flowed like lava over the mountains of coconut, and Mari and I took turns scraping the sides of the pot. Then the mixing began. We added vanilla and salt, carefully blending the chocolate and coconut into a gooey, molten mess. My mother's role shifted to referee since my sister and I had an acute sense of justice regarding who stirred the most.

The dough was heavy and sloppy, and we formed the cookies by dropping small spoonfuls onto our well-loved and slightly warped cookie pans. By the time we had laid out the first pan of cookies, our hands and faces were smeared with chocolate. The cookies went into the oven for ten minutes, and then took a few more minutes to set up; waiting was agony!

At the exact moment the cookies were ready to eat, our four brothers burst through the kitchen door, their school and sports paraphernalia filling the room.

Mild mayhem ensued. "Whoa!" they yelled. "Nana's coconut cookies! Did you leave any for us?"

My sister and I regarded these gangly interlopers with pity. They had, after all, missed two of the best parts of the experience — mixing the dough and scraping the leftover chocolate from the bowl.

My mother carefully handed each of us a cookie. They were still warm and gooey, with just enough shape to hold the coconut enrobed in rich dark chocolate. The soft fudgy texture was perfectly complemented by the sweet crunch of the chewy coconut. We swooned with pleasure, all the while keeping a careful watch on the equitable distribution of the cookies. When you're one of six children, your very survival depends on tracking such things.

The first pan of cookies disappeared quickly, and our mother shooed us out of the kitchen to do homework. We bounded away, giddy with the knowledge that the holiday season had begun, courtesy of a double boiler.

Nana's Chocolate Coconut Cookies

1 can sweetened condensed milk (Be careful not to confuse evaporated milk with sweetened condensed milk.)
2 oz. unsweetened chocolate
8 oz. shredded coconut
1 tsp. vanilla
Pinch of salt

Gently melt milk and chocolate in double boiler until chocolate melts and contents blend smoothly. Do not overheat, and make sure there is absolutely no water in the pot.
Mix chocolate mixture into coconut, add vanilla and salt.
Mix and drop large teaspoons-full onto baking sheet.

Bake at 350° for 10–12 minutes.
Let stand for 5–7 minutes to set up.
Stash a couple of cookies in a plastic baggie to hide from brothers.

— Maureen Tyrrell Simons —

Matt, Mitts and Magic

Never ever doubt magic. The purest honest thoughts
come from children. Ask any child if they believe in
magic, and they will tell you the truth.
~Scott Dixon

M y husband Matt doesn't believe in magic. So when my mother sent an Elf on the Shelf to our family four years ago, Matt wasn't exactly thrilled. Our son Luke was four years old at the time, and he named our elf Waffles.

Waffles wasn't the type of elf to get into too much trouble. The mere fact that he flew to the North Pole every night to report on Luke and his younger brother Evan and returned in the morning was enough to dazzle their young imaginations. Every Elf on the Shelf comes with rules, and Waffles was no exception. For instance, Waffles does not speak, but can be spoken to. But the most important rule is that Waffles will lose his magic if he is touched by human hands.

This year, Luke and Evan learned that Daddy didn't believe in Christmas magic. They were okay with that, but reminded him that Santa has elves and brings presents, so they would continue to believe. But it bothered me that Matt was so open and decisive about magic not existing. Christmas is such a magical time for me, and I wanted my children to grow up feeling the same way. Over the past year, Matt and I had had several heated arguments regarding faith and science, and what our kids should or shouldn't be exposed to. I didn't know to what extent Matt would tell the children about his beliefs, or whether he'd try to convince them to feel the same way.

I continued showing my belief in magic. One morning, Waffles had pinned himself to our bulletin board in the kitchen. Luke moved a pinned page to get a better look when the tack fell out, and Waffles dropped to the floor. We stood, mouths agape. I worried the gig was up, but Luke didn't miss a beat.

"We have to move him somewhere else," he said. "Somewhere safer."

"Okay," I said, my brain whirring. I needed a way to pick up Waffles that wouldn't break the most important rule. I grabbed the oven mitts and scooped Waffles up in my hands. With the care one would give transporting a Fabergé egg, I delicately placed Waffles on a higher perch on the mantel. Matt watched me with I'm-married-to-a-crazy-lady eyes, thinking the whole thing silly. I, on the other hand, felt I had averted a Christmas disaster.

The next morning, Waffles sat on top of a light in our chandelier above the dining-room table. We only used the table for company, and the boys knew to never go in there, so Waffles chose a safe enough place. That evening, I sat down at the kitchen table with my children. Matt grabbed the food from the stove to transition to the table.

"I smell smoke," Evan said.

Immediately, I looked at the stove and sniffed the air. "I smell something, too." From my seat, I had a clear view into the dining room. The lights were on and had been on for a while.

"It's Waffles!" I froze in my chair as smoke billowed from Waffles.

My husband stepped toward the dining room and froze for a split second. He backtracked to the stove and grabbed oven mitts.

My heart pounded as my husband ran to Waffles, mitted up, and freed him from the scorching light bulb. He ran the elf patient, who was still smoking with one leg dangling by a thread, through the kitchen to the back deck.

Our hero returned and saw the fear in Luke's eyes.

"It's okay, Luke." He hugged our son. "The cold air should cool him off."

We sat in silence, looking at each other. I couldn't hold it in any longer: I burst out laughing. Evan followed, and then Luke. Matt laughed and shook his head. "Waffles needs to be more careful," he said.

After the kids went to bed, I retrieved Waffles from the back deck. His right leg fell off completely, and his left hung on by mere threads. His bottom was inverted, taking the shape of the light bulb. Burnt red fabric covered the top of the light bulb.

Waffles recovered on ice in our freezer for two nights until he was stable enough to go back to the North Pole. His surgery was a success, and he made a full recovery. After insurance, his medical expenses only cost $29.99 out of pocket.

Our relatives and friends followed the Waffles saga on social media. Many added their prayers for Waffles to pull through, along with their jokes and personal elf experiences. While we still laugh at the ordeal and say it seems like something out of a television show or movie, there is one part of the incident that struck me: the oven mitts.

Let me be clear. Waffles may have been smoking, but he was not up in flames. He could have easily been picked up by his head and moved outside or under the faucet. The mitts were not retrieved for safety. Matt, the grown man who adamantly claims magic is not real, wore those mitts in order to save the elfin magic.

It may seem a small gesture, but it meant the world to me. Matt made the decision that it didn't matter what he believed. Magic brought such joy to our children's lives that it would have been wrong to take it away from them so young. And the fact that a Christmas elf gave that gift to our family is, in itself, magical.

—Mary Shotwell—

The Reindeer Dance

Reindeer are the very twinkling in the eye
of the holiday that we call Christmas.
~Author Unknown

"What do reindeer eat?" My three-year-old nephew hopped from foot to foot with excitement and wonder. "How do they fly? How do they pull the sleigh?"

"Maybe you should ask Santa all of that in your letter," I said.

"Okay," he replied. "But where will they land?"

I pointed toward the ceiling. "The roof, I suppose."

"But what if they fall off?"

"Don't worry," I said. "They know what they're doing. If the roof is too slippery, they'll land on the front lawn."

Connor paused and pursed his lips. "How do I make sure Santa doesn't miss my house?"

That was a trickier question. Connor has always been a sweet and well-behaved boy, so he was already on Santa's nice list. Telling him to be kind to his sister and eat his vegetables wasn't going to help convince him that Santa would find the house. There had to be a better way to ease his concern that Santa might pass him by.

Connor and his older sister, Kyra, brought the answer back from preschool a week before Christmas. One of their teachers sent them home with small plastic bags of magic reindeer food and instructions for "The Reindeer Dance." According to the handout, the dance was to be performed on Christmas Eve right before bedtime. It was guaranteed to attract Santa's reindeer to their house and show them exactly where to land. The food would reward them for stopping by and help replenish their energy.

We had never heard of the reindeer dance before, but it sounded perfect—a Christmas Eve activity to release a last burst of energy before bedtime, as well as to relieve nervous tension about the big guy's visit. Not only would my niece and nephew be taking care of the reindeers' needs, but they would go to bed confident that Santa would visit while they slept. He couldn't miss their house if the reindeer knew where to go. We decided to give the dance a try.

It's cold where we live, so that Christmas Eve we all bundled up in our coats and scarves before heading out the front door. The kids gripped their little bags of reindeer food in their bare hands.

"Where do you think the reindeer will land?" I asked.

Connor shuffled through the snow that had fallen that afternoon. "Right here." He stopped at the end of the walkway.

Kyra joined him, and they turned to their mother. They listened intently as she read the instructions for the dance out loud, her breath making puffs of steam in the frigid air.

"Stamp your feet five times."

The kids stamped their boots in the snow. Connor had a bit of trouble with the counting and wanted to keep stamping past five, but Kyra counted loudly enough for both of them, and he followed her lead.

"Clap your hands four times," their mother continued.

The kids counted, "One, two, three, four." Even the adults clapped along.

"Now flap your arms three times."

The kids' arms waved up and down, the reindeer food shaking in the bags.

"Turn around two times."

Even though they counted to two, both only spun around once, anxious to get to the last part of the dance. They stared at their mother, waiting for the last instruction.

"And, finally, blink once," she said.

The kids' heads bobbed as they scrunched their eyes closed and then opened them again.

"Now sprinkle your reindeer food," said their mother.

This was the fun part, throwing oats and seeds all over the stones of the walkway. The children grabbed handfuls from their little bags and sprinkled them all around their feet. The pieces glittered in the porch light like magic.

"This is for Rudolph," said Connor, dropping an extra-large pile on the ground in front of him.

Kyra shook the last crumbs from her empty bag. "Santa can't miss us now."

As we went back inside, the kids' eyes sparkled with eager anticipation. They had done everything they could to ensure Santa would come. They had been on their best behavior for weeks, Santa's cookies were laid out in the living room, and the reindeer had their snack. There was nothing left to do except head to bed for a story from Daddy before a good night's sleep.

The next morning, before emptying their stockings and tearing open their gifts from Santa, the kids ran to the front door to make sure the reindeer had eaten all their treats the night before.

"It's all gone," Connor said, his eyes wide with wonder.

"Wow," said Kyra. "The dance really worked."

They were thrilled with the evidence that Rudolph and his crew had stopped for a nighttime snack. The adults were thrilled with the joy and enchantment this delightful Christmas ritual had given us all, along with the comfort it had given a little boy who was nervous about being forgotten. A new holiday tradition had been born, and I'm grateful to that preschool teacher for giving us another way to celebrate.

This past Christmas Eve, we all did the reindeer dance for the eighth year in a row. Even Kyra, now a teen, joined in as we spun, clapped, flapped our arms, and doubled over with laughter before tossing our homemade reindeer food into the snow. And just as it always has, the fun and charming reindeer dance gave the evening an extra bit of special holiday magic.

— Stephanie Gibeault —

59

The Accidental Christmas Caper

The rate at which a person can mature is directly
proportional to the embarrassment he can tolerate.
~Douglas Engelbart

In fourth grade, I started a new school in Scottsdale, Arizona, right after Christmas vacation. When I arrived at my new classroom, I tried to tell the teacher I was new. She couldn't hear me because I was shy. So, she bent down to hear me squeak out, "I'm new."

She lowered her ear to me and said, "What did you say, dear?"

I took a big breath and said quite loudly, "I'm NEW!"

"Oh, welcome! Come in, dear," she said as she walked with me to the front of the class, taking my paperwork from me. "Class, this is our new student. Please tell the class your name, dear."

I mumbled, "Punkin."

Silence. She stooped down and asked me in a loud voice, "*Punkin?* Your name is Punkin?"

As she started riffling through the papers that I had handed her, I realized my big blunder: I had told her my nickname. I spoke up loudly, "Oh, I meant Jeri. My name is Jeri."

To try to get to know me a little better, she asked, "Did you get lots of presents from Santa?"

Hmmm. This is a trick question, I thought. *I just know it.* She was trying to see if I was still a little kid. In my family, once you were older you got your presents from your parents. I *had* actually gotten presents from Santa, but I wanted to seem older, so I said, "No. I did not get *any* presents from *Santa* this year."

"Oh! Poor dear! I am so sorry to hear that! Class, why don't we all bring in a little present for Jeri when we come back to class tomorrow, okay?" Turning back to me, she said, "Let's sit you down in this desk over here by me so we can get you caught up with our class."

The next day, totally forgetting all about the Santa talk the day before, I came into my classroom hoping to remember which desk was mine. I stood there looking around and noticed that all the students were carrying something and looking at me with puppy-dog eyes. I glanced around some more, wondering if I had forgotten that I was supposed to bring something to school. Then they started piling things up on my desk, and when there was no more room, they set things on the teacher's desk, too.

Oh, man! It must be a classroom sharing thing! I felt so bad that I didn't bring whatever it was that I was supposed to bring. The teacher, beaming, called me to the front of the class and said, "Jeri, because Santa didn't bring you any presents, all the students have brought you a Christmas gift! Isn't that wonderful?"

Uh, oh. "These are all for me?" I asked sheepishly.

The teacher was so pleased with all the other children for being so "giving" that she started handing me one gift after the other. I opened them while standing at the front of the class by her desk. "Gee, uh, thanks, guys. I have always wanted marbles." Or, "Uh, thanks, everyone, I have always wanted a ball and jacks." This continued until every last gift was opened. The teacher stood there with her head tipped sideways and her lips pooched out as she patted me on the shoulder. She was probably thinking I was a poor child raised by alligators from the deep bayou who never got Christmas presents.

I couldn't explain my misunderstanding of the question she asked me the day before because, frankly, I couldn't understand my weird reasoning when I answered her. I only thought it was a trick question that would bring a chorus of laughter if I had said "yes" to getting presents from Santa. So, I just smiled and pretended that I had never had presents before and began trying to concoct a story to tell my mom when I arrived home with a sleigh full of gifts. By the end of the day, I had my story all figured out.

When my mom pulled up at the school to pick me up, she saw me trying to lug this big bag to the car and jumped out to help me. "What is all this?" she asked with a smile of puzzlement on her beautiful face — the face I was going to fib to in a matter of moments. My guilt made her smile look all the more angelic to me. So, after we got settled in the car, I stared straight ahead for courage. Then I blurted out the story I had prepared all day.

"You won't believe this, Mom! This is the best school *ever*! When you are new, they are so glad to have you in their classroom that all the other kids bring you a present to celebrate!"

She just stared at me with an odd expression. She said, "Really?"

"Uh-huh!" I answered innocently. *What had I done?*

That night, I felt so guilty for getting all those presents and then lying to my mom that I told my older sister Cindi what happened at school. After laughing at another one of my grand goof-ups, she said, "The teacher just wanted to know if you got any presents for Christmas."

"Oops. But do I have to give all the presents back?" I asked her.

"No. You would hurt their feelings. Just keep them… and don't tell Mom," she answered as she yawned. "Don't worry about it."

We didn't talk about my little secret for a long time. Forty years later, I brought up the momentous bonding moment to my sister. The light bulb hadn't come on yet that everything that goes on in one's life isn't as momentous in a sibling's life. When I shared the story of our incredible bond in our childhood, she looked at me across the table at the restaurant and said, "You did that? And I said that? Doesn't ring a bell. Sorry, I don't remember the incident."

Through her response, I realized that her childhood world didn't revolve around my continuous calamities. Even though she didn't remember the incident, I did. At the time, she knew the right answers for this nine-year-old… and to me, that's all that matters.

—JL LeGerrette—

60

The Most Special
Fire of the Year

What one loves in childhood stays in the heart forever.
~Mary Jo Putney

When my husband and I were searching for our first family home, what was my highest priority? It had to have an open-log fireplace. The warmth on my cheeks, the familiar crackle of slightly mossy logs and the dancing flames remain one of my most vivid memories of Christmas — a feeling I like to re-ignite (literally) every time the season comes around.

But for many years, it was the extinguishing of the fire, not the lighting of it, that most comforted me. Only after it was put out completely could Santa get down the chimney safely. My Christmas spirit depended on it!

Every Christmas Eve, my dad would prepare the fire late in the afternoon as it was getting dark. I would hear the *scrape, scrape* of the iron shovel on the grate, clearing the ashes. Then Dad would shuffle in with the log basket and set it on a newspaper carefully laid down on the carpet by my mum to prevent a mess.

Fire lighter first, then the crunching of newspaper, which was carefully placed around it — exactly six pieces of kindling, stacked around the edge and meeting in the middle like a little tepee. Then the ebony coal, and finally the fat, mossy logs around the edge of the grate. "It's an art," my dad would say, "that mustn't be rushed — especially for the most special fire of the year" — the Christmas Eve fire.

Mum would carefully place the stockings and the decorative ivy, so they were out of the range of any stray sparks, and move back the rug. My brother and I would stand well back as the ceremonial match was lit, while Mum turned off the lights and the magical notes of "Silent Night" would start up.

The moment was magical. But it would soon be surpassed by another slightly weirder but necessary ritual. After a warm mince pie and a hot chocolate, my thoughts would soon turn to the health and safety of Santa. Despite Mum and Dad's assurances that our house was very late in his schedule, I would worry relentlessly about that fire still being hot when Santa came down the chimney.

The chimney was plenty wide enough. I'd done the calculations, based on my illustrated *The Night Before Christmas* book. No, that wasn't my worry. My anxiety was about after I'd gone to bed. What if Mum and Dad put on more logs, and the fire stayed hot for hours? My cousins had told me they thought Santa came to them about midnight, and they only lived in the next town, so we wouldn't be long after that, right?

I knew that Santa would only come once my brother and I were both asleep — properly asleep. But how could I sleep knowing that Santa could come feet-first down our chimney, straight into those hot, mossy logs, or worse, flickering flames? What if he actually needed bandages, or worse, and couldn't get to any other children that night? We could be responsible for ruining Christmas! No, the worry was all too much and enough to put me off my mince pie, even Christmas, full stop.

One Christmas, it got so bad that my dad found me trying to climb up the outside wall of our house, taking all sorts of silly risks attempting to scale the drain pipes. I had a note in my hand that I had handwritten, warning Santa of the dangers of coming down our chimney.

I informed him that he must look for any smoke first, as it would indicate that something was still smouldering, and he should put his head down to check for any flames. My note concluded that if he was in any doubt at all, he should not come down our chimney. My brother and I would understand about the presents.

I don't think my brother was at all impressed with my warning note. He assured me, as did Dad, that Santa would find a way. But after many tears, and Christmas at risk of being spoilt, my dad had the solution.

He shuffled out to the kitchen and returned with a bowl of water. We all stood back as he very slowly and gently poured a little water under the grate. He closed all the air vents in the hearth. Sure enough, after a few minutes, the fire fizzled out — first to a tiny, dull flame, then nothing. He scraped the hot ashes onto a shovel and cleared the hearth. No more fire. I smiled at last, overcome with relief that Santa would be safe.

Looking back, I'm sure that the next few hours of Christmas Eve for Mum and Dad weren't nearly so cozy without that log fire. But they were happy to pay the price for my peace of mind. And, weirdly enough, it did become a tradition of its own in our family.

Every year, after the lighting ritual, a mince pie, a hot chocolate, and "Silent Night" came the extinguishing ritual. And we continued that extinguishing ritual right until I left home at age eighteen!

My husband and I have our own home with a log fire that our kids enjoy, and Mum and Dad live close by. Every Christmas Eve now, we light "the most special fire of the year" in the same way, with the same ritual: kindling, logs, hot chocolate. "Silent Night" is played, although my kids also insist on their own ritual of watching *The Polar Express*.

My kids don't seem to share my childhood worries about Santa's safety. They seem to know that he will always find a safe way to deliver all the presents. Besides, they've worked out his route using the Internet and are confident that our fire will be well out by the time he gets to us.

Still, after the kids have gone to bed, do you know what we do anyway? Mum and Dad come round for a little something stronger than hot chocolate, and we have the extinguishing ceremony! That way, we know that all the children will be visited, Santa will be safe, and the Christmas spark will stay alive for all us children, big and small!

Ho, ho, ho!

— Sal Patel —

Mom's Sneaky Tree

Blessed is the season which engages the whole world
in a conspiracy of love.
~Hamilton Wright Mabie

Both my parents grew up Jewish, but by the time I was about ten, I could already tell that only my dad's side of the family actively practiced. My parents were divorced, and I lived with my mom, but for Jewish holidays I went to services with my dad and his mother, whom I called "Bubbie."

Bubbie was the perfect grandmother. She knitted blankets and sweaters. She told stories and sang lullabies. She taught us to play double solitaire and *Rummikub*, and she could get the right answers before every contestant on every game show. She cooked beef brisket (I was never allowed to reveal that her secret ingredient was orange juice), and made applesauce with the apples and plums from the trees in her back yard.

Bubbie was a founding member of her synagogue. She kept kosher at home and observed the Sabbath. She spoke Yiddish and said her Hebrew the old way: *Shabbes* instead of *Shabbat*.

My mother was never observant or religious, but she liked strings of lights. She liked trees. She liked, for a few weeks every winter, having a tree adorned with strings of lights in the living room.

It wasn't a Hanukkah bush; it was an unapologetic Christmas tree. It had lights, tinsel, and shiny glass balls, along with the rough glitter-and-glue ornaments I'd made in preschool arts and crafts.

Through the Eyes of a Child | 207

One winter, after a nice Hanukkah weekend at Bubbie's house, when Dad got ready to drive me home, he invited Bubbie to come along for the ride. To my surprise, Bubbie said, "Yes."

Playing it casual, Dad said, "Why don't you call your mom and let her know we're all leaving soon?"

Bubbie's phones were all the big, heavy black rotary phones. I loved the weight of them, even though I sometimes lost my place in a phone number while I was dialing because the higher numbers took so long.

Mom answered.

"Hi, Mom. We're heading home, and Bubbie's coming with us. What do we do?"

Mom didn't answer to her former mother-in-law, but she still liked her and respected her. She knew that any fallout from having a Christmas tree in the house would land squarely on me, the unfortunate victim of her heretical parenting.

"Don't worry," Mom said. "I'll take care of it."

I didn't know what "taking care of it" looked like, and I didn't know how to make myself not worry. Mom sounded casual, and Dad was playing it casual, so I tried to be casual, too. It was twilight when we set out, and though we mostly took the big highways, we could see the lights outlining the windows and roofs of the houses we passed.

"I like the twinkly lights. They're like fireflies," I said, testing Bubbie's reaction. She told me about the fireflies she used to see at the lake when she was my age. She didn't say anything about liking, or being tolerant of, Christmas lights, and even at such a young age, I knew better than to press or she might get suspicious.

Traffic was light, and in about thirty minutes we were pulling into the parking lot at my mom's apartment building. I took a long time getting my backpack out of the trunk, double-checking as if something might have spilled out between the teeth of the closed zipper.

Dad finally cleared his throat, and I had to act as if I'd found whatever it was and put it back. I straightened, smiling weakly. Bubbie was going to see the tree and have a fit. She would say that it was bad for my Jewish upbringing, and maybe even that my mom shouldn't be the parent to raise me. Worry lumped up in my stomach and made my feet as heavy as lead.

"Come on. Your grandmother's standing out here in the cold," Dad called, and I followed, trudging up the steps and leading the way inside.

Mom opened the door, gave me a hug, and stepped aside to invite Dad and Bubbie in. I looked around the living room.

The tree — the big, brushing-the-ceiling, light-strewn and tinsel-dripped tree — was gone, without even a shred of silver strands or a speck of glitter to show that it had ever been there.

Dad and Bubbie stayed long enough to each use the bathroom before their return drive, and to listen to me play a couple of songs on the piano. They gave me warm hugs when they left and said, "Happy Hanukkah." They said they'd see me in two weeks, but that I should call Bubbie in between. I said I would.

When the door closed behind them, their footsteps padded out of earshot, and the car finally pulled away, Mom and I looked at each other.

"But… the tree!" I said. "How did you make an entire tree disappear in half an hour?"

She winked at me and led me out the sliding-glass doors to the apartment's balcony. There, sitting dark and clandestine like a thief in the shadows, was the tree. She flipped a switch, and the lights came on, twinkling in slow patterns and shining brilliant colors on the glass ornaments.

"You moved it out here all by yourself?" I asked her. Trees were heavy, and my mom was not very tall.

"Sure," she said. "It wasn't that hard. If Bubbie wants to visit again, just let me know, and I'll move the tree again. I know it would upset her to know that we had one, and the whole point of having the tree is that it makes people happy."

"It wouldn't have made Bubbie happy," I agreed. "I'm glad you moved it. But since she's gone now, can we move it back? It's really cold out here."

— Gabrielle Harbowy —

On Comet, On Cupid, On Fwank

Grandfathers are for loving and fixing things.
~Author Unknown

Seven-year-old Daniel grabbed the box of reindeer parts from the giant stack of Christmas boxes that we had just hauled down from the attic. "I'll do the reindeer!" he said.

When Daniel was a toddler, I had received two reindeer made from logs and sticks. They were presumably handmade and purchased from a craft sale. So, for as long as Daniel remembers, the reindeer have made their home on our front porch at Christmastime.

A little while later, Daniel returned with the empty box. He went straight to Papa and asked him to return to the porch with him. Not wanting to interfere with Grandpa-business, I listened from afar. Daniel told Papa of his concern that those reindeer needed a baby.

Always interested in a good project, and not wanting to disappoint his grandson, they set off into the woods together in search of sticks for appropriate legs, antlers and head for a baby reindeer. They worked all afternoon on their creation until Daniel put the finishing touch on the newborn—a big painted smile.

"What shall we name him?" Papa asked as they stood him up on his thin-branch legs next to his more sturdy parents.

"Fwank," Daniel announced with certainty.

Fwank will be celebrating his tenth Christmas on our front porch this year. Daniel still nods in approval as we take him out and place him in his prominent place between his parents.

—Jesse Neve—

Grandma's Special Cranberry Bread

I know what it is like to be brought up with
unconditional love. In my life that came
from my grandmother.
~André Leon Talley

"Here you go, Barry... just for you." A smile spread across my grandmother's face as she handed me a loaf of cranberry bread wrapped in silver foil. My loaf. I don't know how the tradition started — in fact, nobody can recall — but as far back as I can remember, my grandmother would present me with my own cranberry loaf each Christmas. Nobody else got one.

Was I her favorite? In my heart, I always hoped so because she was my favorite grandma, and I was lucky to grow up with multiple grandmas and great-grandmas. But she never made it known I was her favorite. She doted on all of her grandchildren, and she had many. But, for whatever reason, at some point in time she decided to start making me my own personal loaf. I may have casually remarked how much I enjoyed her cranberry bread, or she may have watched me eat an entire plate of it before anyone else could sneak a thick, moist slice. Did it cause jealousy among my siblings? Yes. And among my countless cousins, aunts and uncles, as well!

My grandmother was not the typical grandma. She was not known for her abilities in the kitchen. Over the years, she knew how to make a roast with little white potatoes and how to broil a steak with little white potatoes. She could open a can of green beans and put a slice of bacon in with them while she mercilessly boiled the beans, and she could make an iceberg lettuce salad with Thousand Island dressing. These were the foods my grandfather and my uncle, who lived with them for most of my early life, wanted to eat. It was always meat and potatoes with the occasional green thing on the side. She was not a baking granny either. She didn't bake cookies, pies or cakes. She just wasn't that crazy about cooking and baking. Except for my special loaf.

Grandma's cranberry bread was amazing! When I say I got my own loaf each Christmas, it wasn't like getting a holiday fruit cake from an old aunt, something you would use as a boat anchor. Grandma's cranberry bread was golden, soft and moist. It was filled with cranberries that were bright red and juicy. The outside was sticky so it would coat my fingers and force me to lick it off. When I cut into it, the knife slid smoothly and easily, revealing the golden spongy wonderfulness inside. Some people would put whipped cream on their slices, but for me, the simple beauty of the sweet, orange-flavored cake and tart, red berries was perfectly satisfying. It needed nothing else. As I got older and began drinking coffee, I learned to love the cranberry loaf even more! It went so well with steaming hot black coffee on Christmas night. I'd eat the loaf rather than pumpkin pie.

The tradition continued through the years and never got old. I'd walk in the house, and hug and kiss Grandma hello, and within moments she would excitedly go to the kitchen and return with my bread. She would always say, "I bet you thought I'd forget to make you your favorite!" Her eyes would sparkle as she laid the heavy loaf into my appreciative hands. "Here you go, Barry… just for you."

Grandma got older, slower and a bit forgetful, but she always remembered the cranberry bread. My kids grew up with the tradition, and my son in particular was always eager to get at my loaf! After a while, I would relent and share — something I never did with my siblings or cousins. It was too special to share with anyone except my kids.

I never watched Grandma make the bread. It was already done

by the time I got to her house. In my mind, I imagined her combining ingredients, carefully pouring them into a loaf pan, and sprinkling magic around it before popping it into the oven. That is, until the year my kids and I entered Grandma's house, and she was slow to come out. Rather than coming from the kitchen, she came from the back of the house where her room was. She looked old and tired. She didn't sleep as much anymore and hadn't been herself. She saw me and smiled, and then a look on her face perplexed me. Was Grandma mad at me? Did I do something wrong? Slowly, she came to me and hugged me. She said, "Barry, dear, I'm sorry. I think I forgot to make your cranberry bread…." Her words trailed off, and she walked to the kitchen. I followed.

"Grandma, don't worry. It's okay. You don't have to make it," I said as I followed her. She motioned for me to get a bowl, and then she went to the pantry and grabbed a small box. "Orange Cranberry Bread Mix" was written in bold letters across the package.

My special cranberry bread was a boxed mix! She struggled to open the box. Her hands were very arthritic, and she couldn't manage. I opened the box and emptied the orange powder with little dried-up red balls into the bowl. I waited, expecting eggs or other ingredients, but she simply put the bowl under the tap and turned on the water.

Not only was the bread a mix, but it was an instant mix! She eyed how much to put in. Then she moved the bowl to the sink, grabbed a spatula and began to stir. She had great difficulty. She could barely hold the spatula and had little strength to stir the thick mixture. I held her wrinkled, swollen hand and helped her stir. When she was satisfied, she poured the batter into the pan and asked me to put it in the oven because she couldn't bend down.

When the timer went off, I retrieved the loaf and placed it on the sink to cool. We took it out of the pan and rolled it in foil. Her old, crooked fingers gripped at the thin metal and folded it around the golden loaf just so. She gave it a pat and then handed it to me, smiling. "Here you go, Barry… just for you." I kissed and hugged Grandma with a tear in my eye, sensing this would be the last special loaf I would ever get.

I was right. Alzheimer's took my grandma away by the next Christmas. I was one of the few people she could still recognize, but she was unable to do much more than sit in a chair and recite the same stories over and over. The first year without Grandma's special cranberry bread was hard. My mom made the exact same mix and baked it for me. It was exactly the same — from a box, with water, folded in aluminum foil — and yet it was not the same. Grandma's had magic.

— Barry Marks —

The Advent of New Holiday Traditions

If they can't learn the way we teach,
we teach the way they learn.
~Ole Ivar Lovaas

By the time my son was two years old, I knew we needed to find different ways to celebrate Christmas. Nicholas's autism diagnosis only validated what we already knew about his sensory issues. Jingle bells didn't make him jingle all the way; they made him cover his ears and dart away, screaming. The long line to see Santa? The excited kids bouncing every which way only made Nicholas want to run straight for the exit. (I couldn't blame him one bit, really.)

Baking cookies for Santa Claus was a no-go, too. I couldn't even get Nicholas to touch the dough, though he did recognize that I was cutting cookies into shapes from his favorite video game. The only aspect that really interested him at all was the baking timer. He wouldn't eat the iced cookies afterward, nor would he even touch any of the usual holiday foods.

So many holiday traditions created sensory overload for him or simply didn't connect to him at all, and trying to make him conform wasn't an option. Why make him — and the rest of the family — miserable?

"We're going to find a way to make Christmas work just for you," I told him one day as we sat in the car after another meltdown.

"Christmas work just for you," he echoed, still hunkered with his hands over his ears.

Sometimes, I felt like I was going through a checklist as we tried out different holiday traditions to find what worked best for him. Holiday music? Great, so long as it wasn't too loud. Being surprised by a live band when out in public caused Nicholas to engage in evasive maneuvers. We found that noise-cancelling headphones made public events a lot more tolerable for him.

Blinking lights and shiny tinsel? He loved it! The lights dazzled his eyes and made him bounce and flap with joy. Telling Santa what he wanted under the tree? Well, that was trickier. As Nicholas entered kindergarten, he was just starting to speak in simple sentences, and he couldn't engage in back-and-forth conversation. It was easiest to have him write down a list to push silently at Santa, whom we had learned to visit at the mall immediately after Thanksgiving when most of the kids in town were at a parade instead.

Then one day when I was out shopping, I stumbled upon the absolutely perfect, most Nicholas thing ever: chocolate Advent calendars! He loved math and numbers, and chocolate candies were one of the few desserts he'd eat. I bought a calendar and brought it out for Nicholas right after school that day.

"See these little paper doors?" I asked him. "You open one each day of December leading up to Christmas. Tiny chocolates are hidden behind each door."

His face crinkled in worry. "Never open day one, two, three?" he asked, his eyes filling with tears.

Oops. We were indeed a few days into December already, and I hadn't even considered that this might be a problem. "You can open them right now and catch up!" I showed him how to pry open the paper door, and I did my part to demonstrate by popping day one's chocolate in my mouth.

"Day four!" he practically yelled as he finally held up the appropriate chocolate for the day.

"Tomorrow will be day five," I said.

He nodded, his eyes bright. "Then day six, seven, eight, nine, ten..." He reached the end of the countdown. "Then Christmas!"

"That's right. When you get to the final chocolate, it'll be Christmas."

The Advent calendar continued to be our ritual each afternoon. He couldn't wait to open those little paper doors to partake in the new day's candy.

On the final day, as he opened up the biggest panel of all, I expected him to be wiggly and about ready to burst with happiness. Instead, he started to cry.

"Advent calendar all done."

"That's because Christmas is here," I said. "Santa's coming, remember?"

He still looked sad. "No more Advent calendar, ever again."

Oh! I felt horrible for not realizing how he'd interpret the end of the calendar. "This one is all done, yes, but we can buy a new one next year, and we can make sure to get it in November, too. That way, you'll be ready to count down starting on December 1st."

"All new Advent calendar!" His face glowed again. "Next year!"

His grin has continued to return every year as he works through a new calendar. Nicholas is twelve now, and almost as tall as me. No matter how early the holiday jingles start playing and the sales start advertising, his Christmas season hasn't officially started until he is counting through December with little chocolates. This remains our special way to celebrate the season using the numbers that he loves so much. His joyous smile lights up our world, brighter than any Christmas tree.

—Beth Cato—

Chapter 8

The Joy of Giving

A Houseful of Spirit

Christmas is the spirit of giving without
a thought of getting.
~Thomas S. Monson

few years ago, Christmas Eve day was snowless, warm and sunny. It looked and felt much like a late fall day. Everything was brown and crisp but with its own coziness. Even though there was no snow, somehow it still felt like Christmas.

Mid-afternoon, my girlfriend Theresa phoned me and said excitedly, "I got a bicycle!"

"A bicycle for Christmas?"

I was confused. She already had a bicycle — a ten-speed. But she explained that her landlady had cleaned out a garage and offered her a child's bicycle. We lived just a few blocks from each other, so I drove over to see it. It was a girl's pink bike with a bell, basket and banana seat. It had pink rubber grips on the handlebars with streamers hanging down. It was not new, but it was in quite good condition.

Theresa was a tall woman, and this was a children's bicycle. There was no way she could ever ride it, but it still excited her.

"What are you going to do with it?"

"I don't know," she said, "I was just so happy to get a bicycle, like when I was a little kid."

"What if we give it away?"

"Yeah…" she said, her eyes lighting up. "Who can we give it to?"

I had been carpooling with a co-worker, John, who was a single father raising three children: an older boy, another around twelve, and an eight-year-old daughter. Life was very hard for the family. His eldest boy looked after the younger kids while John was still at work. I knew that buying food and getting gifts for Christmas had been difficult. But John was very private and never complained.

Theresa and I loaded the bike into her car and drove it to a local gas station. We were pleased to discover that the flat back tire held air. I put some oil on the chain and turned it. It was a standard single-speed bicycle. Giving it to John's daughter seemed an obvious choice.

Now that we knew it was in working condition, I texted a picture of it to John with the message, "Do you want this for your daughter?"

He responded, "How much?"

I answered, "Nothing. We got it for free."

We made arrangements to take it to him that evening.

When we dropped off the bike, John insisted that we come inside. The door opened into the kitchen. It was an older house, neat and clean, but also worn. A TV played a Christmas movie in the background. The kitchen table was covered with various baking dishes, ingredients and lots of flour. The kitchen was oven-warm and smelled of baked goods. There were several different trays of cupcakes around, some cooling, but most already covered in colored icing and sprinkles. The house was sparsely furnished, but it felt like a home.

John's kids immediately pressed cupcakes into our hands. They were confident and shy, happy yet respectful, much like John.

John explained that they were having their big Christmas dinner the next day. Tonight was about cupcakes, and they had been baking and eating cupcakes all night. We didn't want to stay too long. This was a private place into which we had been invited. They packed us a bag of cupcakes, and we left with a "Merry Christmas."

On the way home, I explained to Theresa just how private John was and how surprised I had been to be invited inside. She said that she had sensed that.

We went back to her place and nestled in. We had gotten some snacks to enjoy. We turned on the TV, found a Christmas movie and curled up on couches with blankets, coffee, cheese and olives.

I felt I had been given a privilege, a chance to help in some small way, an opportunity to give a young girl a bicycle. What had been amazing was that they hadn't really needed us. The bicycle was only icing; they already had cupcakes and a house full of goodwill and cheer. John and his children had made their own Christmas despite difficult circumstances.

Theresa and I agreed it was our best Christmas ever.

— Bill Suboski —

Index-Card Christmas

Creativity is thinking up new things.
Innovation is doing new things.
~Theodore Levitt

"O Holy Night" played quietly in the background, and the lights in our log cabin were dimmed to showcase the soft glow of the Christmas tree. My husband had prepared a lavish dinner for our group of eight — the two of us and six of our friends. It was an evening filled with warm conversation and comfortable laughter. We had all been blessed with successful careers, carefully planned retirements, and a special friendship that we had enjoyed for many years.

Our tradition was to each bring one gift to the dinner and then draw names. Each person brought a gift and each person received a gift. Armed with a healthy spending limit, we trolled stores and online websites for jewelry, wine, electronics and designer clothes.

Then, four years ago, I looked at the largesse — the presents, brightly colored wrapping paper and fancy bows — and was overwhelmed by the shallowness of the tradition. "I've got a proposal to make," I said to seven curious faces. "What if we do something that makes a difference next year? What if we still draw names, but instead of shopping for more 'stuff,' we shop for a cause?"

I grew more excited after everyone expressed enthusiasm for the idea. "We can't just throw money at a random charity; it has to be something that touches us. We could all use the coming year to find a need that resonates with each of us. Once we confirm that the charity is reputable and responsible, we can make a donation in the name of the person whose name we draw. The gift-giver can write a short paragraph on an index card that tells about the contribution and why. After dinner next year, the person receiving the index card will read the story aloud." With everyone's agreement, "Index-Card Christmas" was born.

My first gift went to my friend Joyce:

While on safari in Tanzania, we parked in the midst of a large herd of elephants. I watched, enthralled, as these gentle creatures interacted. I saw a mother gently step between two roughhousing babies to separate and calm them. As another herd approached, they greeted one another by entwining their trunks as if shaking hands. One of the babies was unable to cross over a mound of dirt, and a slightly older elephant, possibly his big brother, "trunked" him gently over the hill. For me, it was love at first sight.

In November, I saw an article that chronicled gangs of men in Western Bengal throwing "flaming tar balls" at living elephants. The accompanying photograph showed an adult and calf engulfed in flames, running for their lives. It looked to me as if the baby was screaming in fear and pain, and it absolutely broke my heart.

A donation will be made in your name to the African Wildlife Foundation — an organization that devotes its efforts to saving endangered species.

I had never felt so good about giving — and receiving — a gift. I know my husband and our friends felt the same. Our small group has always been inspired by, and often moved to tears during, the reading of the cards. We've come to look forward to the evening with an excited anticipation we had never felt in the days of our traditional gift exchange. We simply don't miss a shiny, new gadget in the face of giving a gift of compassion that makes a small difference in the life of another.

Naturally, the tradition grew.

We now draw a second name, and the object of this gift is to pick a good cause for which we must devote some hours of our time. Giving money can be easier than actually stepping into the trenches, so we wanted to challenge ourselves to donate some of our free retirement hours. In addition, we must involve at least one other person, so that we encourage the circle of giving to grow. A few examples of the volunteer activities on the index cards have been:

- Organizing neighbors to sign up to ring the bell for the Salvation Army
- A book club was recruited to participate in the Samaritan's Purse Operation Christmas Child shoebox gift drive
- A group of golf buddies now gives several hours every week to help prepare meals at a church that feeds the hungry in their community
- My personal favorite was when our friend organized her yoga class to institute an Index-Card Christmas with their own circle of friends.

We found that giving is a lot like a fire; inject a little oxygen into it, and it will grow and spread.

For the coming year, we are exploring a third Index-Card option in which we, as couples, are to offer our homes or possessions for a special purpose or good cause. One couple plans to open their empty mother-in-law's apartment to someone who has need of temporary housing. One pair will be hosting a cocktail party to raise funds for their local animal shelter. Another gave a car they no longer used to a newly widowed mother of three who was without transportation. My husband I have not yet determined how we will use our home for our contribution, but we are excited by the challenge.

—Vicki Kitchner—

67

Chicken Soup for the Soul

Christmas Eve 1944

For it is in giving that we receive.
~Saint Francis

I t was December 1944, somewhere in southern France. It was the final winter of World War II — in fact, the chilliest winter that Europe had experienced in fifty years. And my dad was right in the center of it.

Shortly after Pearl Harbor, my father left the farm in Nebraska and joined the military. As a United States Army combat engineer, he soon rose to the rank of sergeant, and then was sent overseas. That year found him in Belgium and France, where he fought in the infamous Battle of the Bulge. Then, as winter set in, Dad and his platoon holed up in a tiny, half-demolished village to ride out the frigid cold, with nothing to eat except C-rations.

"C-rations" were small, portable meals in a can, designed by the American armed forces for use by foot soldiers during wartime and other maneuvers. These older versions of the modern MREs (meals ready to eat) were not fine cuisine. However, two "entrees" were rumored to be edible — the sliced peaches in syrup and the chocolate brownies.

And so, as the cruel war came to a grinding, creaking, frozen-solid halt — at least for a short and blessed while — and Christmas approached, my dad came up with a plan. In essence, he "encouraged" his troops to start saving their tin cans of peaches and brownies for a very special reason.

Now, knowing my father the way I do, he probably did not deliver a direct command to his men, especially considering the circumstances. However, he likely said more with a few choice words and a "look" than any order ever could.

The holy day arrived, and everyone was invited to the village plaza for a Christmas Eve celebration. All the townsfolk came, and some of the farm families, too. The soldiers built a bonfire, Dad organized the singing of Christmas carols, and the humble presents of C-rations were passed out to the French girls and boys. Some of those children didn't receive any other Christmas gifts that year. And all of them had endured three long years of wartime deprivation, hunger, and horror.

How their eyes must have glowed in the pure light of the Yuletide flames.

As the blessed ceremony came to a close, and the people began to head for home, the pitch-black night seemed somehow brighter, the bitter cold winter seemed somewhat warmer, and the awful, brutal war seemed suddenly survivable. There had been so much pain, but now there was a bit of hope, too.

"*Merci beaucoup,*" said the French families, as they left the village square that night. "Thank you very much."

To which the suddenly blessed American soldiers replied, "You're very welcome."

— Curt Melliger —

68

Who Knew?

Nothing else in all life is such a maker of joy
and cheer as the privilege of doing good.
~James Russell

My five-year-old son Taylor and I were making a quick stop at the grocery store on our way home from carpool duty. We needed sauce for that night's spaghetti dinner. Taylor was at the age when he wanted to read every sign out loud, so I was worried about how to get in and out of the store quickly.

When we arrived, I noticed the Marines conducting their annual Toys for Tots drive. Two men and one woman outfitted in their spectacular uniforms stood in front of the store. Although I'd experienced this many times before, this was the first time for my son. As we walked from our car to the store, I could see the amazement on his face. The Marines were his toy soldiers coming to life, guarding the front of our Kroger. The formality and sharpness of their uniforms were impressive enough, but when one of the Marines touched the tip of his hat and nodded, Taylor was speechless.

We started pushing our cart through the store when he asked, "What does Toys for Tots mean? Is it like Toys"R"Us?" I explained how the Marines collected toys for children of needy families. Knowing my son would be feeling pretty "needy" himself with all the creative end-cap displays, I explained a needy child was someone whose parents couldn't afford to buy him toys very often. The Marines were here today asking people to help out by donating an extra toy to ensure every child received a nice present for Christmas.

"Like Santa?" he asked.

"Exactly like Santa," I nodded. "Today, they are Santa's helpers." We continued shopping, and it wasn't until the canned-food aisle did I realize how quiet Taylor had become. He wasn't his usual chatty self, even staying quiet with the bright display signs set up by the chocolate milk. I asked if everything was okay.

"Why do people collect canned food? Is it the same as with the toys?"

I stopped walking, struck by the depth of his thinking and question. We'd received a food-drive flier in the mail the day before, letting us know our mail carrier would be collecting canned goods during her delivery route that weekend to provide to the local food bank. Apparently, he had also read the flier.

"Yes, I believe it is."

"Some moms can't buy food for their kids?" He looked at the rows of canned food lining the aisle.

Again, I nodded.

"Can we get some?" He looked up at me with those big brown eyes, and I melted.

"Yes, we can. Do you want to pick out a couple of your favorites?"

With a huge grin, he nodded and headed straight to the corn. We left the aisle, our cart loaded with twenty cans of corn and five cans of pineapple rings. He was excited about the idea of more than one family getting to eat his favorite fruit and favorite vegetable. Finished with our shopping, we headed to the checkout counter. I knew we would be passing the toy section on our way, and I wondered idly what new item would draw his attention.

"Mom, you said no toys today, but can we get some for the soldiers?"

Again, I paused. "For Toys for Tots?" I asked. When he nodded, so did I. "Sure, buddy. Why don't you pick out one toy for a girl and one toy for a boy?"

His smile was priceless. First, he ran to one of the big trucks he'd admired over the past couple of weeks, but shook his head. "Nope, too big for the soldiers to carry."

I was pleased at the thoughtfulness he put into the selection for each item. He didn't dawdle, and he didn't argue when I said "no" to the gaming console. My grocery budget didn't have that much wiggle room.

Finally, with two perfect gifts in the cart, we headed to the register. When we checked out, he could barely stand still. With bags in hand, he ran straight to the front doors and directly to the Marine who had tipped his hat at him when we walked in.

"Excuse me, soldier. Can you put these in the box?" He looked and sounded so grown up.

The Marine knelt down and asked, "What do we have here?"

"We got Toys for Tots." Taylor held up the bags.

The soldier nodded as if this made perfect sense. "How about I give you a little boost, and you can put them in yourself?"

Taylor nodded, again speechless at conversing with a live soldier. At that moment, I couldn't have been more impressed with my son and the lesson he'd just learned. The young Marine lifted him and helped Taylor place the bags in the box, and then set him back on his feet.

Taylor grinned at the man. "Thanks!"

The Marine replied, "Thank you for helping out." Then he raised his hand in a quick salute.

That night at dinner, Taylor explained the whole Toys for Tots program to his dad. And when Saturday morning arrived, he also reminded me to put the bags of canned goods outside when the mail carrier came by.

As the months rolled by, Taylor didn't mention these incidents again, so I pushed them to the back of my memory. Then one day, as we were driving through town, Taylor saw a set of colorful, flashing lights in a store window. "Mom! Is it Toys for Tots time?"

I was stunned. My son hadn't asked if it was Christmas or if it was the time of year for presents. He'd asked if it was time for Toys for Tots. For years, I'd tried to find something that was special for our new family. At that moment, I realized this was "it." This was the beginning of our family tradition. As the years passed, our tradition of giving grew stronger, and Taylor found more innovative ways to help others throughout the year. I was proud of the young man he was becoming.

Fourteen years later, I stood outside on a cold January morning and remembered this exchange like it was yesterday. I fought to hold back tears, pride warring with pain, as a big gray bus drove out of the same Kroger parking lot. Inside was my grown-up boy, heading off to basic training. My baby was taking his next steps to becoming a man. Who knew a forgotten jar of spaghetti sauce would lead to a treasured family tradition? Who knew a new tradition would shape a young man's future?

— Tami Brothers —

69

Saving Christmas

Rich or poor, we will keep together
and be happy in one another.
~Louisa May Alcott, Little Women

A s Christmas decorations appeared in town, our parents called my two younger brothers and me together. At first, I thought someone had died, because I had never seen my parents look so sad. My brothers and I stood waiting for the awful news.

Mom hugged me as she murmured, "Christmas is going to be different this year. We won't be having a tree or presents. We can barely afford food."

Dad, resting on the couch, beckoned the boys into his arms. "Things will change when I get back to work."

It was 1947. My family was poorer than dirt. We lived on the main street of a small Norman Rockwell town in Pennsylvania where the American flag waved atop a flagpole centered in a town square, faced by a bank, a grocery store, a drugstore, a privately owned department store, and an antiquated hotel. Kids walked safely to town and went out to play in the neighborhood all day.

When Dad worked, it was in a coal mine. Mom's job was to wash his sooty clothes, clean our small apartment, create new ways to serve bologna as a hot meal, and teach us right from wrong. Soon after returning to work at the end of a long strike, Dad was hurt in a rock fall that broke bones in his foot. Languishing on the couch with the swollen foot propped high on pillows, he didn't talk or smile much. There was little to smile about. No work, no income.

At nine years old, I mothered my younger brothers: Rodney, age six, and Stevie, three. We shared a small bedroom. They slept in a double bed and I had a twin. That night, after our parents' announcement, we talked.

Rodney began. "Em, didja see how sad Mommy and Daddy looked?" Silence.

"I thought Mommy was gonna cry," he added.

"Me, too," whispered Stevie.

"Yeah… We're in hard times," I said. "It makes Mommy and Daddy sad."

Heavy stillness.

"But we don't have to be sad," I added, hoping to brighten the mood.

"I don't care about Christmas gifts," mumbled Rodney.

"I don't care," Stevie mimicked.

"I only feel sorry… for Mommy and Daddy," Rodney moaned, emphasizing Mommy and Daddy.

"Daddy's foot's… this big!" Stevie held out his arms.

"Yeah… It hurts him bad." I could hear the tears in Rodney's voice.

Gloomy silence.

"Maybe we can do something to cheer them up," I said with overdone enthusiasm. The boys sat up. "We can take the money from our piggy bank… earn some more… and surprise them with gifts!"

"Yeah!" "Oh, boy!" "Good idea!" They chirped.

The gloom was broken.

"Button it down in there!" Dad called from the living room. "Go to sleep!"

Stealthily, I crept into my brothers' bed. Sitting close, we softened our whispers.

"I can run errands for Aunt Em and neighbors to earn money," I offered.

"Yeah," Rodney added, "me and Stevie can return pop bottles and save the deposit money… instead of buying candy!" He nudged Stevie.

"Yeah!" Stevie clutched his hands together.

"We'll have to hide it!" Rodney exclaimed. Then wondered, "Where?"

"In… piggy!" Stevie pointed to the ceramic pig on the dresser.

"Not there," I said. "Mommy'll notice if it gets heavier."

"I know!" Rodney raised a finger and pointed it downward. "In the cowboy box!"

Under the big bed were stored boxes of all sorts containing wind-up toys, marbles, an erector set, games, and two items that would meet our needs: a shoebox filled with plastic cowboys and Indians, and a flashlight.

"Good idea!"

"Yeah!" chimed Stevie.

We had a plan!

Until they nodded off, I coached my little brothers (especially Stevie) in ways to guard our secret. "Don't talk about it during the day." "Act natural." "Don't let coins jingle."

We awoke in the morning, transformed. No longer poor, sad children, we were secret agents on an important mission!

The following weeks saw me dashing home from school each day determined to earn a nickel or dime. I was usually greeted by furtive winks and grins — one with a missing tooth, and the other with tiny, straight teeth — both assuring me our secret was safe.

At night, after hearing our parents' door close, we quietly held our secret meetings. With animated sign language and the slightest of whispers, we'd remove the cowboy box and add any new coins that we had stashed in a pocket or sock.

Every two or three nights, one of my brothers held the flashlight while I, the official treasurer (the only one who could add), counted all the coins before my audience of two with the dramatic passion of a diva. My important role endowed me with unquestioned authority, which I, of course, used unscrupulously at times.

"When we get twenty more cents, we'll have four dollars," I announced one night, failing to mention I had secretly bought candy with one of the pennies I'd earned.

Silently exclaiming "FOUR DOLLARS!" Rodney threw up his thin arms and rolled his large brown eyes. Stevie squinted and squealed softly.

A few days before Christmas, we gleefully went shopping. We had less than five dollars, but with the unforgettable charity of Mrs. Wilson of Wilson's Florist, and Mr. Burger of Burger and Roth's Department Store, we bought Mom a ceramic pink flamingo balanced on one thin leg, and for Dad, a pair of fur-lined leather slippers.

The night of Christmas Eve seemed endless. At turns, I awoke, or one of my brothers woke me asking, "How long 'til daylight?"

On Christmas morning, we scurried into the living room bearing our gifts and a homemade card. A skinny, lighted pine tree with three newspaper-wrapped presents underneath surprised us briefly.

Eagerly, we handed Mommy and Daddy the card and their gifts. They were more than surprised. They were stunned!

Opening the boxes, they became *more* stunned — looking almost scared!

Sort of babbling, they asked confusing questions.

"How did you…?" "Where did you…?" "Who gave you…?"

As we explained how we'd schemed and earned and saved our money, their faces relaxed into expressions of astonishment. Then, through glistening tears, Mom and Dad gazed at us as if they were seeing a sunrise.

The scent of Christmas pine from the scraggly tree (donated from the leftover pile) infused the room. Its colored lights cast a magical glow on happy faces, including Dad's. The five of us hugged, talked, laughed and listened with fresh affection and gratitude.

Years later, Mom confessed that the ceramic flamingo was not an item she would have chosen; Dad admitted that the slippers were two sizes too large. Regardless, they always referred to them as the most precious and unforgettable gifts they'd ever received.

They were for me, too.

I can't remember what was in my own newspaper-wrapped present.

— Emily Rodavich —

70

A Christmas Surprise for Friends

*Without a sense of caring, there can
be no sense of community.*
~Anthony J. D'Angelo

"Let's do something different this year," I told my husband. "I'm tired of all the hoopla with trying to find the most and best and biggest gifts for our kids. They're old enough to learn more about the true meaning of giving at Christmas. Don't you think?"

"Uh, sure, I guess so." He looked puzzled.

I took a deep breath. "Well, why don't we limit our gift-giving to one gift for each child, and then buy the Jones kids some clothes. They've had such a hard year, what with little Cathy's surgeries and Larry out of work."

"Great idea," he agreed, surprising me with such a quick answer. "And let's get our kids involved."

When we told the kids they wouldn't be getting as much this year because we were going to help a needy family, they responded with excitement — another surprise for me. And since the Jones kids and ours were good friends, we decided not to tell them who our recipients would be, only that the family was in dire need.

"If you needed some new clothes, what kind would you want?"

I asked my children. Their responses were heartfelt.

"Warm jeans like ours. With flannel inside."

"And flannel shirts. We want them to be warm."

"Yeah, and warm socks. And mittens. And stocking hats to keep out the chilly wind. And boots to keep their feet warm and dry."

My daughter added, "And girlie blouses and jeans for their girls!"

I guessed at the size of each of the Jones family's four kids, and we went to work, list in hand. We shopped during the school's Christmas vacation, choosing a department store that carried children's clothing. Our kids danced from table to rack, *oohing* and *aahing* over the choices. With their enthusiastic input, we bought flannel shirts and flannel-lined jeans for the boys, pretty blouses for the girls, and socks and underwear, warm hats, and mittens for everyone.

I had lots of help wrapping the four boxes with gift paper. Our dining room table had never seen such bounty. Each gift box sported a different color and print — one with Santas, one with reindeer, another with candy canes, and the fourth with snowmen. After the kids went upstairs to bed, I printed each name on a special tag and finished the gift boxes with ribbons and bows.

"Wow, they look so festive," my husband said, smiling. "We have to make sure this is done in secret. We don't want the Joneses to feel embarrassed or beholden to us."

On Christmas morning before sunrise, after a quick prayer, we placed the gifts into two shopping bags and left for the Joneses' house. When we arrived, we parked down the road so they wouldn't see our car, and we carried the bags up their snowy drive. I prayed they wouldn't hear our squeaky footsteps and their back-porch door opening. We deposited the bags right in front of their kitchen door.

We hurried back to our car, breathing a sigh of relief. Just as we started down the road, I saw a light go on in the house. I smiled, happy and thankful our surprise Christmas remained a surprise for our friends.

Never have I experienced such a satisfying Christmas. Nor have our children, who reveled in giving a surprise Christmas to others rather than themselves. They now follow our example of giving to those in need.

—Sally Bair—

From Kentucky to Kenya and Back

Small acts of kindness can make a difference in other
people's lives more than we can imagine.
~Catherine Pulsifer

The chaos of the Christmas season was in full swing as I got out of the car and ran into the store. I glanced at my never-ending to-do list, hoping to quickly check off yet another errand. I had done this every Christmas for the last few years: shop for small toys, school supplies, and toothbrushes, pack them in a shoebox, and donate them to a ministry called Operation Christmas Child. The boxes are delivered to some of the poorest children in the world.

This year, I was filling a shoebox for a little girl between five and nine years old. I had no idea exactly how old she would be, where she lived, or what her life circumstances were. So as I perused the aisles and gathered the items, I tried to imagine what the little girl from far away might enjoy receiving when she opened my box. Suddenly, I noticed a small tea set with little cups, saucers, and a teapot with a lid. It was small, pink, and would fit easily into the shoebox. I added it to my cart and quickly made my way to the checkout lane. Another item could be checked off the holiday errand list!

As I finished packing the shoebox, I remembered to add our annual Christmas card, which was a family photo. Then I stuck an address label on the back, attached the "Girl, age 5–9" label on the lid, and dropped off the box at a local collection site. Another item checked off my list.

And that was that… or so I thought.

A few weeks later, a mysterious letter arrived from overseas. The letter was addressed to me. Perplexed, I began reading about an Irish woman who had visited an orphanage in Kenya while on a short-term mission trip. She described in detail a very special day while she was there, when the children were surprised by the arrival of boxes from an American humanitarian agency. Each box was filled with toys, candy and school supplies. An eight-year-old girl named Rhoda was there. The letter went on to explain that of all the children in the orphanage, Rhoda was the only one who had recently tested positive for HIV. And it was she who was given a box from a family in Kentucky who had included a card with their picture and address on it. My eyes filled with tears as I read the next words:

The box you sent brought her such joy… She felt like a princess. She knows about her condition, and that sometimes makes her very sad. When she showed me your family in the picture and she was smiling, I knew I had to write you. I want you and your family to know that today you made a difference to an eight-year-old girl. You may not have moved any mountains or even changed the world, but today you made a difference to Rhoda because today she smiled brighter than before.

The letter included two pictures of this little girl from Kenya. In one, she was holding a photo of my family in her hands. In the other, she was playing with that little pink tea set. I couldn't hold back the tears.

I realized at that moment that my mundane holiday errand was a life-changing moment for a child in need. The label attached to the top of the shoebox marked "Girl, age 5–9" was suddenly no longer vague and impersonal. Her name was Rhoda, and the simple gifts I had packed for her brought her joy. It made me want to be more generous and intentional with giving, knowing the difference that a simple act of kindness could make.

I read the letter to my kids and showed them where Kenya was located on the map. We prayed for the little girl who was holding our family photo in her hands. That night, Kenya and Kentucky didn't seem so far apart. And the world seemed a little smaller than before.

—Suzannah Kiper—

Armfuls of Happiness

*An effort made for the happiness of others
lifts us above ourselves.*
~Lydia M. Child

She squealed with glee when she saw them: thirty-two teddy bears spread out all over the couch. When I told her what they were for, she couldn't contain herself. Between sobs, she could hardly get out the words. "Thank you. Thank you. This is the best Christmas gift that anyone could have ever given me."

The idea came to me when I read an article in the morning paper on Christmas Eve. It described a "free store" that would be open all day, hosted by a local homeless shelter. People who could not afford a gift for their kids could come by and take whatever they wanted.

I decided to buy a bunch of toys and donate them to the free store in my mother's name! I'd already picked up a couple of small gifts for her, but this would be an extra special present. Since she had been an elementary school teacher for years and had such a soft heart for children, this would be the perfect Christmas surprise.

It had been a pretty rough winter for her so far. She had surgery in early November, and she was exhausted and weak. Although it had been nearly six weeks since she was released from the hospital, recovery can be extra slow at age eighty-four. We really needed an infusion of the Christmas spirit. And this could do it!

I called the number listed in the paper, but all the gifts had been taken, and they were starting to close up shop. It was only noon, so a lot of people must have really needed those toys for their kids.

But my idea was still percolating when I went to Walgreens just a few minutes later to pick up a prescription. I passed a display filled with teddy bears of every size and shape, and I knew just what to do! I would buy a bunch of teddy bears for the shelter.

I started pulling teddy bears from the shelves. I commandeered two shopping carts and filled both to the brim with brown, beige, and white teddies ranging from about nine inches to three feet tall. Quite a variety!

When I got to the checkout counter, a boy — he must have been no more than ten or eleven — kindly offered to help me push the carts and unload the teddies into the car.

Once I arrived home, the teddies stayed in the hatchback overnight. I would set them up early Christmas morning.

The next morning, after exchanging Christmas greetings, I brought my mother into the living room where the teddy bears were arrayed on the couch.

"Merry Christmas!" I announced. "This afternoon, all of these teddy bears are going to homeless children in your name."

Her face filled with a mixture of astonishment and delight, and the tears began to flow.

We took a picture of the teddies on the couch with Lola, my mother's Cockapoo, posing right next to them.

Later that morning, I took them over to a local shelter, where they were graciously accepted and distributed to the kids who had the least under their Christmas trees.

That night, thirty-two children would have something special to hold and comfort them.

— Harry Pickens —

You Shouldn't Have

The manner of giving is worth more than the gift.
~Pierre Corneille

French cooking class with a world-renowned chef, a stunning haute couture dress, and a sleek black negligee that made me feel like a Victoria's Secret model. Those were the gifts my oh-so-in-love husband bestowed on me during the early years of our marriage. Tom knew me so well — my size, my style, my passions.

As we settled into married life, the gifts were still wonderful but gradually became less inspired — a food processor, a terrycloth bathrobe, a jam of the month club membership. The same was true on my end. After all, how many watches does a guy need?

At around year twelve, I suggested that we stop getting each other gifts and consider our annual winter vacation our Christmas gift to each other. Tom agreed. Or so I thought.

Instead, he went underground. Plotting and planning super secret surprise gifts. I'd check in again and again. "We're not getting each other anything this year, right?"

"Right," he'd say.

So imagine my surprise that Christmas, when he disappeared into the basement and emerged with a giant wrapped rectangle for me. "You said no gifts!" I complained weakly even though I was completely delighted.

"I know," he said, "but this is something I really want you to have."

The Joy of Giving | 235

He sat close to me as I carefully pulled back the red and white snowflake paper to expose the limited edition numbered and autographed print from renowned artist Jacob Lawrence. We had met him the year before he died. Unfortunately, my husband had glued the valuable print into a $4.99 poster frame from Target.

"You shouldn't have," was all I could say as I tried to keep my face composed. I knew that rescuing this piece of art was going to cost us hundreds.

A few years later, when I was going through the hot flashes of menopause, Tom bought me long-sleeved quilted pajamas. "You shouldn't have," I said.

"Why don't you ever wear them?" he wondered a few weeks later.

Another year, we were at a discount store in the aisle of special gift ideas for people who have everything. There were electric foot massagers, fondue sets, and an "instant hot tub" device that you put into your bathtub to make it like a jacuzzi. I saw Tom looking at it wistfully. He knows how much I enjoy a hot tub. "I know what you're thinking," I said. "Do not get this for me. Listen to me. I do not want it. And I am not trying to use reverse psychology hoping that you'll get it for me anyway. I really do not want this."

So, I was not surprised one little bit when he presented me with a brick shaped box wrapped in Goofy Santa paper with a big green bow.

"Wow! I wonder what he got you this year," said my excited mother-in-law who was sitting with me on the love seat.

I channeled my inner actress, tore off the paper and exclaimed, "Oh how wonderful! But you shouldn't have…"

After everyone left, Tom said, "That was a good performance. I'll take it back tomorrow."

"From now on, no gifts, right?" I said, relieved that the message had finally gotten through.

"Right."

This year he gave me an aerobic dance CD. Why?

— Elaine Maly —

Chapter 9

Perfectly Imperfect

74

Keeping Christmas Past

Some Christmas tree ornaments do more than glitter
and glow, they represent a gift of love
given a long time ago.
~Tom Baker

They had to go. I had made up my mind that December. I was definitely getting rid of them. I opened the red and green storage boxes with determination, mentally declaring, "I think I can. I think I can. I know I can. I know I will. This Christmas, I will get rid of the shabby holiday decorations that have been tacky-ing up my house for years!"

The first box I opened revealed two elves — much earlier versions of the Elf on the Shelf. They were slightly creepy pixie dolls with no hands or feet that my husband and I had bought early in our marriage when "cheap" made everything attractive. With or without the ability to tattle on us to Santa, those shoddy elves were goners.

Packed away near the bottom of the box was an Old World Santa. For some reason, this particular Saint Nicholas had ditched his sleigh and reindeer and chosen to travel through our Christmas seasons behind the wheel of a metal steamboat. His presence in our decor had embarrassed me long enough. I was sending him and his sorry excuse for enchanted transit to The Salvation Army.

In the other boxes, I found our horribly mismatched stockings, the stuffed Santa bear that no longer played music when its paws were squeezed, and the Christmas potholders we used for coasters because they were so pitifully small. I set aside those things and others like them. Even the faded and frayed Santa Claus that I had saved from my childhood, whose plastic face fell off when he toppled over, was destined to retire to a corner of the attic. They were all going to be replaced.

I felt a sense of accomplishment in making those decisions and much pleasure in knowing that I would finally have a tacky-free holiday. I was satisfied.

"It's good to finally get rid of all that stuff."

I sat back and applauded myself.

"I knew I could do it."

Then my eyes fell on the substantial discard pile.

"Wow, there is a lot of stuff there."

I leaned in.

"Did I mean to throw out all of this?"

I looked closer.

"You know… some of it isn't all that bad."

I doubted myself.

"Should I really get rid of everything?"

My good intentions stepped in to guard against the signs of sentiment.

"Are you crazy? You should throw out every single one!"

They fought valiantly to stave off the enemy.

"Stand firm! Be strong! You can do this!"

But as I ran my eyes over those ratty, old decorations, I saw the memories that were attached to them. Those memories were the death of my good intentions.

The elves had joined our Christmases when our children were young. They were new and exciting (albeit creepy), and our kids thought they were wonderful. How could I get rid of my children's wonderment?

The mismatched stockings had been laid by our fireplace every Christmas morning since we became a family. Our oldest daughter had spent hours making those tiny potholders. And the faded, frayed

Santa whose face falls off came from my own childhood. He deserved to keep his prominent place on the mantel in our living room.

In the end, those Christmas decorations did not go anywhere. The elves, the potholders, the stockings, Santa and his steamboat — they're still on display during our holiday seasons. They keep company with many other trinkets that should have been thrown out long ago.

But this December, when the general state of tackiness overwhelms me, I will remind myself that my home is not decorated in bad taste. It is adorned with Christmas memories.

— Leigh Ann Northcutt —

75

Fruitcake: A Love Story

But some secrets are too delicious not to share.
~Suzanne Collins

Years ago, while living on the island of Guam, I found cooking holiday favorites a challenge. Everything had to be flown to the island. Therefore, we learned to be creative with recipes, and that was especially the case with baking a fruitcake.

This was long before the Internet and Google; my research involved the library, frantic letters home, and a lot of experimenting by substituting readily available ingredients for the ones I couldn't get on Guam. One day, I found the perfect recipe using local ingredients. Imagine my joy when it tasted delicious, too. My husband and I and the neighbors enjoyed it, and it helped us imagine it was really Christmas — even though we were on a tropical island and it was 85 degrees!

That recipe became my standard for fruitcake. For the next twenty-nine years, I made at least one or two because, once back in the States, I discovered that my extended family really liked it. I shared the recipe and had it printed in church cookbooks. I wrapped it and gave it as a gift. Even friends who "hated" fruitcake liked my version.

Later, during the years when it was just my son and me for holidays, he soon learned that, like a "real" tree and special Santa gifts, the fruitcake was Christmas. Every year, he shared the first piece with me and assured me that it was good.

"Even better than last year, Mom," he'd say. It continued to be part of our family tradition.

Christmas 2005 was different. Our country was involved in the Iraq War, and my son, now grown up and in the Air Force, was far away and would not be home for Christmas. My heart was heavy as I shopped for Christmas presents for him and wondered what I could send that would not spoil and would be useful in the small quarters he shared with his teammates at the Baghdad airport.

As I prepared the package, I wrapped everything festively, thinking that even the wrapping paper would bring a feeling of Christmas and home to him. I added a small Christmas tree, some battery lights, and then the last thing in the box: a large piece of the fruitcake, wrapped tightly in tinfoil and then Christmas wrapping paper with a big red bow. I paid extra postage and said a prayer that it would get there in time and before anything spoiled... especially the fruitcake.

Before Christmas, I received a rare phone call. My son was safe and, yes, the package had arrived in good shape. He thanked me for the "goodies" and wished me a Merry Christmas. I felt good that I had been able to share a little of home and the holidays with him although he was a world away and in a war zone. I did not want to think about that too much; instead, I concentrated on the fact that the things I had sent had made his holiday a little better and was glad that he had enjoyed the fruitcake.

Oh, if I had only known!

The following year at Christmas, my son was home, and I was happily preparing his favorite foods. As we were talking, I mentioned the fact that I was baking the fruitcake. It must have been something on my son's face that caused me to stop and ask him what he was thinking. It was only then that he started to laugh and agreed to tell me the story of the fruitcake and Christmas at the Baghdad airport!

He started out quietly, hesitating a little and looking at me with a cautious expression. "Well, Mom, you see, I never really liked that fruitcake."

Puzzled, I stopped what I was doing and said, "What? You have liked that fruitcake all of your life!"

Laughing, he said, "No, I haven't. But I didn't want to hurt your feelings — you were so proud of it. I didn't want you to know that I didn't like it. I don't like any fruitcake!"

So, I asked, "What on earth did you do with the cake I sent you for Christmas?" I was thinking to myself, *I paid all that extra postage… only to have him trash the cake!*

At this point, he could not contain himself. He laughed loudly and said, "Oh, it was really hard to get rid of. I tried to trade with the other guys, but they all laughed at me. No one wanted fruitcake. I told them it was really good — if you liked fruitcake. But no one likes fruitcake."

By this time, I, too, was laughing hysterically as I listened to him describe going from cot to cot trying to make a trade with each of his teammates. Then, when he was unsuccessful, he went next door to the Army tent and tried to find someone, anyone, who would trade with him or at least take the cake so he would not have to trash it. At one point, the guys were taking the fruitcake and tossing it back and forth, teasing my son about getting fruitcake in his care package.

Fortunately, he is a good sport and was determined to make the best of a "gift from Mother" situation. He did finally find a soldier who liked fruitcake and made his trade, even though the treasured piece of fruitcake was no longer in the best condition.

The story of the fruitcake is one I will treasure forever. My son is a good storyteller, and as I listened to him, I could "see" the scene as the piece of holiday-wrapped fruitcake was tossed back and forth by the young airmen, giving them a few minutes of fun in the midst of a dangerous, lonely situation.

But more important than that funny scene was the knowledge that since he was a very little boy, my son had eaten the obligatory piece of fruitcake and never told me he did not like it. He ate it because he knew it was important to me. That was his gift to me, and it was the best gift of all.

Today, I still bake the fruitcake and always tease him that I am making one just for him. He and I laugh and remember his story of the fruitcake at the Baghdad airport, and again I am thankful for the gift of his love (and that he made it back from that assignment safely). The cake, which came to be a part of my Christmas celebration out of necessity so long ago, had come full circle — from an island in the Pacific to a desert airfield in Iraq and back home to Florida. It is my symbol of the best of Christmas.

— Glenda Wood —

76

The Doorknob

Every man's memory is his private literature.
~Aldous Huxley

When I was twenty-eight, my parents asked, like they did every year, "What would you like for Christmas?" At the time, I really didn't need much. I had a good job, a girlfriend who loved me, and generally all the material things I needed to function and survive in this life. But I told them I would think about it, as they always wanted to give me and my siblings something meaningful. At the time of their request, they were having the exterior of the house redone: new siding, windows and doors. Especially doors. Thirty-four years of slams and jams had worn out the old hinges and knobs.

Then it hit me.

I thought about all the people I had ever known and loved... about how every single one of them had turned that one knob on the door that led into our garage to where the main kitchen entrance was. All my family, all my friends, all my relatives... special visits, happy visits, sad visits. Even the only grandparent who I knew touched that doorknob. So many people and so many memories. I thought I would like to have that old doorknob. But, strangely enough, I didn't ask them to give it to me for Christmas; I just asked them to save it for me for the above reasons. It represented everything I could remember about my house being a home.

I turned it with excitement when I came home from school...

especially on a Friday. I turned it with trepidation if I was late or I thought I was in trouble for something. I turned it and jostled it with great ferocity when I was afraid and wanted to get away from a storm or some imagined bogeyman that surely lurked in the darkness. When inside, I pushed in the knob and felt confident that the old lock would keep everyone in my family safe.

The trusty, old doorknob. So many twists. So many turns… just like my life.

That Christmas, my siblings and I gathered to celebrate the holidays with our parents once more. We marveled at the exterior makeover of our old home. It was almost unrecognizable with its new look. The roof was sturdy and reliable once again. The siding was a bright and welcoming white. The new windows gleamed, and all the doors opened without a creak.

I was a bit sad thinking I would never again see the house the way I remembered it, but the change was good for my parents. They had always worried about "the roof caving in" so they were very pleased with the finished result. I could see the positive effect it had on their morale, and I felt good that they were once again comfortable in their home. It marked the beginning of a new chapter for them and all of us. Old and, one day, new hands would touch the new doorknob at the garage entrance.

On Christmas morning, after opening all our gifts, my mom pointed to one gift hidden way back under the tree. One of my sisters retrieved it for me. It was a small but weighty box. My mom would always say, "Don't rush! Make it fun! Shake it! See if you can guess!" So I placated my mom with the ritual Christmas present-guessing game. "Is it a gold bar? A chunk of lead? Perhaps a replacement part for my crumbling junker of a car?" I failed the guessing game, but was not penalized and given permission to open the box, which I did so with earnest.

Inside was the old doorknob, covered in gouges and scratches from untold thousands of attempts to find the keyhole. Its brass had given way to a silver and copper looking patina, well worn and weathered. I held the knob in my hands and like the sap I am, bawled my eyes out. It was probably the most beautiful gift I'd ever received. To me, it represented all the love and joy of family and friends that I was so fortunate to receive and share while growing up in that wonderful, old house.

Whereas that knob once opened the door to the welcoming warmth of our home, it now opened a door to the depths of my heart.

— Michael J. Cunningham —

77

The Perfect Christmas Tree

The perfect Christmas tree?
All Christmas trees are perfect.
~Charles N. Barnard

My husband and I have raised three children together, and like any married couple, have survived disappointments and bumps in the marital road. Many of those bumps were encountered at Christmas, when we set out to find the perfect Christmas tree. We never, not even once, agreed on which tree to buy. Inevitably, whichever one of us won the argument was then confronted by defects of the chosen tree once we set it up at home. Nevertheless, the tree always looked beautiful once it was adorned with lights and ornaments. But not perfect.

After the children left home and had their own Christmas trees, we bought an artificial tree. Surely, a fake tree would be perfect. But it wasn't. It was pathetic. For once, both of us agreed. The artificial tree wasn't for us, and we gave it to a friend.

And so the annual search for the perfect tree continued, and even became a joke. As we headed to the tree lot, one of us would mutter, "Off for the traditional fight."

Until this year. Perhaps after fifty-six years of marriage we finally developed some common sense, or perhaps we are just too old to argue. Or maybe, miracle of miracles, we finally realized that nothing is perfect.

We went to our favorite Christmas tree lot and examined the trees, which were all encased in netting. "Do you like these?" my husband asked, pointing to a bin of trees. I did. He picked one out. We did not ask the salesperson to take off the netting, or fluff out the branches, or spin the tree around. We declined his offer to show us other trees. He looked perplexed. Perhaps he remembered us from prior years.

We bought the tree without an argument. We took it home, set it up, and admired it together.

Ah, I sighed. At last, the perfect imperfect Christmas tree.

—Josephine Fitzpatrick—

A Pony in the Living Room

A horse doesn't care how much you know until
he knows how much you care.
~Pat Parelli

I was getting a pony for Christmas! I knew it! I held the proof in my hand!

At our house, Santa often left presents a few days early. Sometimes, it was just to remind us he was watching us. Sometimes, they didn't fit into his sleigh. Sometimes, they were a clue as to what we could expect to find under the tree. Always, they came with a note in Santa's large, curly handwriting.

Santa had left me a manure fork beside our Christmas tree five days before Christmas in 1968. The note read:

If you really want a pony, you'll have to learn how to use this.
Love, Santa.
P.S. Couldn't fit this in my sleigh with everything else this year.

"A pony would be a lot of work," my father reminded me, echoing Santa's warning. Was I ready to take on the responsibility?

"Yes! Yes! Yes!" was my answer as I danced around the kitchen with the manure fork with the big red bow.

All I saw in that manure fork was a bright-eyed pony who would love me as much as I already loved her or him. However, Santa saw road apples and wet straw that were beyond my sight.

It was Friday and the last day of school before Christmas break. I wanted to take my manure fork to school to show everyone the proof that this was my year to get a pony! But my mom insisted that if a manure fork didn't fit in a magic sleigh, it definitely would not fit on a school bus.

So, I had to settle for telling everyone that I was getting a pony because Santa left me a manure fork. No one believed me. They were mostly city kids and did not understand that a manure fork was proof-positive I was getting a pony for Christmas. But I knew. In my mind, I could see my pony already, standing by the Christmas tree in our living room, waiting for me.

The five days leading up to Christmas were the longest of my eight-year-old life. Christmas Eve was torture. I knew I wouldn't sleep. I heard hoofbeats and sleigh bells outside my window, along with a pony's whinny and a reindeer's snort. I smelled hay and carrots, molasses feed and apples. The night before Christmas was the cruelest night, and I squeezed my eyes shut as a last resort.

A moment later, the sun was peeking through the curtains. I heard sleigh bells for real and rushed to the window. Nothing. Then my father called up the stairs, "Santa's been here!"

I was the first one down the steps, ahead of both brothers and both sisters — all older and faster than me. In mid-flight, I realized the door to the living room was closed. It could only mean one thing: A pony was in the living room, and my parents didn't want it wandering around the house.

"We are going to church before we open presents," my dad explained. "We are not going to be late for Mass again this year."

My mom was at the stove smiling as she made breakfast, and I knew my dad had winked at her over my head.

There was definitely a pony in the living room!

We were early for Mass — the longest Mass in the entire history of the Catholic Church. All I could think of was my poor pony standing all alone in our living room beside the Christmas tree with a big red bow (even larger than the one on the manure fork) wondering where I was and why I didn't come and bring her an apple to eat.

I sang the last hymn as loudly as I could so everyone would hurry up. People walk faster after they sing real loud, but they still wasted a lot of time wishing each other "Merry Christmas" over and over. I pestered my dad to drive faster on the way home, but it only made him drive slower. When he finally pulled in the driveway, I could hardly wait for the car to stop so I could jump out.

My pony wasn't in the living room. She was sticking her head out of the barn door, and I ran to her. Her name was Lucky, and to this day, the name gives me chills.

She was a brown-and-white paint straight off the cover of *Misty of Chincoteague* by Marguerite Henry, a book I had read so many times I nearly had it memorized. A secondhand saddle and bridle were under the Christmas tree, and my parents said I could take my first ride as soon as I changed my clothes. Five minutes later, apple in hand, I was ready to ride off into the December sunset on Lucky.

I settled into the saddle like a pro, all smiles and proud as only a kid with her first pony can be. My brother led us once around the barnyard before he let me go solo. As soon as he released her, Lucky ducked her head and lit into one of the finest bucking horse exhibitions our county had ever witnessed. She sent me sailing into the soft mud. Well, it wasn't so soft either; there was frozen ground beneath the mud. When I started breathing again and crawled to my feet, I got back on the pony.

I have read in all the best books on riding that only those who never ride, never fall. By that definition, I "rode" that Christmas. I climbed back into the saddle five times, and five times that loco pony bucked like a champion and sent me flying for a crash landing. I would have kept climbing back on, too, if my parents hadn't called timeout.

The following day, I learned that ponies kick and bite, too. The gentle mare my parents had watched the previous owner's children pile on bareback in the pasture and ride with nothing more than a halter turned into a terror.

When I limped into class after the New Year, I told everyone that

Lucky was from Chincoteague and still a little wild—not being very used to people and the strange sights of Ohio.

Two weeks later, Lucky's old owner took her back and refunded my dad his forty-five dollars. It turned out that Lucky was incredibly homesick for her old family. As soon as she returned to them, so did her gentle ways, and "her kids" piled aboard bareback and rode off on her with nothing but a halter and lead rope to steer their steed. I felt betrayed.

I disowned Lucky as my first pony and gave that honor to a little black pony named Star who made up for what he lacked in stature with a horse-sized sense of humor. I thought of Star as more of a big dog than a pony. Like all of our dogs, Star was a rescue. His former owner had bought him for a granddaughter who quickly lost interest. Star was a waste of feed on a beef farm, so my dad bought him for twenty-five dollars.

Star was only forty-two inches tall and boring black with a big white spot in the middle of his forehead. He didn't look like a pony from the cover of a book, and I really treated him more like a dog than a pony. After getting thrown so many times by Lucky, I wasn't eager to climb aboard Star. So I gladly cleaned his stall and then spent most of my time teaching him tricks—counting, shaking hands, bowing, standing on a heavy box my dad made for him, and shaking his head "yes" and "no." Star would steal my hat and gloves and run off with them. Like a dog, Star would do most anything for a carrot or sugar cube.

I didn't ride Star until my dad threatened to sell him if I didn't. I loved Star too much to let that happen. Star wasn't very well broken, but he wasn't mean. He would nip me if I forgot to give him a treat when he thought he had earned it, and he was inclined to rub me off on a tree if I didn't pay attention while riding in the woods. Star taught me to ride better than any human instructor. I took a few tumbles from Star, but he waited for me to climb back on and found the way home when I got us lost in the hills.

In summer, I let Star loose in the yard to eat grass. When he got full and bored, he would come up on the front porch and peer into the living room through the screen door. I was always tempted to let him into the living room — just once.

Star wasn't a storybook horse like Misty or Flicka, but he was the first of many horses in my life that came with road apples and wet straw — the sort of real horses that Santa knew I wanted when he left me a manure fork in 1968. I got my first blister from that fork and bent a prong cleaning a frozen stall one year. Fifty years later, I still tie a red ribbon around it every Christmas.

—Linda K. Hren—

The Cut-Rate Poinsettia

Christmas isn't a season. It's a feeling.
~Edna Ferber

As Christmas approached one year, my mother exclaimed out of the blue, "Why is it that other women are given beautiful flowers by their so-called loved ones for no reason whatsoever, and I don't even warrant a poinsettia at Christmas? It doesn't seem like a lot to ask. I don't want some fancy plant from the florist. Any broken-stemmed reject from a discount department store would do."

I may or may not have rolled my eyes at her. *Fine,* I thought, with all the disdain that only a teenage daughter can command. *If that's what she wants, that's what she'll get.* That evening, I trotted off to the local cut-rate emporium and picked out the most disreputable specimen of seasonal flora I could find.

"Here," I said when I got home, slamming down the plastic bag triumphantly before her. "You asked for it, you got it."

My mother opened it, saw the woebegone little plant inside and promptly burst into tears.

"It's lovely," she cried, hugging me (and the plant) to her ample bosom. The poor thing, with its single red leaf, was placed in the most coveted spot on the mantel. Throughout the season, she pointed the gift out to all as if it were a diamond tiara.

Somehow a tradition had been started, and every year after that it became a point of honour for me to present her with the most bedraggled little plant I could find. She never failed to exclaim over it or express her disdain for what she referred to as the soulless pots of perfection with which her friends were forced to decorate their homes.

As time passed, the yearly poinsettia seemed to become a kind of surrogate daughter. She was able to lavish the attention on it that my prickly nature refused to accept. I remember the Christmas Day my husband and I endured a nasty eight-hour drive home from the distant city we had moved to. That was another year she cried when I gave her the plant I'd brought along with me, confessing how worried she'd been all day that "it" wouldn't survive the trip.

The situation was reversed a few years later when my parents flew out to spend Christmas with us in our new home even farther away. I picked them up at the airport late at night and brought them home to a house that was almost fully decorated. The next morning, I went out to buy the poinsettia and gave it to my mother's adored eighteen-month-old granddaughter to present when she came down for breakfast. Again, there were tears.

My mother was obviously unwell that Christmas, but I didn't realize how ill. Nor did I realize that it would be the last poinsettia I would ever give her. She died the following June.

The next year, my father flew out alone to spend Christmas with us. We knew it would be difficult, but enough time had passed since my mother's death to take the edge off our grief. He came quite early in December, so he was able to get involved with all the decorating and preparation for the season. We baked cookies, shopped, cut down the tree and generally threw ourselves determinedly into the trappings of the season.

One day, the three of them — my father, husband and daughter — came home from shopping with tentative smiles and a carefully protected package held in front of them. Inside was a poinsettia. It was large and showy, and that difference was the only thing that kept the tears in check as I gave it a place of honour on the mantel.

That was many Christmases ago. My father has been gone for several years, and we have moved once again. Many other things have changed as well. But every Christmas, my husband and long-suffering teenage daughter come home with the most disreputable looking poinsettia they can find. Sometimes, its only stem is bent. When we were living out in the country, it often needed first aid for frostbite after enduring a forty-minute drive in our inadequately heated pickup truck. But its arrival is as much a tradition as any other ceremony of the season.

—Denise Flint—

80

The Gift of Love

The greatest gift that you can give anyone
is your pure love.
~Debasish Mridha

Teenagers. Some say it's hard to live with them. I say it's sad to live without them. That is where my heart was the Christmas our son Chris was nineteen and our daughter Melissa was seventeen. I was overwhelmed by the reality that in just a few short years, they would both be off pursuing their own lives. I decided I wanted to tell them how much I loved them in a way they would never forget.

I came up with a plan. Being a good kindergarten teacher, I chose to use the five senses as my way of accomplishing this important assignment. It would require a separate gift for each sense for them to open on Christmas morning.

For the sense of sight, I gave each of them a framed photo of the three of us. This was no easy task since I was usually behind the camera. I did manage to find one nice one of us in our front yard, so that would have to do.

The sense of taste was accomplished through the compiling of a recipe book for each of them containing some of their favorite dishes I had made over the years. I really had to think through some of these recipes since I don't usually measure everything as I cook.

When it came to the sense of smell, I bought each of them a small bottle of my favorite perfume. I figured if they were missing me, they could smell the cologne, and it would bring me closer to them.

A CD called *The Line Between the Two* by Mark Harris containing the song "Find Your Wings" was how I wrapped up their sense of hearing. This song said everything I wanted them to know. I gave them roots, and now I wanted to give them wings!

This just left the sense of touch. For this one, I had to get a little more creative. I decided to make each of them a fleece blanket. On the blanket I hand-appliquéd a cutout of my hand with a red heart in the palm. The idea was that when they wrapped the blanket around themselves, my hand would be over their heart. I know it sounds a little cheesy, but I was all in by that point.

Christmas morning finally came. I was so excited to give them their special gifts of love. I saved these special gifts until the end. When it was time, I explained how much I wanted them to always know my love, and I was using these five gifts to convey that message.

I had them open the CD first so we could all listen to the song together. They proceeded through the rest of the gifts, saving the blanket for last. As they opened the blanket, they looked at each other, and then looked at me with tears in their eyes. Our daughter Melissa asked finally, "Mom, are you dying?"

Well, I didn't see that coming!

— Janell Michael —

81

The Christmas of My Dreams

Christmas now surrounds us, happiness is everywhere.
Our hands are busy with many tasks
as carols fill the air.
~Shirley Sallay

I have a recurring stress dream about Christmas. It always starts the same way. *Suddenly, I realize that it's Christmas Eve, and nothing is done. There are no trees, gifts, or groceries ready to be cooked into a holiday feast. The halls are decidedly un-decked. I panic and* rush to the store, but the shelves are bare. There's no food left. All the presents, decorations, and rolls of wrapping paper are sold out. There aren't even any Christmas trees. Christmas is ruined, and somehow it's all my fault. Then I wake up in a cold sweat.

I know exactly where this dream comes from. My family never did Christmas "right." We were those slackers who finally got around to getting a tree on December twenty-third. I have no memories of my mom ever hanging a wreath, and we had zero lights around our windows. Sure, we had a nice dinner. My mom was a great cook, but the turkey and candied sweet potatoes were served on paper plates because she liked everything casual. No fuss. That was why she never wrapped our gifts. My sister and I would get our gifts — tags still dangling — in the bags they came in. And since Mom hated surprises, she could never wait until Christmas morning to give them to us. It drove me insane. As a kid, all I wanted was to be in charge so I could "fix" Christmas and make ours like the ones I saw on TV.

I vowed that when I grew up, I'd never put together such shoddy holidays. I'd watched a Martha Stewart Christmas special when I was about twelve, and the elegant tables, handcrafted ornaments, families in matching plaid, candles glimmering in real crystal holders, holly sprigs, and homemade eggnog enchanted me. That was a real Christmas, I thought, and that's what I wanted.

Motherhood finally gave me the chance I'd been waiting for. It had been two and a half decades since I'd first seen Martha artfully arrange those poinsettias, but the image had been burned into my memory forever, and I recalled every detail. My daughter was four now, and she'd be able to remember this year. I felt like I owed her the picturesque Christmases I never had, so as soon as Black Friday was over, I embarked on what can only be described as a Christmas blitzkrieg. I was going to do everything, and it was going to be perfect. My little one was going to be so happy.

Except… things didn't go exactly as planned. What was supposed to be a magical morning spent decorating the tree while sipping hot chocolate (homemade, with organic artisan cocoa powder), and listening to classic carols ended up with my daughter in tears in a heap on the living-room floor, while a blackened pan of snickerdoodles smoked in the oven. This wasn't exactly what I'd imagined.

I don't know what music was playing at the time, but it wasn't the Mormon Tabernacle Choir version of "O Come, All Ye Faithful." I'm pretty sure it was heavy metal. My daughter thought the holiday choir music was "scary" and wanted to play her favorite movie soundtrack (which was highly annoying). Then she seemed uninterested in trimming the tree and wanted to make cookies. When they were done, she tossed sprinkles all over them, completely destroying the tasteful, minimalist Scandinavian look I was going for, which I'd seen in an issue of *Martha Stewart Living*.

When she finally wanted to decorate the tree, it seemed we had very different ideas about what that entailed. She liked a low grouping of ornaments clustered within a single, ten-inch radius while leaving the rest of the tree stark naked. This fir was nowhere near magazine-worthy. To tell the truth, I was embarrassed to even post it on Instagram. We weren't wearing our matching plaid jumpers anyway, and that's because we didn't have matching plaid jumpers. We were still wearing our pajamas.

It got worse when I tried to make a gingerbread house. Apparently, to really do it right, one needs an advanced degree in cookie architecture. My house collapsed. Its roof slid, and the chimney was crooked. Once I finally got the thing to stand up, my daughter attacked it with a zeal and fervor that was frankly alarming. It looked like a Jackson Pollock painting when she was done. I kept trying to tell her where to place the Skittles and marshmallows, but the kid was having none of it.

"Mommy, it's beautiful," she sighed, with a clump of dried frosting stuck in her left eyebrow.

It was not beautiful. It was the stuff of nightmares — my recurring nightmares, to be exact. Maybe I was psychic, and now my dreams were coming true. The holidays were going to be ruined because I couldn't get my act together. I felt like the tragic heroine of every made-for-TV holiday film — it was up to me to save Christmas, and I was failing.

"Honey, the gingerbread house looks a mess. Let's try to make it look like this one I saw on Pinterest," I suggested.

My daughter looked crestfallen.

"Why, Mommy? I like my gingerbread house. I think it's pretty like this. You don't like what I did?" she asked.

I didn't know what to say.

"You thought the tree was ugly, too, and I was trying to help you make it nice," she said.

She got up from the kitchen table, wiped her hands, and went into her bedroom to watch her iPad while I cleaned up.

That's when I remembered a story my mom had once told me about her own childhood.

"My mom always had to have everything perfect," she said. "We weren't even allowed to go into our living room when we were kids, and on Christmas we'd be in hot water if we got anywhere close to the tree. My mom wouldn't let anyone touch it."

My mother told me that their Christmas tree was a showpiece that stood proudly in their picture window so all the neighbors could see it. There'd been no festive tree-trimming parties because my grandmother had meticulously decorated every branch herself, usually when the kids were at school.

"She knew we'd mess it up. The ornaments wouldn't be spaced evenly. We'd put too much tinsel in one spot, not enough in another, and probably break a piece she loved. She wanted it to look just so, and you know how children are. Little kids can't make it look perfect," Mom told me.

"That's so sad," I said.

"As kids, we never cared about that stuff anyway. It didn't matter to us what the tree looked like. You know what we cared about?" Mom asked.

"Toys?" I guessed.

Mom smiled and shook her head.

"We were poor, so we didn't get a lot of toys. A doll and a new dress maybe."

"What was it then?" I asked.

"We cared about people. My brothers and sister and I loved visiting my grandparents. We loved having a big dinner with our family. My grandmother made every kind of pie you can imagine, and everyone was happy and talking and hugging. I'll never forget how special it felt. That's why when you were growing up, I never stressed out about the garlands and bows. I focused on being with you kids, having fun, and being relaxed."

Mom was telling the truth, and because I was too busy complaining that our family holidays didn't look like a scene from Currier & Ives, I'd overlooked what had mattered most — the fun we'd had, the memories we made, and the laughter we shared. Our Christmases were a blast. Sure, Mom may have slacked on the decorations, but she gave her all when it came to love and generosity.

Our family had never missed out on togetherness, and neither would my daughter. I knew now how ridiculous I'd been. It was time to relax and prioritize my *presence* with my daughter instead of perfectly wrapped *presents* for her. Kids don't want a tree that's a museum piece. They just like the process of decorating it with people they love.

I owed my little girl an apology for being such a perfectionist, which she happily accepted with a hug. This yuletide wasn't a nightmare after all. It was the real Christmas of my dreams.

That year, our tree may have been a little wonky, and our gingerbread house a bit slipshod. The snickerdoodles went in the trash. In the end, when I finally let go of my ridiculous expectations and really started having fun, I realized what truly matters during the holiday season: spending time with the people we love most.

—Victoria Fedden—

A Rockin' New Year's Eve Indeed

Life begins at the end of your comfort zone.
~Neale Donald Walsch

"Three, two, one. Happy New Year!" I screamed the words as loud as I could, for a second not worrying about how hoarse my voice was going to be the next day or how tired my legs were from standing for fifteen hours straight. The confetti fell from every direction. The crowd cheered with a collective voice louder than any I'd ever heard, and I finally understood what it felt like to be gathered, in such a state of joy, in the heart of the Big Apple with tens of thousands of people from all over the world.

My best friend leaned on my shoulder with a look of pure happiness on her face as we all began to sing. Whatever exhaustion we'd previously felt had been forgotten, and for just one moment, life felt truly magical.

That year we'd hardly seen each other. We were both in college, struggling through exams and schoolwork. That's why we needed to do something fun and adventurous together.

Ever since we had met in high school, we had spent New Year's Eve together. And every year we watched the ball drop in Times Square on TV, and said we would go there one day from our small town in the South.

Our parents thought we were crazy, and our friends did, too. But we didn't let that stop us. We planned, planned, and then planned some more. We met up on random weekends to work out our schedule, to buy tickets for everything we wanted to do and, most importantly, to plan just how to stand in Times Square for fifteen hours straight.

When the big day finally arrived, everyone thought we were going to back out. The weather had changed drastically, from being in the upper thirties to being snowy and colder than any cold we had ever experienced. It was one of the coldest New Year's Eves in New York City on record. Whereas my mom had once said, "Make sure you dress warm enough," she now said, "You're going to freeze. Are you sure you have to go?"

Of course, we didn't make it that far to back out, and so we did go. And, of course, we did freeze, but only a little. After settling into our hotel and then spending a few days in the city, we set our alarms for seven o'clock in the morning, tried to forget about the fact that our feet were already hurting, and went to sleep.

When we woke up in the morning, things moved rather quickly. We wanted the best spot possible, so we had to get there early. We heard it was going to be crowded, and there's only so much space in Times Square, right? So, we threw on layer after layer of clothes — two pairs of pants, two pairs of socks, boots, two undershirts, a sweater, a coat, a heavy-duty jacket, a hat, gloves, a scarf, and a neck warmer. It was hard to walk!

Still, we made it work, and before we knew it, we were on a bus from our hotel in New Jersey and headed toward the Big Apple. Once we got there, we found our way to the line pretty quickly, considering everyone else was pushing their way in the same direction. Once we got in line, we waited to finally get into our gated area, which was pretty spacious and close to the actual ball, something that we were very excited about. While we waited for the festivities to start, we met people from all walks of life and all over the world.

Halfway through the day, my friend and I couldn't feel our toes. We sat down on the ground in Times Square, took off each other's shoes, and shoved in some hand-warmers. We ate cheese sticks covered in turkey, jumped up and down, and did pretty much anything we could think of to stay warm. The temperature kept dropping, but our spirits never did, at least not enough to make us actually want to leave.

Before we knew it, performers were singing, and we were singing along. About an hour before the ball dropped, I vividly remember thinking about leaving because I had never been that tired or cold in my life. But then I remembered everything we had gone through to get there and how amazing it all was.

Even though I can't really remember the last hour of the event — I think at that point sleep deprivation had finally gotten the best of me — I don't think my best friend and I will ever forget the moment the clock struck midnight, and we knew, really knew, we had done something amazing.

— Ashley Oldham —

Homemade Holidays

83

Pop Pop's Workshop

Gifts of time and love are surely the basic ingredients
of a truly merry Christmas.
~Peg Bracken

Pint-sized carpenter aprons hang on a hook in the basement, silently revealing the passage of time. The need for the aprons began two decades ago. One cold, late-November evening, after the last turkey casserole from Thanksgiving had been eaten, my husband Chris said to me, "Wouldn't it be fun to have the boys make something special for their parents for Christmas?"

"They're preschoolers. Aren't they a little young?" I asked. "What in the world could they make?" It was a foolish question for my highly inventive husband. He was already brimming with ideas.

Since Pop Pop had his own carpenter apron, I thought our little grandsons needed theirs, too. I purchased some sturdy denim fabric and created mini-aprons with deep pockets for tools of the trade: bottles of craft paint, sponge brushes, tubes of glitter, and lots of glue.

When Pop Pop's "Christmas workshop" opened, Joey and Christian could barely see over the top of the workbench as they worked on their gifts for their parents. As the years passed, they were joined by their cousins, Kevin and Erin. All four of them donned their aprons every December and made gifts in Pop Pop's workshop.

In the early years, the gifts were simple wooden trivets and napkin holders embellished with the tiny handprints of their creators. We also purchased unpainted wooden trays from the craft store and the grandkids painted them, and then decoupaged on their favorite family photos.

Over time, the gifts grew more complicated. Pop Pop took great joy in teaching Kevin, Christian, and Joey how to safely use a scroll saw to design intricate Christmas tree ornaments. As the three boys moved further into their teen years, another rite of passage began. The older boys wanted to create metal art gifts by learning to weld — as their grandfather does. I must admit I had to stay out of the workshop for those lessons. Apparently, grandfathers are more daring than grandmothers. Protective headgear replaced the childhood aprons.

During scroll-saw and welding lessons, I could be found in the kitchen with Erin. As the sounds of machinery emanated from the basement workshop, Erin and I sat together at the newspaper-covered kitchen table with mountains of glitter, sequins, craft-store jewels, and trays filled with undecorated glass ornaments. Erin turned them into works of art.

The elder boys are now twenty-six and twenty-four. When they went away to college, I had said to my husband, "I'm sure they will be far too busy to come to Pop Pop's Christmas workshop now." Wrong! When final exams ended each December, they would squeeze in time to visit the workshop. The first Christmas they were both away, they made wooden ornaments with their college logos decoupaged in place.

Time has a way of switching roles within a family. Our four grandchildren now challenge their grandfather with increasingly sophisticated visions for their homemade gifts. They still seem just as excited about creating them as they were when they were little kids.

The tiny carpenter aprons that started it all still hang from their hooks in the basement. Although they have been washed many times, the paint, glue, and glitter stains of Christmases past grace them. Pop Pop's Christmas workshop created treasured, homemade memories for three generations of our family.

— Judy Harch —

84

An Unorthodox Thanksgiving

Home is where love resides, memories are created,
friends always belong, and laughter never ends.
~Author Unknown

We nuns were allowed to go home for Thanksgiving dinner with our families. Since my family lived in Pittston, Pennsylvania, a small coal-mining town a short ride away from our school-and-convent in Dunmore, I chose to spend Thanksgiving with Mom and Dad.

Dad had phoned me with this hesitant apology: "Honey, would you mind if just this once we have the Thanksgiving dinner that Mom and I like now that we live alone? All our lives, we wanted you kids to feel 'American' and not out of place, so we had turkey dinners. Mom and I actually hate turkey, cranberry sauce and pumpkin pie, but we didn't want you kids to feel 'different.' However, if you want a traditional Thanksgiving, no problem."

I assured him that I loved Italian food. "May I invite some nuns whose families live far away? A few of them will be alone in the convent." I heard silence on the other end. "Don't worry," I insisted. "They'll know the menu." Dad agreed, so I slipped this note under the bedroom doors of the other Sisters:

Dear Sister:

You are invited to Thanksgiving Dinner with the Palmeri Family, IF you like this Thanksgiving menu: Homemade Italian Lentil soup with tiny pasta, chopped carrots-celery-onions-garlic & smothered with fresh Parmesan cheese, grated right off the "block." "Polpetti," Italian hamburger/meatballs ground at home from fresh steak straight from the local butcher, seasoned with minced garlic-cheese-onion-mint-and homemade cheese-seasoned breadcrumbs. Tossed Italian salad with extra-virgin olive oil: Garden tomatoes, cukes, minced celery, onions, radishes, carrots, apple-cider vinegar-black olives. Homemade Italian bread covered with sesame seeds, dipped in olive oil.

I remember my second-grade teacher chirping conversationally, "How many of you children are having turkey for Thanksgiving?" Most of my little classmates' Italian mamas would be preparing ravioli, lasagna and braciole. I was proud to raise my hand. We were having turkey! Only after Dad's call did I learn that my Italian-American parents wanted us to "fit in," and had made the sacrifice of eating food they disliked just so their children could feel "American."

I remembered my little friend Joanie whispering sadly, "We're only having rabbit. My father raises them. We have seven kids. We either have fried rabbit or baked rabbit, but we always have rabbit!"

Now my Dad was getting nervous, as a number of my fellow Sisters had accepted my invitation. He kept phoning: "Are you sure the nuns won't mind? What will they think of us? Your mother's getting nervous. It's not too late for us to order a turkey and the trimmings."

"Daddy, the nuns chose to come. They're thrilled that they're 'going out' and don't have to cook it themselves," I assured him.

On Thanksgiving Day, the table gleamed with Mom's wedding china with the pretty little rosebuds, the "company glasses," a snow-white linen tablecloth, and a big wedge of Italian cheese right next to the cheese grater, for each guest to grate her own fresh Parmesan on her to-die-for thick lentil soup.

The nuns raved over the meal! They asked for seconds and thirds, and wrote down the recipes. My mother confessed, "Sisters, up until last night, I was ready to send out for the turkey."

"Never!" they protested. "This was out of this world!"

Time for dessert. Alas, Dad had weakened the night before and bought a pumpkin pie instead of Italian spumoni. "Just to show you that we have at least a little American tradition in us, we're having pumpkin pie with ice cream for dessert."

The Sisters howled with laughter at the stories of Dad, a professional emcee and entertainer, as well as the town's most popular barber. Mom gazed lovingly at the nuns and thanked them for gracing our home with their presence.

Years passed, and we were all assigned to different schools in faraway places. Mom and Dad passed away, but I received notes from the Sisters many Novembers, recalling that meal as "one of my loveliest Thanksgivings."

— Sister Josephine Palmeri —

85

Chicken Soup
for the Soul

Celebrating a Southern Christmas

In my South, the most treasured things passed down
from generation to generation are the family recipes.
~Robert St. John

Although I was born and raised in the Midwest, both of my kids were born in the South. We lived down there for a good portion of their childhood. When we relocated back to the Midwest, I felt that it was really important to include their Southern heritage in our family traditions.

When we do holiday meals, I almost always try to include at least one Southern-inspired dish. For example, on Thanksgiving and Christmas, it is a long-standing tradition in our family that we serve sweet-potato casserole. It's a family favorite.

On Thanksgiving, we also make Southern cornbread dressing, which is much different from what Southerners would call "Yankee Stuffing." Where I grew up, we called it "stuffing" and made it from traditional white bread. But I grew to love and become loyal to cornbread dressing over the years.

New Year's Day is different, too. In the Midwest, the holiday is mostly about New Year's Eve, rather than New Year's Day. But, in the South, it's all about New Year's Day. A big meal is cooked on New Year's Day, just like on any other significant holiday, and it often includes ham, black-eyed peas, mashed potatoes and collard greens. True Southerners will hide a dime in the black-eyed peas, and the collard greens also have a special meaning to them on the holiday. There is also a superstition that whatever you do on New Year's Day, you will do all year long, so we also choose not to do anything but relax and watch football, like all good Southerners. The women are also adamant about not cleaning or doing any laundry on New Year's Day because of this superstition!

Although we don't hide a dime in our black-eyed peas or cook collard greens, we do cook a ham and a holiday meal. We aren't really superstitious, but we love the idea of having a day to relax with family. We often include board games in our New Year's Eve and New Year's Day traditions, especially longer board games that can't be completed in a normal allotment of time that we would have on a regular weekend game night.

What I love most about this tradition is that it always stirs up conversation in our kitchen. The time-honored recipes bring back fond memories. For those who would like to add something a little Southern to their holidays, I thought I would share one of my own family recipes that I've adapted over the years.

My Family's Georgia Sweet-Potato Casserole Recipe

1/2 c. butter or margarine
3/4 c. sugar
1/3 c. milk
2 eggs
1 large and 1 small can sweet potatoes (drained)

Topping:
1/3 c. flour
1 c. brown sugar
1 c. chopped pecans
1/2 c. melted butter

Beat all ingredients together well, except toppings. Pour into buttered 9 x 13 casserole dish. Mix remaining flour and brown sugar. Top casserole with chopped pecans, then add flour mixture. Pour melted butter on top. Bake at 350° for 45 minutes or until browned and bubbly.

— Stephanie Davenport —

86

Truly Appreciated

*That's the thing with handmade items. They still have
the person's mark on them, and when you hold them,
you feel less alone.*
~Aimee Bender, The Color Master: Stories

I t was only the last week of November, but everybody had agreed that we should get together early. December was bound to be crazy, and we'd never be able to set a date and time when everybody would be free.

I was feeling good. For the first time in years, I was actually able to indulge and buy myself a new dress instead of searching through the thrift store. My gifts were also store bought. No more mentally cringing as my recipients opened my presents and too-brightly exclaimed over the homemade items.

After a flurry of hugs and air kisses, we started exchanging presents. We'd learned to put presents in separate bags for each family to avoid confusion. I'd decided to hit one high-end store and bought everything for this group from there. I had seven impressive shopping bags, duly labeled and ready for handing out.

I got a few curious looks as I distributed them. One of my friends, who was a bit notorious for speaking the truth, said, "You didn't make these gifts; you bought them!"

Another friend added, "You look different, too! Trendier!"

I had no idea it would be that noticeable. Or that they would call me out on it. I began to stammer a reply, but somebody else cut in first. "It's because you guys wanted to have this party so early. We all had to rush to buy presents. Ivy obviously didn't have enough time to make stuff this year."

Well, that gave me an excuse. "Yeah," I agreed weakly.

One of the sweeter friends tried to smooth over the two bumblers' gaffes. "I'm sure we'll love this year's presents, but we always look forward to your homemade treats. My personal favorite is your banana-carrot cake with cream-cheese frosting."

That mollified me a bit. Another friend helped by saying, "And you look lovely as usual, just a bit more restrained. You're usually more flamboyant, which we love."

"Yeah," the one who had originally exclaimed about my new look chimed in. "You're more hippie vintage than — you know." She named the store from which I'd bought my outfit.

I'd always been crafty and preferred to make things from scratch when I had the time. Even when I had been financially comfortable, I had a penchant for hitting thrift stores.

Then, when our income halved just at the time our family grew, my DIY projects and thrift-store shopping became a necessity instead of just a preference. Somehow, my attitude changed and I starting thinking that my homemade goodies were inferior to store-bought items, and that my vintage clothing was embarrassing instead of fun and creative.

I had been convinced that our friends felt sorry for our family and merely tolerated our presents since they knew that we were going through leaner times. I tried to compensate by coming up with suitable items that I knew they would enjoy and hoped that the thought behind them would be appreciated. Nonetheless, the minute my husband found a better paying job and I was able to score a work-from-home gig, I foolishly bent over backwards to show that I was no longer penny-pinching.

I didn't get the reaction I was expecting. It turned out that everyone had truly liked my homemade presents. And they had thought my thrift store outfits reflected my personal style and not my budget. I was ashamed that I had let my focus on money make me feel embarrassed and apologetic.

I lifted my chin and looked around our little party. I saw everybody in a different light, even the two non-candidates for the diplomatic corps. They hadn't meant any harm in calling me out.

I raised an appeasing hand. "Okay, okay. Next year, I'll start crafting and baking for Christmas in June just in case we decide to beat the holiday rush again and hold our get-together on some crazy early date."

Everybody laughed. I felt a hundred times lighter as my perception became so much clearer.

Since then, no matter my financial status, I've continued to give mostly homemade presents. I have certainly enjoyed the labor of love more, unhampered by ridiculous notions. I'm glad I regained my senses before I completely lost the joy in my traditional way of holiday gift giving.

— Ivy Papa-Goze —

Oma's White Christmas Cookies

If baking is any labor at all, it's a labor of love.
A love that gets passed from generation to generation.
~Regina Brett

My grandmother, whom we called Oma, died at Christmastime in 2002. Afterward, when my mom asked if there was anything of hers I wanted, I asked for comforting things: her rocking chair and her cookie cutters. Oma was famous for her white Christmas cookies and I wanted to continue making them for our family. Using her cookie cutters made me feel connected to her while I carried on her legacy.

Oma was one amazing lady. She'd come to Canada from Germany as a young bride with a baby, having survived firsthand the terrors of World War II. Many years later, I travelled with her and my mother back to Germany and got to hear her speak about that difficult time in her life as we stood where it had all happened so long ago.

Her life in Canada wasn't easy either, but she always worked hard and took care of her family first. When my family of five moved from Manitoba to Ontario, we lived with her for several months while my mom tried to build a better life for my disabled brother. And after we had our own house, I continued to visit Oma regularly. As a child, I thought Oma was the coolest grown-up I knew. We'd sit on her couch and watch *The People's Court* together while eating heaping bowls of ice cream. Once, when Opa commented on how much ice cream she'd given me, Oma remarked, "It's not so much if it melts." And the matter was settled.

When I got married, my aunt threw me a shower and asked everyone to bring a recipe. The one she gave me was for Oma's white Christmas cookies. Not the exact recipe, of course, since Oma never wrote it down. But my aunt got it almost perfect. This little recipe was easily the best wedding gift I received. With it, I'd gained not just the chance to make a great cookie, but also the ability to carry forward a tradition that had deep significance to my family. I didn't realize until just a couple years ago when I posted a partial picture of the recipe on social media that most of my relatives didn't yet have any idea how to make the cookies. Suddenly, I was bombarded with requests for the whole recipe from members of my extended family.

It would've been easy to keep the recipe to myself, but that would have run counter to the way Oma lived her life. Everything she did was for her family. She made these cookies for us year after year, and in sharing this recipe I could gift my family with a little bit of her presence long after she'd left us.

My own kids didn't know her, but they do know her cookies. Despite all the baking I do during the holidays, the white cookies are still the favourites in my house. Once the cookies are cooled, the kids like to wait while I carefully spread the white icing, and then they gleefully scatter the coloured sprinkles over the top just like I used to do as a child.

Now there are a few of us who make these cookies every year in memory of my Oma. Each time, I wait until the beginning of December, and I crank up the Christmas carols so that I'm working with optimum Christmas spirit. And as I roll out that dough, adding some flour and then a bit more, the act of doing generates more than just mere memories; it seems to somehow recall her presence. And then, when the cookies are ready, I share them with my children, extended family and close friends.

Every year, it takes me the better part of a day to make just one batch of these cookies. Oma had eight children and fourteen grandchildren, and anyone who wanted white cookies got a bucketful. That's how much she loved us all.

I want to pass this special recipe on to as many people as I can. The cookies are meant to be given and passed around — shared with your family, your children, your friends.

Oma's White Christmas Cookies

1-1/4 c. sugar
1 c. butter
1/8 c. shortening
1/4 c. milk
2 beaten eggs
1 tsp. vanilla
3-4 c. flour (plus more for rolling out dough)
3 tsp. baking powder
pinch of salt
icing sugar
warm milk

Mix together the sugar, butter, shortening, eggs, and vanilla and beat with mixer on low. In a separate bowl, mix together the flour, baking powder, and salt. Add the flour mixture slowly to the batter, alternating with the 1/4 cup of milk. Keep adding flour until the dough is "not too wet" to roll out. Dump onto floured surface and knead. Roll about 1/3 of dough at a time gently to about 1/4" thickness. Lightly grease pans or line with parchment paper. Cut out shapes with cookie cutters and bake at 375° for 6–8 minutes or until lightly brown around the edges. Transfer to cooling racks until completely cool. Ice with mixture of icing sugar and warm milk, and top with sprinkles. Share with those you love!

— Andrea Marlene —

Tamale Memories

A good cook is like a sorceress
who dispenses happiness.
~Elsa Schiaparelli

"We should make tamales for New Year's!" my daughter suggested enthusiastically on New Year's Eve.

"Nope!" was my response.

"Please, we've never done them before! We only have to make a little bit."

Being a second-generation Mexican-American, my daughter Christina has never had to suffer through the difficult work that is making tamales. Unlike her, I have been traumatized to no end by the countless times my mother's kitchen and dining room became a tamale sweatshop for her eight children and husband.

In the Mexican culture, posadas are five days of rosary praying and celebrating in which we recreate the plight of Mary and Joseph as they looked for shelter on the night of Jesus's birth. The entire neighborhood walks along a chosen path of five homes and stops to ask for "posada" or shelter. They are denied entrance and move on to the next home, all the while carrying statuettes of Mary and Joseph and praying a station of the rosary.

At the fifth stop, the hosts gladly accept the pilgrims and their hordes of hangers-on. They enter the home to finish off the rosary, get goody bags, play games, break piñatas and eat like there is no tomorrow. Each day, a new home hosts this feast. Ours was always the last one.

It was a point of pride to be chosen to host one of the neighborhood posada stops, and my mother wanted hers to be the best.

That brings me back to the tamale mill my mother ran for an entire Saturday. While other children got to play outside, the Hernandez children put in a day of hard labor. My mother would wake us at the crack of dawn for a trip to Juárez, the sister city to our border town of El Paso, where we lived. We would pile into my father's blue station wagon and go over the bridge to the *mercado,* or market, in Juárez. There, my mother would have us carry bags of dried-up corn husks, red chiles, pig lard, and whatever other magical spices made her tamales taste delicious. My mother would make her way through the crowded market, flinging sacks and bags at us while my father took out his old leather wallet and paid. I don't know who suffered more — us with the heavy loads, or my poor dad as he saw his small paycheck vanish with each purchase.

Once we arrived back home, we unloaded, and the real work began. Our first task was to pile the dining-room chairs in a corner of the living room, leaving the dining-room table in the middle for everyone to work on. The only chair at the table was my mother's. From there, she would hand out orders like a tiny Mexican ringleader making sure her tamale circus ran smoothly.

The rest of the day was spent helping my mother create her mini corn pillows of deliciousness and pain. We each had a job. Mine was soaking the cornhusks in warm water to soften them. The problem with getting goods from Juárez is that they are farm-to-table goods, and these cornhusks usually came with dead worms. I would spend most of my time pulling out the black, furry worms and throwing them away. As I got older, I was promoted to spreading the corn dough, or *masa,* on the cornhusks. Little did I know when I first started what I was in for. It didn't take long for me to miss the worms.

Those who were tasked with the job of spreading the *masa* were in for a miserable day. The trick with tamales is that the dough has to be spread on a certain side. If it's spread on the wrong side, the *masa* just slips off and ends up everywhere. By the end of the day, we were covered. It was in our hair, our eyelashes, and all over our arms. Top that off with the wrinkled fingers from all the moist cornhusks, and we were a sight to behold.

The biggest problem was that tamale *masa* has magical powers. It would multiply in its bowl. We'd look down and see the bowl half empty and start to plan our escape, but when we looked again, that darn dough was back twice as high as before! Our hopes of freedom were dashed as that *masa* mound grew to new heights.

Halfway through the day, our backs were aching, our fingers were wrinkled, and our heads hurt from the smell. But my mother would keep us going. I would secretly wish I could throw some of the *masa* away, but then I'd notice that she had the trashcan right by her side. After all those years, she knew what would go through our minds.

Our hard labor would carry on, one tamale at a time. Finally, the *masa* had reached the end of its magical powers, and my oldest brother would put the giant tamale pot on the stove. While delicious-smelling steam permeated our home, we would wash the dishes in my mother's tiny kitchen sink. Our furniture would be back in order, and we would all take turns at our only shower, trying desperately to wash off chunks of dried corn dough without tearing out our hair and skin in the process.

That evening, we would eagerly await the familiar singing as it approached our door. The anticipation was palpable. After some long, torturous final prayers, the celebration would start. My mother would flitter about, sparkling in the adulation she received for her delicious tamales.

After my mother passed away, it was so much easier to buy the tamales at the bakery down the street. Those posadas were my mother's time to shine, and making tamales without her was like a recipe without its key ingredient. It just didn't work.

That brings me back to this past New Year's Eve and my daughter's enthusiasm for making tamales. Reluctantly, I agreed, dreading the process and the heartbreak it would stir up. My intent was to make a tiny batch, which of course didn't happen because of the magical *masa* and its growth power.

My daughter learned that spreading *masa* is tedious and back-aching work. She too, got to experience her fingers wrinkling like prunes. Luckily, our cornhusks were worm-free.

Our tamales weren't as good as my mother's. The memories, however — the old ones in my mind and the new ones forming in my daughter's — will continue to grow as she gets older, much like the magical *masa* in its bowl.

— Lorraine Hernandez —

89

The Hanukkah Gift that Keeps Glowing

*We light candles in testament that faith
makes miracles possible.*
~Nachum Braverman

Although my parents usually visited us on Succoth (also known as the Feast of Tabernacles), that year my daughter's bat mitzvah was on the seventh night of Hanukkah. It was also my father's birthday and the beginning of his retirement from his successful dental practice. Thus, we were challenged to find the perfect gift to commemorate these events for him, and a watch wasn't going to do it.

For months, my family tried to find an appropriate gift. I began to realize that the best gift we could give would have to enlist everyone's talents, skills and creativity to truly be something personal and unique. We rejected making a pillow or a photo album, and then I had the perfect idea. "Grandpa collects menorahs. Let's make a menorah incorporating all the grandchildren's names in it!"

One of my daughters jumped right in. "We'll use Fimo (colorful clay) to make figurines to go with each candle. Grandpa has nine grandchildren, and there are nine candles (if you count the shamash — the candle used to light the others). Each child will be one of the candles."

We decided to use each child's Hebrew name, and since those names have meanings we would make a figurine representing each one. My husband found a beautiful piece of wood that was big enough to hold nine little figurines and nine glass oil holders. We wanted to use oil instead of candles to make it even more special.

The boys took turns sanding down the base, which became smooth like velvet. Then they varnished it with a soft pink color and the wood gave off a warm glow. We drilled holes in it and then the girls got to work on the figurines.

Penina was a pearl in an oyster shell. Jacob had a ladder. Asher, one of the sons of Jacob in the Bible, was blessed with olive oil, which was symbolized with a pitcher of oil. A female sheep represented Rachel. Ilana was a beautiful tree. Noah was, of course, an ark filled with giraffes, lions, snakes and more. The animals were indeed challenging and needed the most colors of Fimo. The girls got to practice making their own colors from mixing the basics. Shai was a gift. My second daughter, whose middle name is Marigolda (named after a great-grandmother), was obviously a marigold flower. Elisheva, the bat mitzvah girl, was a menorah with seven lights burning as well as the shamash (which became her spot on the menorah itself).

It took weeks to prepare the menorah, and it truly became a gift from the entire family. We could barely restrain ourselves from presenting it to my father as my parents walked in the door. Since they arrived right before the beginning of Hanukkah, it was difficult to wait for the bat mitzvah day to give the gift. But the finale was breathtaking.

He was flabbergasted. With tears in his eyes, he promised this menorah would sit in honor among all his collection. And it did. It is a gift that keeps glowing.

— Debbie Hirsch —

90

It Wouldn't Be Christmas Without Them

You don't have to cook fancy or complicated
masterpieces — just good food from fresh ingredients.
~Julia Child

We saw our breath as we got out of the car. Daddy got the floppy, old blanket from the trunk and spread it out on the ground. "Now, I'm gonna climb up there and shake 'em down. Stand clear."

Up he went — higher and higher until he reached what he thought was the perfect point. Then, he leaned down and started to jiggle the branches, gently at first, then harder and harder, until at last the nuts broke free and rained down onto the old quilt.

As the storm of pecans showered down, my brothers and I scampered around, flipping the strays onto the spread. All the while, I imagined all the cookies and treats that our mother would make with them, not to mention the pecan pie that would provide a spectacular finale for our Thanksgiving and Christmas dinners.

We brought the clumpy blanket home and dumped the huge pile of nuts under the carport. Then we bagged our treasure in brown paper bags and hauled them into the furnace room to dry out.

The next step was the cracking. After Moma got them all cracked, it was my job to dance around the kitchen with a cookie tin, shaking it like a maraca to get the shells to fall off. When I opened it to check my progress, somehow more than a few nuggets found their way into my mouth.

After I finished, we both knew what came next — BUTTER BALLS!

We filled the big, metal mixing bowl with softened butter, sugar and flour. In went my freshly washed little hands to squish the ingredients together. Moma stood beside me, dropping handfuls of chopped pecans into the dough.

Then, we lined the cookie sheets on the countertop, rolled the dough into little balls, put them on the sheets and popped them in the oven. The sweet, buttery scent drifted all through the house. When the cookies came out, we rolled them in powdered sugar, and I delivered them to Daddy and the boys, who were in the living room pretending to be watching TV. I knew they were really waiting for the cookies. With the first bite, we knew that the Christmas season had officially arrived.

This Christmas, baking butter balls will be one of my favorite ways to celebrate the season of love and good cheer, even though the pecans will come from Sam's Club instead of us harvesting them ourselves.

But still, I'll love making those powdered-sugared, pecan-laden delicacies to share with my family and friends. And as I eat more than my share, I will savor the memories of those Christmases long ago. You see, butter balls are more than mere family tradition; the truth is — it wouldn't be Christmas for me without them.

Butter Balls: A Harper Family Christmas Tradition

1 c. butter
5 T. sugar
3–3½ c. flour
2 tsp. vanilla
1 c. chopped pecans

Mix ingredients by hand in the order shown. Roll into small balls. Line up on ungreased cookie sheets. Bake at 350° for 12 to 15 minutes. Cool for a few minutes. Shake in a plastic bag with powdered sugar. Prepare to eat and smile!

— Kay Harper —

Mom's Little Helper

*The people who give you their food
give you their heart.*
~Cesar Chavez

We were refugees from Vietnam, living in California with a lot of hope and drive, realizing the American Dream. We didn't have much money, so my parents had to channel their creativity when it came to gift giving, especially during the holidays. Since my mother was the world's greatest cook, the natural solution was to give their friends something delightfully edible.

But what could be easily transported without fear of spilling, spoiling, or melting? And what could my mother produce in mass quantities? Eggrolls! Mom's eggrolls were the stuff of legends. To this day, people still talk about how great they were. Most people preferred to partake of eggrolls with a dipping sauce, but they didn't need any kind of sauce with my mom's. They were that good.

Mom assembled bowl after bowl of pork, carrots, crabmeat, shrimp, mushrooms, and everything else that was good in the world. Due to the huge quantity needed to satisfy all of their salivating friends, she had to cook the eggrolls in several batches, using an oversized, electric frying pan that had to be placed on the floor. As such, we lined the floor with newspaper to prevent any cooking oil spillage. Our kitchen was simply not big enough to accommodate this massive deep-frying project. Thus, the family room was turned into a veritable eggroll assembly line.

Given my complete lack of culinary skills, I was named the wonton-wrapper peeler. I never managed a promotion to the role of egg wash sealer or even the prestigious position of the eggroll roller. The role of wonton-wrapper peeler merely involved peeling the sticky wonton wrappers apart. Even though someone else might have considered this to be monotonous work, it was kind of fun for me.

Once her individually peeled wonton-wrappers awaited her, Mom would reach for one and generously spoon the scrumptious filling into a tube-like shape. Her sense of proportion was frighteningly exact. Before I knew it, I was looking at rows and rows of perfectly shaped tubes, ready for the next stage: frying!

My mother definitely knew her way around a frying pan. As she gingerly placed the tubes into the pan of hot oil, the immediate sizzling sound almost instantly gave way to a delectable and distinctive scent. The entire house soon became enveloped in the mouth-watering aroma of cooking deliciousness. Because Mom knew how to fry eggrolls to absolute perfection, the result would be golden brown, crispy tubes of savory goodness.

Occasionally, some of the eggrolls would suffer from what I shall refer to as "exploding filling syndrome" whereby the filling would seep out of the wonton-wrapper during the frying process. "We'll eat the ugly ones," she would say as she smiled, setting aside those aesthetically unpleasing rolls for me or another family member to devour. Mom never wanted to deliver her friends anything less than perfection. I think her attitude was that if she couldn't give them something valuable, she would at least give them something beautiful.

Once the frying was complete, she would transfer the golden tubes to a paper-towel-lined plate so that the excess oil would be absorbed. Mom's eggrolls were never greasy.

As a child, I barely ate any Vietnamese food because my tastes heavily favored American food. Despite my predisposition to pizza and hamburgers, I couldn't resist her delectable crispy-on-the-outside, savory-on-the-inside tubes of fried, flavorful tastiness.

By the time the frying was finished, I usually smelled like I had done a few breaststrokes in the pan myself. After they cooled, we would place them onto display plates, and wrap them in foil for delivery. Then my parents would be off in the car, delivering eggrolls to their friends.

The eggroll production line operated for many holiday seasons, until our financial situation improved to the point where Mom no longer "had to" make eggrolls as Christmas gifts. My parents began to give "proper" gifts that were purchased from a department store. Apparently, this was an indication that we had finally moved up in the world.

Mom is gone now, and so are her precious eggrolls. I never even tried to make them myself. But I'm left with the tender memory of being Mom's Little Helper all those years ago, watching her share her love of her traditional food with her friends in her new country. And that memory warms my heart every Christmas.

— Kristen Mai Pham —

Chapter 11

It Takes a Village

92

The New Folks

*Christmas is most truly Christmas when we celebrate
it by giving the light of love to those who need it most.*
~Ruth Carter Stapleton

n mid-December, we had moved to a little cluster of four
houses outside an isolated rural village. Ours was a blended
family, rebuilt from two previous marriages, and at the time the
location seemed like a kind of exile set apart from traditional
families. The only neighbor we had met so far was Mary. Ten minutes
after moving in, our children were playing with her two children. We
soon learned that their father had recently moved somewhere else.

On Christmas Eve, the temperature plunged to -22 degrees and
stayed there. Then came the snow, which would amount to thirteen
inches by morning. I fed the wood stove to supplement the heat from
the furnace, and we were cozy as the kids gleefully opened their presents and the cats scrabbled through the wrapping paper. By the time
we stuffed the twenty-pound turkey and popped it in the oven, we
seemed to be having a pretty traditional holiday.

"Something's wrong," Leslie said. "The oven's not getting hot."
None of the burners worked either. The outdoor propane tank was
half-full, but as I came back inside I noticed that the propane line ran
exposed to the sub-zero air for twenty-five feet.

"How am I going to cook Christmas dinner?" my wife said. "We
can't start our first holiday like this."

Leslie phoned Mary. "I hate to ask," she said, explaining the situation.

Mary's propane line was buried, and her stove worked. She told us to bring over our turkey, so I wallowed through the knee-deep snow with it. That's when I realized the road had not been plowed. Intense cold burned my lungs, and I panted while stamping my boots in her entryway. "Thank you so much!"

"Hot chocolate before you go back?" she asked. I accepted gladly, hoping it might wake up my fingers and toes. Besides, maybe she'd like the company. She must have been feeling lonely.

"Do you have enough room in the oven for your dinner now?" I asked.

"Oh, yeah. We're supposed to eat at my mother's, and I was assigned mashed potatoes and veggies." She laughed and glanced outside at the road. "That's not happening."

As I began inviting her to join us, the Christmas tree lights and kitchen lights flickered, went out, returned for two seconds and then died for good. Mary sighed. "I bet a tree took out the lines. It'll be hours." The gas stove would work, but our furnaces would not.

"We have a wood stove. Please join us."

"Okay. But I'm worried about Clarence — the last house before the mountain. He's near eighty," she whispered. "His wife died last year, and he's gotten frail."

"Well, let's bring him along. Leslie and I should meet him."

"He can't hike through that deep snow." She hesitated. Cars were out of the question. "Let me call Tex and Dot. They live on the other side of you." Ten minutes later, we spotted a big John Deere farm tractor rolling down the road and pulling a wagon with a beaming woman standing in it like George Washington crossing the Delaware. Laying down the first tracks in the road, the man I would soon know as Tex circled through Clarence's front yard, where a bent man scrambled into the wagon, and then chugged back to pick up Mary, her children and me.

Tex wore a red ski cap and grinned back at the wagonload of people. "Fifty-six reindeer under this hood!"

"Does that look like Santa Claus, kids?" Dot asked.

"No!" they shouted.

"I think he is," Mary said. The tractor puttered across the deserted road and climbed our driveway. We all spilled out and stamped into my kitchen, shouting, "Merry Christmas!" to my befuddled wife. Everyone carried bags, and the counter and table were soon full. Snow-dusted coats, hats and boots were piled on the floor.

Dot brought two pies she had baked earlier. Mary had some oranges and promised her mashed potatoes and veggies when we went back for the turkey. Clarence offered a bag of hazelnuts and beechnuts from his trees. Tex produced a lantern and a dozen candles.

I introduced Leslie and myself, but Clarence said, "Ah, we know who you are. This is a small town. Let me at your wood stove — I got ten icicles for fingers."

Tex said, "Remember 1977 when the birds collected on chimney tops to get warm?"

Dot said, "Every time the power died, the Ingrahams invited us over. We had some wonderful times. I brought the cards. It'll be like the old days."

"How long you two been married?" Tex asked.

"Three months," Leslie said. All eyes shifted to our children, ages five through eight, and I felt myself tense. Now the knowing looks would start. Dot and Tex seemed like the all-American couple, probably married fifty years.

Dot merely said, "Oh, that's nice. Newlyweds. The Ingrahams were newlyweds here, too."

A few hours later, we retrieved the turkey, potatoes and vegetables from Mary's kitchen, and I carved the turkey on the table where there was light. The candles and lantern glittered off the glasses and silverware and cast shadows on the walls from each person, as if there were extra people or ghosts in the room. In a way, there were — watching us continue a long tradition — and not just the shadows of the Ingrahams either. Whoever welcomes strangers, whoever welcomes those who have not had the smoothest lives, was in our house, blessing our second chance. This was the day to find room for everyone.

Dot gave our kids some of her handmade ornaments to hang on the Christmas tree. Clarence offered to go home for some of his possum stew, but Tex winked at me, so I knew he was teasing the children. Mary and Leslie plotted ways to coordinate their work schedules so our six kids would always have someone around for school-bus departures and arrivals. "If you need wood to feed that stove," Clarence told me, "I've got a dead beech you can take down."

The snow was piling up on the window ledges, and prisms of frost crisscrossed the windows. But the room was warm, and the shadows seemed to nod with the flickering candlelight. I held Leslie's hand under the table, just like a newlywed should. After the turkey came Dot's mince and apple pies. As she stood poised to cut them, she asked, "What are you folks doing for New Year's?"

— Garrett Bauman —

93

The Broken-Wing Party

Christmas is doing a little something extra
for someone.
~Charles M. Schulz

My brother-in-law had just been told he had cancer. Emotionally shaken by the diagnosis, both he and my sister were unsure how to cope with the rigors of the treatments and help their young son deal with it all, let alone think about Christmas. "Don't bother including us in any plans," was their message.

Another friend shook her head. "I dread Christmas this year. The church family has been great — they mean well — but we just don't feel like facing everybody and all their questions," she said. I understood. Her husband was the most beloved pastor for miles around, the kind of man who knew everyone by name. Both of them were willing to help anyone who ever knocked on their door. But this year their son had hit a low point and attempted suicide. In a story that is a miracle in itself, his life was spared. But the whole family was wounded and in a raw state. They needed some privacy away from the crowd.

I heard the same refrain from many of our friends and family members. "We can't really plan much this year." "We don't quite feel up to celebrating." I felt like everyone I knew was grieving or going through some other kind of trouble. For them, celebrating the holidays was like trying to fly with a broken wing.

That's when I made up my mind. Since our family had lost our father to a heart attack on Christmas Eve a few years before, we understood that Christmas is difficult for folks who are suffering or lonely. We knew that broken-wing feeling. We all grieved, but we also knew that no one had loved Christmas more than our dad. Being gloomy on Christmas was not the way to honor his spirit.

So I made my lists. I called all the hurting people in my circle and invited them to just drop by on Christmas Eve. On each call I made, along with a plea to "just show up for a few minutes at least," I offered a bit of an explanation. "You don't have to put up a good front because everyone invited is coping with something heavy right now. No one is flying high. In fact, everyone has, in essence, a broken wing. You don't have to be in the mood to celebrate. We'll just get together for a while."

I invited people who were not going to be able to go home, as well. There was a couple that was temporarily living in Guatemala working with the underprivileged. They couldn't be in their own house for their holiday furlough because they had tenants. Then there were my daughter's college friends from all over the world who couldn't go home for the holidays because they lived too far away.

Christmas Eve arrived. I had decorated, bought little gifts, and made a feast for our guests. I slipped off the apron covering my satin skirt and emerald-green blouse. "Green is for hope," I prayed silently, "and I hope this night goes well." The doorbell rang. I had deliberately set up a crooked little spruce tree in the front foyer and decorated it with tiny stuffed animals and gingerbread boys dangling from loops of red twine. It was the first thing our guests saw as they stomped the snow off their boots. Everyone laughed. "It's a Charlie Brown tree!" they said.

I smiled at the lopsided thing with its missing branch. "Even the tree has a broken wing," I added.

One by one, they traipsed in, chuckled over the tree, inhaled the aromas coming from the kitchen, and gathered in the room with the fire roaring in the stone fireplace. The woodsy scent of the fire mingled with the aroma of the savory dishes weighing down the sideboard. No one needed coaxing to load their plates.

Between the main course and dessert, I tugged on my son's sleeve and gave him the sign. There was a red suit laid out for him upstairs, and the patio door would be left ajar. The giant sack of gifts was waiting on the deck. As the pumpkin pies were lifted hot out of the oven and the coffee percolator gurgled, I heard the rattle of bells and the booming "Ho ho ho!" Laughter rang out through the house to cries of "Look! Look! It's Santa Claus!"

"Now come sit on my knee, little boy!" coaxed Santa. A young man who had not smiled for weeks obliged and laughed out loud as he put on a funny elf hat. A college student from Kenya wiggled his red, green and yellow toes in his new socks. My brother-in-law played a few notes on the toy harmonica he received, and everyone applauded.

As all good things must, the party ended, and we bid our friends farewell. As we opened the door, the streetlights shone through the white confetti of a gentle snowfall. The feathery flakes fell on the sleeves of their coats as, one by one, my special guests hugged me and said, despite the circumstances, it was their best Christmas Eve ever.

Sometimes, when we are unable to fly, it helps to just perch together, leaning our broken wings against the warmth of another person.

— Phyllis McKinley —

Angels Among Us

This time of year means being kind to everyone
we meet, to share a smile with strangers
we may pass along the street.
~Betty Black

As a single mother to a beautiful eight-year-old daughter, I was struggling to provide the essentials on just one salary while also paying off my student loans. I was fortunate to have found a good job as a secretary so that I was able to be home in the evenings and on weekends. Since I had been at the same job for seven years and my parents had given me a parcel of land as a down payment, I had been approved for a mortgage. I was so excited to be able to purchase a previously owned mini-home and place it on the land where I had played as a child!

By the time I got the land cleared and prepared, the well and septic installed, and my home moved onto it, I felt like I had climbed Mt. Everest. It was a tougher process than I ever could have foreseen, and it seemed like there were complications at every turn. I was relieved to get the furniture moved in and get settled. It didn't matter that it was all secondhand, nothing matched, and I still had rooms to paint. I got so much satisfaction just being able to lay my head down at night in my own home.

The first winter was tough. With no skirting around the base of the house, the bitter arctic winds that blew under the house kept the floors cold. And with no wood stove installed yet, the electric bill was daunting. The next summer, my dad got me an old wood stove at a yard sale and installed it. My family helped me put insulation and skirting around the base of the home. My uncle brought me some wood, and I was feeling much more prepared for my second winter!

In the deep freeze of December that year, I was disappointed when the old fridge that I had rescued from my mother's basement gave one final shudder and quit. Of course, I didn't have the means to go out and buy a new fridge, living paycheck to paycheck as I was, but I was determined not to get discouraged. I decided to think like a pioneer. It was December in Canada, so anything left outside would freeze solid in a matter of hours! I took the food out of the freezer section, put it in an old cooler and set it out in the snow. I collected empty containers, filled them with water and put them outside. Once they froze, I put a few in the fridge to keep it cool, switching them out as they thawed.

When my mother saw what I was up to, I joked to her that it was like an old-fashioned icebox. One day, she was talking to a friend of hers and told him about my "icebox." This gentleman was concerned for me and formulated a plan. He contacted a local appliance store and, explaining my situation, got a discount off their already rock-bottom price, and the delivery fee waived. He then contacted a few of his friends and gathered donations to pay for the fridge! As if that wasn't enough, he arranged to have a truckload of firewood delivered to my home to ensure that we were warm enough.

At Christmas that year, I realized he had approached even more generous contributors and arranged for some lovely gifts to put under our tree to make the season even brighter for us. My heart swelled with gratitude and joy at his kindness and generosity. I had a brand-new fridge, enough wood to keep us warm for the duration of the winter, and a blessed Christmas for my little girl. We may not recognize them in our day-to-day lives, but there are truly angels among us!

— Lisa D. MacDougall —

Christmas Eve
in the ER

*Body and soul cannot be separated for purposes of
treatment, for they are one and indivisible. Sick minds
must be healed as well as sick bodies.*
~Jeff Miller

Christmas in Steamboat Springs, Colorado, is right out of
Currier & Ives — knee-deep snow, white lights twinkling on
aspen trees, and families shopping on our small-town main
street. Less than a mile away, we're working as usual in the
emergency room, because illness and trauma don't respect a holiday
schedule. Cars crash in the snowy mountains, skiers fall, bellies hurt
and the flu comes a-calling. Holidays are often very busy times in
emergency rooms, maybe because the underlying frenzy of expectations triggers the weak and weary.

Now that my own boys are grown, with families of their own, I
volunteer to work almost any holiday but Thanksgiving. That's a sacred
day of gratitude (and football), and one where I always yearn to be at
a table with family. As for the others — from Christmas through New
Year's Day — I'd rather let a co-worker enjoy a day off so I can focus on
helping people who feel terrible on what's supposed to be a day of joy.

On one particular Christmas Eve, we were handling the normal
workload. It's my job as the tech to help the doctor and nurses in any
way I can, from cutting off clothes on a broken limb to taking vital signs,

inserting IVs, cleaning up rooms, interacting with other departments and keeping the patient flow going smoothly. I also listen to the radio for news about skier transports and ambulances.

I knew there was a serious injury when, with a slight catch in his voice, I heard a patroller report, "Young male down, impact to head, no helmet, non-responsive." When the paramedics came rushing in with this young kid on the gurney, still as the night, I thought, as I often do, *He is somebody's son.*

Why is it that the holidays seem to heighten suffering and also joy? Why does everything feel more poignant, or perhaps real, on Christmas Eve or New Year's Day? In this case, I knew that this boy's family would never see Christmas Eve the same way again. It would always be marked — hopefully with relief ("Remember when David got so hurt on the mountain on Christmas Eve?") — but likely with deep sadness. No matter the outcome, this time of year would be altered forever for David's family.

We clicked into high gear, everyone quietly and very intensely doing his or her job. There is such focus in these moments that everything else falls away — the lights, music, decorations, the loud clanking of the ER machines and curtains, carts and monitors. Everything was tunnel-silent, except for what we needed to do to keep David alive. His family stood in a circle, quaking like aspen trees. We stabilized him and flew him to Denver for more specialized care, and then we resumed going through the line of waiting patients.

On my security camera, I saw another young man, doubled over in pain. We specialize in triage — the process of getting to the most critical patients quickly — and I ran out to the admissions area. A guard helped me get this young guy into a wheelchair, and I put a towel in front of him as he was retching violently. When we got him back to a bed, I saw his suffering up close. An insulin-dependent diabetic, this twenty-two-year-old managed to tell us (between violent bouts of sickness) that he had run out of his medication and his insurance two weeks earlier. He had hoped his body would make it another week or so until he started his new job. He had no family or friends in the area. For some reason, again, because it was Christmas Eve, I felt his sadness deeply.

We helped Sean as quickly as possible: warm blankets for his shaking and an IV with nausea meds. Within thirty minutes, he was feeling better. This, too, is a miracle of medicine in the US, something we take for granted every single day.

Sean was so sick, but in the back of his mind he was frantic about money. With no insurance, he'd have to find a way to pay for this ER visit and the meds he would need to make it through the next few weeks. Nearly every day, I am reminded of how many people struggle to have basic needs met. Between caring for Sean and David, despite the decorations and all the cookies in the nurses' station, I was feeling blue that night.

And then came the metaphorical "Mary and Joseph"—a young couple from Texas, looking terrified. Sophia, the young wife, was about twelve weeks pregnant and bleeding. Her husband Steven was a paraplegic, confined to a wheelchair. They were stricken with grief and fear. There is always a back story to each patient in the ER, and theirs was particularly heartbreaking. Because of Steven's condition, they had used in vitro fertilization (IVF). So far, Sophia had had four miscarriages. What they wanted, more than anything, was a baby. And now, on Christmas Eve, it looked like their nightmare was continuing.

These are the boundaries that stretch our compassion, the times when our hearts break with the patients'. We quickly got them comfortable and, frankly, we all prepared for the worst. When Sophia was wheeled to the ultrasound room, Steven was wheeling himself right behind her. With alarms going off, kids crying, and the radio yelping, it's tough to pray, but that's what I did—just for a second—as the ultrasound tech turned the corner with Sophia and Steven.

I'm not sure folks understand how deeply clinicians are affected by these daily stories of tragedy, love, and joy. But they show up every day, committed to helping, whether it's Christmas Eve or some nondescript winter morning. I love and admire doctors and nurses who just keep showing up.

So, we kept splinting broken legs and running tests for abdominal pain and flu, all the while waiting to hear about Sophia. The icon on her electronic chart indicated the test was finished. We collectively held our breath waiting for the radiologist to give us the results. *Please, please don't let them suffer another miscarriage.* If there was anything we could have bartered with the health gods that night, we would have gladly given it over for Sophia and Steven.

And then the phone rang, and I remember it now as the happiest Christmas carol ever, more joyful than any news on any day: Sophia was fine. The pregnancy was good and healthy. Our "Mary and Joseph" were going to be parents after all. Our doc practically ran down the hall to their room to tell them the good news, and she told us later that the three of them cried for joy. Imagine Steven, with all the challenges he faces every day just trying to negotiate the simplest tasks, imagine the happiness filling his heart. And that's the love of Christmas.

This is what humans do. We get knocked down; then we get back up. Bad news comes, bad things happen, and we endure. It turns out David lived through his devastating brain injury and, though somewhat impaired, returned happily to his life. We discharged Sean with enough insulin to ensure his safety, fingers crossed that insurance kicked in soon and he would never let himself get that sick again. And just about everyone hugged Sophia and Steven as they left our ER glowing with relief and happiness.

Why is everything so much brighter on Christmas Eve? Why do our hearts sing (and break) bigger on December twenty-fourth and twenty-fifth than, perhaps, any other day of the year? Something about the holidays reminds us of our shared humanity, our common basic goodness, and our faith that we are all in this together. I'm lucky to be a part of the Christmas story in real life, in real service to people who end up that day (or any day) in the ER—certainly a place no one wants to be.

I am blessed to work with a crew of dedicated experts who bring their best to that room every day, who keep showing up with kindness and skill when folks bring us their broken selves and, often, their broken spirits. David, Sean, and Sophia—all Christmas miracles to me — are just part of the tapestry of our beautiful everyday lives. When the caroling ceases and the lights come down, we are all still deeply bound by the miracles of Christmas.

— Phyllis Coletta —

Pick One Person

The joy of brightening other lives, bearing each other's
burdens, easing other's loads and supplanting empty
hearts and lives with generous gifts becomes
for us the magic of the holidays.
~W.C. Jones

We had been living in Palermo, Sicily for over a year, and I was getting used to Italian customs and the rhythm of everyday life. One thing I never got used to, though, was the number of poor people and beggars on the streets. I always wanted to help them. Mother told me we couldn't possibly help all of them, but she would think of something.

One night, Mother called my sisters and me into the kitchen. She told us we could each pick one person we knew to receive our help. When we chose our person, she would decide whether to give money or clothing or food.

I made a list of all the people I knew who could use some help. The next day, I went around my neighborhood and visited everyone on my list. I visited Signore Mateo, who played cards in the park with his friends. He was the only person I knew with one arm, and I had often seen him struggle with his handicap. Next, I visited the old lady who sold chestnuts. She had gnarled fingers and she was bent over with a hump on her back. She wore ragged clothes, and her weathered cart was falling apart.

The last person on my list was Giuseppe. He worked in the

incinerator room of our apartment building. That was where all of the garbage ended up, and Giuseppe was the person who burned it all. Every floor of our building had a chute that went all the way down to the incinerator room. I never paid much attention to the stinky chutes, and I never thought about where the things people stuffed into them landed.

One day, I was in the basement of our building. I was waiting for the elevator when a door in the corner opened and out walked a heavyset man wearing a stained shirt and brown pants.

He said, "What are you doing down here? Are you lost? No one ever comes here."

"I guess I am lost," I answered.

As soon as Giuseppe opened the door, a horrible stench had filled the hall. It was more than I could stand, and I pinched my nose shut with my fingers. He laughed and said, "I'm used to the smell."

I kept my fingers pressed against my nostrils and asked him what was behind the door. He told me it was the incinerator, and he would show it to me.

The incinerator was a large oven. It was built into the wall, and it had an enormous door on the front. When Giuseppe opened the door, I could see flames dancing around.

There were piles and piles of garbage that he had to shovel into that oven, and the smell was so strong it brought tears to my eyes. There were no windows in the room, and the floors were covered with slime. It was the most horrible place I'd ever seen — even worse than the catacombs in Rome.

I asked Giuseppe if his wife made him shower the moment he got home. He looked down at the floor and said, "No. No wife. My wife and my baby girl died in the big war."

He told me he had lost his wife and his only child when Palermo was bombed during World War II. I looked at Giuseppe and said, "You work down here by yourself all day, and then you go home at night and are by yourself at home?"

Giuseppe answered, "Yes, that's true."

I asked, "Don't you get lonely?"

He nodded and said, "I do."

I thought about that and asked, "Would you mind if I came to visit you sometime when you're here at work?"

Giuseppe sounded grateful and said, "You would do that? You would come here to visit me? That's so nice. You come to visit."

After that day, I went to visit Giuseppe at least once a week. He always seemed happy to have a little company.

I liked spending time with Giuseppe, but hated the smell. I had to hold my nose when I was in the incinerator room. One day, Giuseppe surprised me with a clamp for my nose. It looked like a piece of equipment used for medical procedures. It had little round pads on each end so it wasn't all that uncomfortable when clamped on my nose. I appreciated Giuseppe's gift because it was so useful.

One day, I asked Giuseppe if he was ready for Christmas. He told me he didn't have a Christmas tree or any Christmas decorations. To him, Christmas was just another day.

We visited for about an hour, and then I had to go home. That night after dinner, Mother called me and my sisters into the living room and asked us who we were going to help. My sisters told Mother their picks. We were going to give food to the person my older sister chose and clothing to the person my younger sister chose. Then it was my turn. I told Mother it was a difficult decision, but I wanted to help Giuseppe.

She asked, "What does he need — food, clothing, or money?"

I replied, "He needs a family."

Mother was pensive and said finally, "I know what we can do. We can be Giuseppe's family for a day. We will invite him to Christmas dinner, and we will be his holiday family."

When Mother opened the front door that Christmas Day, she was surprised to see that Giuseppe was a middle-aged man. He kissed Mother on both cheeks and thanked her profusely for inviting him to dinner. Next, he kissed my father on both cheeks and asked him if he was proud to have daughters.

My father said, "I am very proud. I am especially proud today."

That was the beginning of our new holiday tradition. Over the years, we have met some fascinating people, but Giuseppe is the only one who ate Christmas dinner with us. He said the blessing at the table that December twenty-fifth, and the word he used most often was "thankful."

— Faye Fulton —

97

Santa's Early Visit

This is the message of Christmas: We are never alone.
~Taylor Caldwell

The winter I was six years old, our family was sitting in the living room watching TV one night near Christmastime when the doorbell rang. My mom and dad told my older sister and me to answer the door. Imagine the look on our faces when we opened the door to see Santa Claus — accompanied by two helpers — standing there with a huge sack of toys slung over his shoulder. It wasn't even Christmas yet, and Santa had come to *our* house to visit us!

A few months earlier, my dad had been outside chopping wood at my grandparents' house when he suddenly came inside looking quite ill. Our normally easygoing father was sweating profusely, said he didn't feel well, and went to rest on the sofa. Within a matter of minutes, everyone was surrounding him as something was obviously wrong. Even though he insisted he just needed to rest for a few minutes, they wisely drove him to the emergency room of the nearest hospital. As they drove down the long dirt road and away from my grandma's house, my sisters and I watched out the window, wondering if we would ever see our dad again.

At the young age of thirty-eight, our dad had suffered a heart attack. He would eventually recover, but he was hospitalized for two weeks.

It turned out the heart attack was stress-related. To make ends meet, my dad had taken on a second full-time job at a retail store, something he been doing since a few months after my birth. Working two jobs had clearly taken a toll on his body, and he would need to rest for several weeks after he was home — which meant he wouldn't be able to work either of his jobs. As he was the sole income earner for our family, times were tight that year, and we didn't expect much.

Somehow, though, Santa had gotten word that we needed some extra Christmas cheer, and he made a point of coming to our house before Christmas Day to drop off some gifts. As we watched in awe, Santa and his helpers unloaded the presents from the sack and handed them to my parents, who put the beautiful gifts under our tree. Mom and Dad even had gifts, even though they had never gotten a gift from Santa any other year.

In addition to the abundance of gifts, Santa's helpers brought the most beautiful, handmade gingerbread house I had ever seen. I imagined Mrs. Claus in her kitchen at the North Pole, carefully frosting the gingerbread and making sure that every gumdrop was exactly in place. The gingerbread house was full of decadent confections that we would never eat because we just couldn't bear the thought of ruining the house.

After Santa had unloaded the gifts, he sat with us. He chatted with us about his work at the North Pole, and about how busy the elves were all working in preparation for Christmas. Even though we no longer needed to tell him what we wanted for Christmas, he let us sit on his lap anyway, and he posed for photos with us, with a distinctive crooked smile that surprised me.

After he had stayed a while, he said he had to be on his way. He hadn't come with the reindeer, who were resting up for Christmas Eve, so he walked outside and got into a blue pickup truck with his helpers and drove away.

Christmas Day was amazing. There were so many gifts — many more than I had ever seen any other Christmas and many more than any other Christmas after — and somehow Santa had known exactly what we all wanted, including the new Barbie doll I had secretly been hoping would be under the tree. My sisters and I opened gifts for what felt like hours.

One day several months later, my sisters and I tagged along with my dad to his job to pick up his paycheck. We passed by the head of store security and he gave us a crooked smile that looked just like Santa's. How funny was that?

It wasn't until years later that we knew the whole story. My dad—a beloved employee at the store he worked at—had been so well liked by his co-workers that when tough times struck our family, they made it their mission that year to make our Christmas extra special. The employees in the store held a potluck where everyone brought food to share, but they had to pay to eat the food they had brought. When all was said and done, there was enough money to buy gifts for my parents, my two sisters, and me, but also extra money left over to help cover other expenses for our family. Their generosity made our Christmas completely magical that year.

The best part, though, was their decision to have Santa deliver the gifts to us ahead of time, driving around town in a big blue pickup truck.

— Resa Delaney —

98

Make a Joyful Noise

It is Christmas in the heart that
puts Christmas in the air.
~W.T. Ellis

I was up to my elbows in sugar-cookie dough one day in early December when my friend Jane called to say she was putting together a group of couples to do some caroling. She invited my husband and me to join.

Although it had been years since I'd sung in any kind of choir, I had always enjoyed singing. I was confident that with the proper songbooks, plenty of rehearsal time, a good director, and maybe a guitar to accompany us, we would be great. I told Jane we would be happy to join her caroling crew.

Jane was thrilled. But as she began to describe her plan, my enthusiasm dipped a little. Jane felt one rehearsal would be plenty, and since no one in the group played a guitar, our voices would be enough. She didn't know what we would be singing, but she'd come up with something.

I had always admired her free spirit, but I was skeptical. I was already regretting my quick decision. But with a house full of kids and Christmas around the corner, I had plenty of distractions so I stopped worrying about it.

Then Jane called one snowy afternoon and said our rehearsal would have to be canceled. One couple was out of town, Jane explained. Another had the flu bug in their house. But it would be fine, she assured me, her enthusiasm never wavering. No music had been selected yet, and we probably wouldn't be very good without rehearsal. But I didn't want to be the humbug in her Christmas, so I kept quiet about my doubts.

Nevertheless, everywhere I went, the world was full of the sounds of Christmas; shopping malls patched it through their loudspeakers, and local radio stations played carols around the clock. How could we possibly compete with so many perfect Christmas songs?

At home, we had transformed our place into a winter wonderland. Joe had spent a weekend carefully trimming the gutters with new white lights until the house glowed. I carried in the fragrant pine boughs and the pretty poinsettias with their scarlet leaves. Together, we hung five stockings along the mantel and then decorated a large tree with all the ornaments we had collected over the years. Carefully, I set up my Christmas village collection, complete with a fluffy blanket of snow.

Our refrigerator was hung with the kids' festive artwork: construction paper reindeer, cotton-ball snowmen, and glittery wreaths. And the children's excitement was contagious. They counted down the days on their Advent calendars, unwrapping a chocolate each morning.

With so much to do, the caroling date I had circled on the calendar arrived quickly. On the allotted day, the eight of us caravanned toward our first destination in a neighborhood just minutes from my own. We would be visiting a homebound woman and her husband.

We turned into a neighborhood I had only driven by on my way to the school or the gym. Now I noticed the modest houses frosted in sparkly snow. I imagined the eight of us clustered in the cold around one of the tiny front stoops.

Soon, we were pulling up to one of those small houses and traipsing through the snow. I remember thinking, *At least we're all in this together*.

A solemn man, not much older than myself, opened the door. To my surprise, he ushered us inside the small house.

At first, we gingerly tried to crowd into the tiny hallway, afraid to mess up the floor with our winter boots. But the man insisted we come all the way into the warm house, and as we packed into their living room, the quiet space seemed to shrink even more. We stood shoulder to shoulder in the cramped room. We were making a mess on the floor, but the man didn't seem to care, telling us not to worry about it.

A woman greeted us quietly from her spot on the couch. The evidence of her chemo treatments was obvious. Her head was wrapped in a colorful scarf that set off the dark pools of her eyes in a pale face. Gray smudges were apparent beneath her eyebrow-less eyes, and the table before her was littered with medical supplies and prescription bottles.

There were no festive flowers or garlands to be seen. In fact, there was no Christmas tree at all.

The man sat down expectantly on the arm of the couch beside his wife. My stomach twisted. With no practice, no harmony, and no accompaniment, I knew we would only add to the couple's disappointing season.

As we launched into our first song, "Joy to the World," the faces of the man and woman transformed. The man leaned over to wrap his arm around his frail wife, their eyes full of gratitude and hope. I wasn't prepared for the tears running down their cheeks as we offered our simple songs. But I was even more surprised to feel my own eyes filling.

And as the snow turned into small puddles on their bare floor, I began to realize something: I had wasted my energy in worrying. The couple before us had no Christmas in the house, but we were bringing them a small bit of it, and that meant the world to them.

I felt a warmth beginning inside me as we said our goodbyes and ducked back into our cars for the short drive to our next destination. Now I understood that the most beautiful songs aren't the most perfect ones, but those that are offered with love and hope to ready hearts.

—C.L. Nehmer—

A Conspiracy of Love

*The future belongs to those who give the next
generation reason for hope.*
~Pierre Teilhard de Chardin

I t had been a rough year for our family. I was only seven years old, but I understood enough to realize how bad it was when I watched my father lock the doors of his business for the last time. That same year, I lost my room to my new baby sister and was forced into the new role of "the middle one."

But now it was Christmastime, and that always meant joy and excitement. As I sat at the foot of the Christmas tree, enveloped by the twinkling lights, I knew in my heart that the barren spot I was occupying would be filled with wondrous things the next morning. I could see beautiful dolls with long, flowing hair to braid. I could feel the soft fuzz of plush animals. I could hear the cheer as I won the board games. It was all so exciting that I could hardly settle myself.

"What are you looking at, sweetie?" said my mother.

"I'm just wondering what will be under the tree tomorrow."

Mama seemed almost in a panic as she quickly turned and called for Daddy. I didn't care. I was too excited to even think of what must be bothering her. Then my eyes caught sight of the nativity we always set out each year. I scooted toward it, and my eyes locked on the little baby Jesus. I gently picked him up and was holding him in my arms when Mom and Dad entered and sat down on the sofa behind me.

"Honey, come here." My daddy put out his arms.

I laid the baby Jesus back down for the wise men and shepherds to worship and crawled into his lap.

"You know we love you, right?"

"I know, Daddy." The Christmas excitement still sparkled in my eyes.

He shifted nervously. "Well, I just want you to know that sometimes we may not get a lot for Christmas, but that doesn't mean that we're not loved."

"Yes, I understand."

"Well, do you have any questions about what I said?"

I rubbed my hands together anxiously. "Yes." I nodded my towhead. "What time does Santa get here?"

My mom released a soft chuckle, and my dad kissed me on the forehead. "Go on to bed, honey."

The next morning, my sister and I darted down the hallway, and when we rounded the corner, my eyes could scarcely take in all the gifts stacked around the tree. It was the most beautiful sight I had ever seen, and we spent the entire day opening gifts, laughing, and chatting.

Many years later, I learned the truth. My poor broken father, devastated by his losses, had never expected what happened that Christmas Eve. People had come from all over to help: the members of our church where my daddy volunteered, former customers from his business, and so many other friends and family had rallied to help my parents keep the magic alive for their children.

Today, I share that story with my own three children to make sure we always remember what Christmas is. It's so much more than just presents. It's the day that daddies find themselves heroes again in the eyes of their children. It's the day that mommies put aside housework to enjoy their families. It's the day that moments with the ones we love are etched into our minds forever. It's friends coming together in love to help others.

— Misty Huelsebusch —

100

The Christmas Day Mitzvah

He who has not Christmas in his heart
will never find it under a tree.
~Roy L. Smith

In truth, this is my son Gil's story. It's a story that begged to be written, and since Gil was a writer, eventually it might have been — had cancer not intervened and ended his life much too early. But a good story should not go untold. For Gil, then, here it is, many years later but etched in my memory as I first heard it from him.

It was Christmas Eve. In his second year at Brown University, Gil was living in a rented house with two roommates, both of whom had already left for the holidays. Since as Jews we didn't celebrate Christmas, Gil felt no need to rush home to our house in Massachusetts. But on December 24th, when he'd planned to leave, New England was hit by a huge snowstorm. Travel was out of the question.

With nightfall, the snow sparkled like crystal under the incandescent moon. Going out for a brief walk, Gil gazed at the houses where the windows framed the vivid colors of lights, garlands and ornaments on the Christmas trees inside. In the yards, little white bulbs strung on bushes shimmered under their halo of snow. When he returned to his house, it seemed all too empty. He called home and confessed to feeling lonesome.

"I'll try to come tomorrow," he said. "Depends on the weather. I'll let you know."

The next morning, the plows had come and gone, having deposited the cleared snow in a huge mound now blocking Gil's driveway. Reluctantly, he bundled up and tackled it, heaving one shovelful of snow after another off to the side. After ten minutes, his back was aching, and he had made barely a dent in the mound. Stopping to rest, he stared down the empty street, where he saw something black moving in the sea of white. The black object gradually took form: It was a man with a beard and long sidelocks, dressed in a long black coat, a fur-covered black hat and black pants tucked into high black shoes. Gil realized that he was from the congregation of Hasidic Jews living in a nearby neighborhood. The man seemed to be looking for something, turning his head from right to left as he negotiated the snowy sidewalks. Spotting Gil, he called out. "Excuse me, young man, maybe you are Jewish?"

Startled, Gil answered, "Well, yes, I am."

"Good. So maybe you would be willing to help us out? You know what is a *minyan*?" the man asked.

Gil nodded. He knew a *minyan* was the term for the ten men required for prayers at Jewish ceremonies, although he didn't know any of the prayers and didn't read Hebrew.

"My brother just had a son, and we are having the bris," the man explained. "Some of the family couldn't come because of the weather...." He interrupted himself. "You know what a bris is?"

"Yes," Gil said, but did not admit that although he knew a bris was the ritual circumcision for Jewish male babies, he'd never been to a traditional one, and his own circumcision had been done by the hospital pediatrician.

"For our *minyan*, we need just one more man. Could you spare maybe an hour to come to my house to make the *minyan*?"

Gil hesitated. Was just being the tenth man enough, or would he have to say prayers? Worst of all, would he have to witness the circumcision from close up?

"It would be a *mitzvah*, a good deed," the man pleaded. "We have food, drinks… You are welcome to join us afterward."

How could he refuse?

As they trudged the several blocks to the house, the man introduced himself as Avram and Gil told him his full name — Gilad. Avram was surprised. "A very good Biblical name. But you are not religious?"

"No," Gil said. "My mother just liked the name." He knew Avram would have preferred an observant Jew, but on Christmas Day following a blizzard, he didn't have much choice for the tenth man.

When they arrived, Avram handed Gil a yarmulke, introduced him to his brother — the proud father of the new baby — and found him a place amidst the other men who stood in the dining room, where there were two empty chairs. The *mohel*, who would do the circumcision, was putting some surgical instruments on a tray on the table. An older woman, probably one of the grandmothers, emerged from the kitchen where the women and children were gathered, carrying a pile of blankets with only a tiny fist sticking up through the folds. As she entered, everyone chanted something in Hebrew.

Gil bent his head and tried to look as if he were praying. The woman handed the baby to the grandfather, who placed him carefully on one of the empty chairs. Again, a prayer was said, but this time by the *mohel*, so Gil was spared from further revealing his ignorance. Avram sat in the other chair and took the baby on to his lap, while the *mohel* held what looked like a terrycloth pacifier soaked in red wine near the baby's mouth, tapping his cheek gently to get him to suck on it.

When the baby had his fill, the *mohel* bent over him and performed the circumcision. Gil breathed a sigh of relief that the *mohel* blocked his view. The baby cried briefly, blessings were said over wine, the *mohel* said more prayers, and then announced the baby's name.

Both Avram and his brother were beaming as the other men came to shake their hands. The mother came in from the kitchen, and when the baby was handed to her, Gil saw that she was crying what he hoped were tears of joy. Avram insisted that he stay for the celebratory refreshments, which included bagels, smoked salmon, pickled herring, fruit platters and several cakes, so Gil indulged in a bagel with lox before he said his goodbyes. At the door, Avram shook his hand. "You know," he said, "what you did today was truly a *mitzvah*. You fulfilled your obligation as a Jew. Thank you."

Outside, the late-afternoon light cast blue-gray shadows on the snow. The noise from the house gave way to that particular quiet that descends as heavy snow muffles all sound. The Christmas lights in most of the houses were lit again. As Gil came to his front steps, his neighbor, who was getting into his car, called out, "I hope you had a nice Christmas!" before driving away.

Gil called us. "Actually, I had a really nice day," he said. "I spent it doing what people are supposed to do on Christmas — celebrating the birth of a baby!"

The next morning, he got up early, finished shoveling the driveway, threw a bunch of things into a suitcase, and drove home.

—Stephanie Schamess—

101

Sang and Yen

*Gratitude can transform common days into
thanksgivings, turn routine jobs into joy,
and change ordinary opportunities into blessings.*
~William Arthur Ward

I n 1975, my family and I celebrated a special Texas Thanksgiving with two men who were refugees from Vietnam. They had aided American troops during the war and faced retribution if they stayed in country. So we volunteered, in Texas, to sponsor the two men and help them get started in the US. They were unrelated to each other, but they gratefully shared a large bedroom in our home.

Sang was a twenty-five-year-old who spoke a few English words. Yen was a reserved thirty-eight-year-old. He spoke no English, but smiled, bowed, and nodded in agreement with whatever was said. He had courtly manners and a straight-backed stance.

When the men first moved in, they were horrified by some of our food. Pizza was a good example. Sang decided to try it after he saw our youngest pulling cheese strings from her piece, but Yen wouldn't touch his until it was smothered in grape jelly, which made my children stare at him in shock.

We introduced the men to the wonders of our bathroom, light fixtures, and bedding. They learned how to use the washer and dryer, and we had "English lessons," naming various mechanical items they might remember.

When I brought out my vacuum for the first time, their eyes didn't leave this strange item until I flicked the "on" switch and its motor came to life. Sang bolted to the other side of the room, shouting words I was glad I didn't understand. Collecting his dignity, he approached the machine, and I let him feel the suction that picked up bits of food and dust. He closed one eye and looked up the vacuum hose until his nose was sucked into the nozzle. Yen slapped his leg and for once laughed without reserve. Sang chased him across the room, trying to vacuum his hair. Yen never made friends with this strange thing, but for some reason Sang took it over, cleaning up crumbs my two-year-old dropped from her highchair.

All four of my children accompanied Sang, Yen and me to the supermarket, where I knew the men would be amazed by the ample fresh foods. What I didn't anticipate was their fear of the doors that suddenly slid open at our approach. Neither man would enter until my older children held their hands, and then they ran in and out until I had to put a stop to the fun.

We bought bicycles for the men, and I took them for practice runs through our small town to make sure they knew how to return home. My husband reminded me that they had been able to find their way out of Vietnam and into a new country, so he was sure they would find their way around.

The men's respect for me was evident when we celebrated our first Christmas together. They bowed and presented me with the gaudiest Valentine's Day cards I'd ever seen, accompanied by a stuffed red-satin heart flowing with blue ribbons. I was proud of my children as they held back guffaws at these strange Christmas presents. I cherished the cards.

Yen was the first to find employment — with the City Parks Department. He worked with zeal until he embarrassed his co-workers who tried to slow him down, but he appreciated the work and wouldn't do less than his best. Sang was hired by American Bridge Company, a subsidiary of U.S. Steel.

As the men became self-sufficient, it was time to find them an apartment and set them up to live on their own. Our special time with them was drawing to a close. Yen told us he was part of our family now, my husband being the papa and I the mama. Our children were brothers and sisters to him. What great strides he had made with English.

The men continued to visit for Sunday dinners, and we were proud as they mingled with other Vietnamese families in neighboring towns.

We've never forgotten our 1975 Thanksgiving. It truly helped all of us understand how blessed we were.

— Denise Hengeli —

Meet Our Contributors

Adrienne A. Aguirre is a graduate of CSU San Marcos, and has a Master of Arts in Theological Studies from Bethel Seminary San Diego. Chaplain Adrienne provides spiritual care through her mobile ministry, and sells her books to support her four sponsor children in Uganda. E-mail her at ChaplainAdrienne@mobileministers.net.

Valerie Testa Almquist authored *Look Back Move Forward*, an inspirational, historical fiction adventure. Her story, "Mother-Daughter Connection," was published in *Chicken Soup for the Soul: Best Mom Ever!* and "Familiar Words" won 1st place and appeared in the March/April 2018 edition of *Writer's Digest*. Learn more at ValerieTestaAlmquist.com.

Kate E. Anderson is the fourth of six children with a carefree dad and an amazing, intelligent, dedicated mother, Clarissa. Kate seeks to emulate her mom by believing anything is possible with hard work. Kate lives in North Logan, UT, with her devastatingly handsome husband, five clever children, and two nosy Beagles.

Sally Bair lives near Lake Superior where she enjoys nature, writing, and visiting family. She is a columnist, speaker, and teacher of writing. She has self-published three adventure books about Alaska, four devotionals, and a memoir about her childhood as an identical twin. E-mail her at sallybair@gmail.com.

Garrett Bauman has been published in fifteen *Chicken Soup for the Soul* books and in *The New York Times*, *Sierra*, *Yankee* and other publications.

A retired college professor, he and his wife of forty-one years still fondly recall their first brutally cold Christmas together and the warm people who shared it with them.

Lil Blosfield fell in love with writing shortly after she learned how to read. She has a vast collection of stories and poems and truly believes that every day is an opportunity for a story with a constantly changing flow of characters. E-mail her at LBlosfield40@msn.com.

Susan Stowell Bowmer wrote many novels as well as newspaper and magazine articles. She enjoyed finding inspiration in everyday life. "Stories are everywhere you look," she said. "You just have to look." Susan passed away before this publication was released but would be so proud and happy to share this experience with others.

By day, **Tami Brothers** is the SuperVisor of a small group of superheroes, working for a well-known logistics company (Aim High!). But during early mornings, lunch breaks, and early evenings she reverts to SuperAuthor with a number of short stories, novellas and full-length books under her cap(e).

Jill Burns lives in the mountains of West Virginia with her wonderful family. She's a retired piano teacher and performer. She enjoys writing, music, gardening, nature, and spending time with her grandchildren.

Erinn C. received her B.A. in Political Science from the University of North Carolina at Chapel Hill and is currently pursuing her M.A. in Bremen, Germany. She loves writing outside in the sunshine with her dog.

Rebecca Calappi has a journalism degree from Oakland University. She's a professional freelance writer in the Detroit area and the mother of twins—a boy and a girl. Free time is scarce, but she enjoys reading, traveling with her husband and binge watching anything not animated.

Greg Cameron has spent a good part of his life in a small prairie town; on the edge of that town stands a forty-foot banana named "Sunny" with a five-foot Blue Jay called "Breezy" in its hand — enough said! He now lives in the core of a city of a million or more and drives a taxi. His story originates from a Christmas Eve fare long ago.

Nebula Award-nominated **Beth Cato** is the author of the *Clockwork Dagger* duology and the *Blood of Earth* trilogy from Harper Voyager. She's a Hanford, CA native transplanted to the Arizona desert, where she lives with her husband, son, and requisite cats. Follow her at BethCato.com and on Twitter @BethCato.

Phyllis Coletta is a recovering litigation attorney, writer, and EMT currently teaching at-risk youth at a recovery high school in Seattle. E-mail her at phylliscoletta@gmail.com.

This is **HM Cook's** second story published in the *Chicken Soup for the Soul* series. A married mother of four children, HM enjoys reading, writing, and spending time with family. Sharing her own experiences with brokenness, she writes on topics related to healing the wounds we carry in our souls. E-mail her at HM_Cook@yahoo.com.

Gary S. Crawford is a published author, editor, blogger, historian, and lecturer. His books include local historical nonfiction as well as horror-fantasy. Trying to be retired, he lives at the Jersey Shore with his wife, daughter, and four grandchildren. Learn more at www.crawsat. wixsite.com/garyscrawford.

Michael J. Cunningham, a previous contributor to the *Chicken Soup for the Soul* series, has also written three screenplays. His first, *Swing Vote*, placed 2nd out of 2,300 entries in the Scriptapalooza Screenwriting Contest. He enjoys family, friends, standup comedy, creating music and film. E-mail him at mrsea@frontiernet.net.

Stephanie Davenport is a freelance writer and resides in Illinois with her family and two cats. She enjoys good books, coffee, and spending time with friends and family.

Resa Delaney is currently an MFA Creative Writing student at Concordia University, and is working on her first novel. She also blogs about the chaos of her everyday life as the single parent of four children (and a very spoiled dog) at convincingchaos.com. E-mail her at msresa@convincingchaos.com.

Michelle DelaPlace received her Bachelor of Music from the University of British Columbia but she has always had a passion for literature. She has a daughter and a son, both whom are a constant source of inspiration to her. She has written a series of children's books as well as an album of lullabies.

James Fasino earned his B.A. degree in Communication from William Paterson University of New Jersey. He is a freelance writer, a retired New York City news and sports television cameraman, and a Cold War–era veteran of the United States Navy Submarine Service. James resides in Myrtle Beach, SC.

Victoria Fedden is a writer and a mom from Fort Lauderdale, FL. Her memoir, *This Is Not My Beautiful Life*, was published June 2016 by Picador USA. She received her MFA in Creative Writing from Florida Atlantic University in 2009, and teaches college writing in South Florida.

Josephine Fitzpatrick is a retired attorney. She has been married to her husband Art for fifty-six years. They have three children and six grandchildren. She loves to write, read, swim, and photograph anything that catches her interest.

Denise Flint is a freelance journalist living on the edge of North America in the middle of the North Atlantic. She's lived in four provinces and three countries and her interests are diverse. Denise's articles have appeared in newspapers and magazines internationally and she has received many awards for her work.

Savannah Flowers received her Master's in Social Work from The University of Texas at Austin. She works as a full-time writer and proofreader. She lives in an RV and travels around the country with her husband, their dog and two cats. She enjoys needlework, reading, and traveling. She is currently working on a children's novel.

Faye Fulton has been a speaker, communications trainer, professional storyteller, and writer for over two decades. She grew up in Sicily and Trinidad and has traveled extensively. She tells stories in educational and corporate settings about her adventures and the diverse group of people she has met over the years.

Nancy Gallimore lives on Tails You Win farm in northeastern Oklahoma. She and her partner Jim share their lives with a collection of dogs, horses, donkeys, and other animals. Nancy enjoys writing, running a rescue for Dalmatians and other breeds, and life on the farm. She hopes to write a book about her animals.

Ginger M. Galloway earned her B.A. in Human Development from Azusa Pacific University. She is a graphic artist, published author, poet, and playwright. She teaches crochet, art, poetry, and theatre classes and lives with her husband Richard and four of their seven children in Southern California.

James A. Gemmell is the proud father of two grown children. His favourite hobby is long distance hiking. James likes to indulge himself each summer by hiking trails in Spain and France. He enjoys playing the guitar, writing short stories, drawing and painting portraits.

Stephanie Gibeault is a freelance writer and certified professional dog trainer with a Master of Science degree in animal behavior. She enjoys tap dancing, escape rooms, and writing stories for children. She is also the official family photographer and never misses moments like the Christmas reindeer dance.

Lynn Gilliland is a retired electrical engineer from a large automotive firm. He and his wife Karen have two daughters and five grandchildren. He has been writing since his retirement twelve years ago. He leads the local Defiance, Ohio Writers Group, and belongs to the Northwest Ohio Writers Forum.

Jeanne Green is retired and content living in Wisconsin. A Minnesota and South Dakota middle and high school English teacher for thirty-five years, she now fills her days with travel, book clubs, scrapbooking and volunteering with P.E.O., a Philanthropic Educational Organization.

Gabrielle Harbowy is a writer, editor, and anthologist with two published novels, a dozen short stories in print, and over seventy-five published editing credits to her name. Learn more at www.gabrielleharbowy.com or on Twitter @gabrielle_h.

Judy Harch is a journalist and book author. *Falling Off the Family Tree* is her first novel. She also co-authored the book, *Alzheimer Solutions: A Personal Guide For Caregivers*. Judy and her husband Chris are grandparents to four wonderful adult grandchildren. They share their home with Gracie, a rescue Labrador Retriever.

Kay Harper loves baking pies, cakes and cookies at Christmas—a skill she learned from her mom. She's an actress and author who blends these talents when speaking at Christian venues. The author of *Stumbling Into Grace*, Kay posts daily on Facebook. Read her blog at kayharpergodisbig.blog.

Charles Earl Harrel served as a pastor for thirty years before stepping aside to pursue writing. His stories, devotionals, and articles have appeared in numerous magazines and anthologies. He is also a six-time contributor to the *Chicken Soup for the Soul* series. Charles enjoys guitar, music, and painting. He is currently writing a novel.

Steve Hecht is a 1972 graduate of Duquesne University. He is retired from the *Pittsburgh Post-Gazette* where he was a writer and copyeditor for thirty years.

A Florida Atlantic University graduate who majored in English, **Denise Hengeli** has published a novel, *I Shawn*, and a poetry book, *My Mind's Manifestations*. Her short stories have been published by Scribes Valley, Fossil Creek, Eber & Wein, and *The Lutheran Digest*. She continues to fine-tune her work.

Lorraine Hernandez received her Bachelor of Interdisciplinary Studies from the University of Texas El Paso in 2003 and her MLIS from the University of North Texas in 2015. She is a school librarian and mom of one daughter and two cats. She spends her free time cooking delicious food, although she refuses to make any more tamales.

A past *Chicken Soup for the Soul* contributor, **Debbie Hirsch**, received a degree in Journalism and years later started writing professionally. She first catered, taught English, and now writes. Debbie lives in Israel with her large family including more than a dozen grandchildren. She writes Jewish stories and blogs at tziyonawrite.wordpress.com.

Joei Carlton Hossack is the author of fourteen adventure travel books, a photographer, an entertaining and inspirational speaker, and has turned her itty-bitty beading hobby into a raging addiction.

Linda K. Hren is the director of a small rural Library in East-Central Ohio. She has been writing stories about the animals in her life since she was eight years old. She is currently working on a series of children's books based on her adventures with her pony Star from "A Pony in the Living Room."

Misty Huelsebusch is a motivational speaker and writer sharing about overcoming challenges and finding hope and happiness in everyday life. She received her Bachelor of Science in 1999 at Southwestern Assemblies of God University, where she and her husband Joseph of eighteen years met. They have three beautiful children.

Jim Jenkins was a retired schoolteacher whose passion was writing about life experiences. An avid sports fan, he played hockey until the age of seventy-five. He enjoyed serving in his church especially in the children's programs. As of March 2019, he is rejoicing in Heaven.

Vicki L. Julian, a University of Kansas alumna and award-winning writer, is the author of four inspirational books, two memoir anthologies, various newspaper and magazine articles, and is a contributor to nine anthologies. She writes a faith-based blog in addition to serving as a freelance editor. Learn more at www.vickijulian.com.

Rachel Katherine is a passionate Pentecostal, currently enrolled at Life Christian University. She enjoys learning languages, playing the ukulele, writing, and various other creative hobbies. E-mail her at rachelkatherine33@gmail.com.

Wendy Kennar is a Los Angeles native who prefers sunflowers to roses. Much of her writing is inspired by her son and from the memories of her twelve-year teaching career. She blogs about books, boys, and bodies — primarily living with an invisible disability — at www. wendykennar.com.

Mary Potter Kenyon graduated from the University of Northern Iowa and is a certified grief counselor. She works as the program coordinator at Shalom Spirituality Center in Dubuque, IA. Mary is the author of seven books, including one on creativity that is to be released by Familius Publishing in 2020. E-mail her at marypotterkenyon@gmail. com.

Wendy Keppley, a Florida native, counseled troubled teens and taught college courses for high school honor students. She enjoys family, playing with her grandsons, and living in the woods near Tampa, FL. Wendy also loves writing, kayaking, reading, yoga, and exploring waterfalls. E-mail her at wendykep@gmail.com.

Sky Khan is an artist, educator, parent, and wife living in Texas Hill Country. Her work has been covered in *The New York Times*, *Time Out*, and *BuzzFeed*. Her life is guided by time spent sitting with the dying, her study of Buddhism principles, and her experience as a parent of a cancer survivor. Learn more at skykhan.com.

Suzannah Kiper graduated with high honors from the University of Louisville and is a seventh generation Kentuckian. She has been married to her husband Tim for twenty-two years and has two amazing kids (Daniel and Lydia) and two Maltese dogs (Bella and Chloe). She has had two stories published in the *Chicken Soup for the Soul* series.

Vicki Kitchner is a retired educator who taught Exceptional Student Education for thirty years. She divides her time between North Carolina and Florida. She and her husband love to travel, hike, garden, and entertain family and friends.

Charles Milton Lee is a retired college professor who has discovered the joy of writing both nonfiction and fiction and the challenge of oil painting. He held his first art show in June 2018 at the age of eighty. He is addicted to his family, chocolate, and anything Christmas. E-mail him at tallychuck@gmail.com.

Karen M. Leet writes from Lexington, KY, heart of the Bluegrass, where she enjoys reading, family time, and writing.

JL LeGerrette's roots began in San Diego, CA as the daughter of musicians. She loves to share stories of her life, write novels, and laugh. She lives in the Pacific Northwest, hating and loving the rain, cherishing spring and fall as old friends, and waiting anxiously for their peaceful visits.

Mark Leiren-Young is the author of two comic memoirs: *Never Shoot a Stampede Queen* and *Free Magic Secrets Revealed*. Based in Victoria, BC, Mark is an advocate for the Southern Resident Orcas. He's the author of *The Killer Whale Who Changed the World*, director of *The Hundred-Year-Old Whale* and host of the Skaana podcast.

Lisa D. MacDougall was a single mom for a lot of years and learned very valuable lessons through her experiences. Trials bring out our strengths and we attract what we focus on. Lisa lives in rural New Brunswick, Canada and enjoys gardening, preserving what she grows, crocheting, and spending time with loved ones.

Elaine Maly teaches the art of creative engagement for meaningful connections with elders, especially those with dementia through her work with TimeSlips. She writes about her life and times as a native Milwaukeean and is an active participant in her local storytelling community, Ex Fabula. She's the grandmother of three spunky grandsons who give her plenty of material.

Dr. Barry Marks is a Chiropractor who earned his DC degree from the Los Angeles College of Chiropractic in 1986. He is an Orange County native and practices chiropractic in Orange, CA. Dr. Marks enjoys cooking, art, and sports car racing.

Andrea Marlene is a mom of three who lives in Ontario, Canada. She currently runs a small hand-stamped jewelry business and is also enrolled in the Graduate Certificate program in Publishing at Ryerson University. She loves to read and enjoys hosting an online book club. Her writing has appeared on several websites.

Irma A. Mason is an accomplished artist who takes great joy in making others smile through her original paintings, photography, and writing. Fishing, hiking, and spending time with her family help keep her creative juices flowing. Irma's goal is to tell her stories through her art and writing talents. E-mail her at Irmas.Art@yahoo.com.

Nicole Ann Rook McAlister has studied journalism and pursues an avid interest in world religion and mythology. Nicole enjoys adventures in camping, sunrises on the beach, painting, crafting and all manner of such things. Several of her pieces have been on exhibit at the Whitesbog Historic Village in Browns Mills, NJ.

Gena B. McCown is a ministry leadership coach, public speaker, and author from South Florida. Married for nearly twenty years to her husband Justin, they have three daughters — Casey, Shelby, and Naomi. Gena has a heart for serving women, developing female leaders, and sharing messages of hope, love, and forgiveness.

Phyllis McKinley has authored five books and won multiple awards for her writing. She loves family, friends, and Christmas. This is her seventh story published in the *Chicken Soup for the Soul* series. A former Canadian, she now lives in Florida. E-mail her at leafybough@hotmail.com.

Curt Melliger worked dozens of different jobs before discovering writing. Since then over 100 of his articles have appeared in print. His recently released first book *Heaven Here on Earth* explores how to access the Ultimate while still alive. Learn more at curtmelliger.com.

Harriet E. Michael is a multi-published author and freelance writer. She has authored seven books, with more under contract, and hundreds of articles, stories, and devotions. Married for over forty years, she has four children and two grandchildren. Find her books on her author page at www.amazon.com/-/e/B00MCID8DE.

Janell Michael's first book, *Fairytales Redeemed: A Woman's Study on the Power of Love, Forgiveness, and Reconciliation*, was published in 2018. Recently, she and her husband moved 2,400 miles to live closer to their children and grandchildren. Since retiring from teaching, Janell hopes to continue her writing career.

C.L. Nehmer lives with her husband and three teenagers in Wisconsin, where she enjoys walking with her hounds, baking cakes, and taking in late-night poetry readings. Her work has been published in *Southern Poetry Review*, *Pedestal Magazine*, *Sunlight Press* and *An Ariel Anthology 2018*. Learn more at clnehmer.com.

Jesse Neve is a wife and mother of four from Minnetrista, MN. She enjoys traveling with her big crowd, and writing about her family's adventures and what she has learned from them. Jesse's life goal is to bring a little smile to everyone she passes. E-mail her at Jessedavidneve@frontiernet.net.

Leigh Ann Northcutt lives in the nicely worn farmhouse in western Kentucky where she raised five children and one husband. Her tacky Christmas decorations continue to adorn her home every December. As a humorist, she has written stories, blog posts, newspaper columns and magazine articles about her life in the farmhouse.

Michael D. Nye studied writing at the University of California Berkeley, but his love of the arts really began when, as a child, he and his parents traveled with the Ringling Bros. and Barnum & Bailey Circus. These days Michael writes short stories and songs, as well as teaches brain games to seniors.

Sara Ohlin's essays can be found at *Mothers Always Write*, *Feminine Collective*, *The Manifest Station*, *Project Hot Mess*, and the anthologies *Are We Feeling Better Yet? Women Speak About Health Care in America* and *Take Care: Tales, Tips, and Love from Women Caregivers*. Read her blog at www.lemonsandroses.com.

Ashley Oldham is an English and Comparative Literature major at the University of North Carolina at Chapel Hill. She is an avid reader and writer, and hopes to pursue a career involving the two in the future. Ashley enjoys traveling, trying new coffees, and attending concerts. She hopes to one day write a novel of her own.

Sister Josephine Palmeri, MPF has been teaching Spanish, Public Speaking, and Theology to teenagers for over five decades. "Teenagers keep me young," she says, "and they teach me some new technology every day." Her hobbies are writing, reading, biking, hiking, and meeting new people.

Nancy Emmick Panko is an award-winning author of *Guiding Missal* and eleven-time contributor to the *Chicken Soup for the Soul* series. She is a member of the Cary Writing Circle and The Military Writers' Society of America. Nancy is a retired pediatric nurse, wife, mother, and grandmother. She loves boating and fishing on Lake Gaston with her family.

Ivy Papa-Goze is a romance author who writes under the pseudonym Margery Santander. Besides writing, she also pursues other interests such as gardening and birding. Once a Spanish teacher at an international school, she now focuses on homeschooling her three children.

Sal Patel lives in Devon, UK, with her family. She works freelance as a communications consultant, specialising in the nonprofit sector. Sal enjoys writing professionally and for pleasure, and has had two short plays produced in London.

Craig Perino is a child of God who has spent time in a federal prison from bad choices he made. He uses writing to express what is in his heart and to hopefully draw others to Christ.

Kristen Mai Pham is an inspirational screenwriter and author. A devoted Christmas enthusiast, she is delighted to have her sixth story published in the *Chicken Soup for the Soul* series. She spends most of her time sending pictures of Corgis to her husband Paul. Follow Kristen on Instagram or e-mail her at Kristenmaipham3@gmail.com.

Lori Phillips lives in Southern California where she enjoys reading, walking, propagating plants, and spending time with her family. She earned both her Bachelor of Arts in Communications and Master's in Education. Currently, Lori is working on children's picture books and juvenile fiction.

Harry Pickens is an award-winning performing artist and educator. He is the author of *In Tune: Lessons in Life from A Life in Music*. Harry's multifaceted musical career has touched the lives of many people around the world.

Jilly Pretzel is a fiction and nonfiction writer from Southern California. She received her M.A. and MFA from Chapman University and now teaches Creative Writing at California School of the Arts—San Gabriel Valley.

Connie Kaseweter Pullen lives in rural Sandy, OR, near her five children and several grandchildren. She earned a B.A. degree, with honors, at the University of Portland in 2006, with a double major in Psychology and Sociology. Connie enjoys writing, photography, and exploring nature. E-mail her at MyGrandmaPullen@aol.com.

Rence Regan is a husband and father of four boys and two girls residing on Long Island, NY. After thirty-five years working in the television industry, Rence now fills his time with extemporaneous writings often centering around his close-knit family. Rence graduated from Siena College in 1982 with a B.A. in History.

When she isn't playing her flute at church or the local nursing home, laughing with her grandchildren, working on a new book, gardening or traveling, **Kathleen Cox Richardson** can be found writing potential stories for the *Chicken Soup for the Soul* series.

Mark Rickerby is a writer, screenwriter and voice actor. His stories have appeared in over twenty *Chicken Soup for the Soul* books. Links to these and his other works can be found on his website: www. markrickerby.com. However, the achievements he is most proud of are, and will forever be, his daughters Marli and Emma.

Emily Rodavich, retired English teacher, mother of three and grandmother of four, patented a hands-on methodology for teaching grammar. In addition to writing lyrics for an original musical, she has written two books, *Mystical Interludes I* and *II*. She enjoys traveling, reading and playing word games.

Stephanie Schamess returned to her first love — writing — after retiring in 2000 from Hampshire College, where she taught child development. She is in the process of moving with her husband to a local retirement community and is excited about beginning a new phase of her life.

Emily Olson Shipley holds a B.A. and M.A. in English from California Polytechnic State University in San Luis Obispo. She has slowly tried to make a living from writing, but has also enjoyed teaching the subject to community college English students. When she's not on campus, Emily enjoys reading, cooking, and weekend hikes.

Mary Shotwell is the author of short stories and debuted her small-town romance novel *Christmas Catch* (Carina Press) in 2018, receiving a starred review from *Library Journal*. She lives in Nashville with her husband and three children and loves holidays — especially Christmas. Learn more at maryshotwell.com.

Maureen Tyrrell Simons attended the University of California, Santa Barbara and the Université Grenoble. She has a beautiful daughter who is studying to be a teacher. After many years in high tech, Maureen is now a writer full-time. She is working on a book about the redemptive power of love and caramel sticky buns.

Debbie Sistare says, "The world may refer to me as disabled, but as long as I can write, I shall refer to myself as enabled." She has multiple eBooks and paperbacks published online. Book 2, *Wisdom,* in her *In Search of the Key of David* trilogy, was published in spring 2019 and book 3, *Power,* comes out in early 2020. E-mail her at debbieblessesu2@ yahoo.com.

Ellie Spence is a retired eighth grade English teacher who found a second career teaching Creative Writing at Marin County Jail.

Margarite R. Stever grew up in Asbury, MO, a tiny town of just over 200 people. She currently lives in a larger town with her husband and fur babies. She writes stories that touch a person's heart. Her work has been published in a variety of collections and seeds of wisdom and joy can be read at ozarksmaven.com.

Bill Suboski is an aspiring writer, mostly science fiction but with forays into other genres. Bill believes, as Stephen King said, "It is the tale, not he who tells it." E-mail him at wsuboski@yahoo.com.

Diana Traeger is a wife, mother, and grandmother. She and her husband run a nonprofit organization in the rural Utah community where they live. She is a devout member of the Church of Jesus Christ of Latter Day Saints and says service is what fuels her reason for living.

Swami Vidyananda is a yoga teacher and a Monk. She teaches yoga postures, meditation and philosophy internationally. She trains teachers in yoga for stress management and loves to sing, write, and walk in the wild Virginia woods.

Samantha Ducloux Waltz is delighted to be part of the *Chicken Soup for the Soul* family. Her writings include anthologized and award-winning essays, several books on parenting, and the Seal Press anthology *Blended: Writers on the Stepfamily Experience*. She lives in Portland, OR where family, pets, writing and dance keep her busy and happy.

David Warren resides in Kettering, OH with his wife Angela. They have a daughter named Marissa. He's a frequent contributor to the *Chicken Soup for the Soul* series and other publications. David is VP of Lutz Blades and enjoys travel, sports, and music.

Glenda Wood is a photographer, writer, and former owner of a media relations consulting firm, specializing in political media. She worked for the U.S. Air Force and Navy and the governor of Florida as a speechwriter/public affairs director. She is a licensed Realtor and college Writing/English tutor at Gulf Coast State.

Meet Amy Newmark

Amy Newmark is the bestselling author, editor-in-chief, and publisher of the *Chicken Soup for the Soul* book series. Since 2008, she has published 160 new books, most of them national bestsellers in the U.S. and Canada, more than doubling the number of Chicken Soup for the Soul titles in print today. She is also the author of *Simply Happy*, a crash course in Chicken Soup for the Soul advice and wisdom that is filled with easy-to-implement, practical tips for enjoying a better life.

Amy is credited with revitalizing the Chicken Soup for the Soul brand, which has been a publishing industry phenomenon since the first book came out in 1993. By compiling inspirational and aspirational true stories curated from ordinary people who have had extraordinary experiences, Amy has kept the twenty-six-year-old Chicken Soup for the Soul brand fresh and relevant.

Amy graduated *magna cum laude* from Harvard University where she majored in Portuguese and minored in French. She then embarked on a three-decade career as a Wall Street analyst, a hedge fund manager, and a corporate executive in the technology field. She is a Chartered Financial Analyst.

Her return to literary pursuits was inevitable, as her honors thesis in college involved traveling throughout Brazil's impoverished northeast region, collecting stories from regular people. She is delighted to have come full circle in her writing career — from collecting stories "from the people" in Brazil as a twenty-year-old to, three decades later, collecting stories "from the people" for Chicken Soup for the Soul.

When Amy and her husband Bill, the CEO of Chicken Soup for the Soul, are not working, they are visiting their four grown children and their grandchildren.

Follow Amy on Twitter @amynewmark. Listen to her free podcast — "Chicken Soup for the Soul with Amy Newmark" — on Apple Podcasts, Google Play, the Podcasts app on iPhone, or by using your favorite podcast app on other devices.

About Toys for Tots

Your purchase of this *Chicken Soup for the Soul* book supports Toys for Tots and helps create Christmas miracles for children who might not receive gifts otherwise! The mission of the U.S. Marine Corps Reserve Toys for Tots Program is to collect new, unwrapped toys during October, November and December each year, and distribute those toys as Christmas gifts to less fortunate children in the community in which the campaign is conducted.

You can contribute to your local Toys for Tots campaign in several ways. You can donate a toy at one of the area toy drop locations, host a Toys for Tots event at your office or other venue and collect toys for Toys for Tots, or volunteer at the local warehouse. You can also donate by visiting toysfortots.org.

Local campaigns are conducted annually in over 800 communities covering all 50 U.S. states, the District of Columbia and Puerto Rico. Local toy collection campaigns begin in October and last until mid to late December. Toy distribution also takes place mid to late December.

Members of the community drop new, unwrapped toys in collection boxes positioned in local businesses. Coordinators pick up these toys and store them in central warehouses where the toys are sorted by age and gender. At Christmas, Coordinators, with the assistance of local social welfare agencies, church groups, and other local community agencies, distribute the toys to the less fortunate children of the community.

Over the years, Marines have established close working relationships with social welfare agencies, churches and other local community agencies which are well qualified to identify the needy children in the community and play important roles in the distribution of the toys. While Toys for Tots Coordinators organize, coordinate and manage the campaign, the ultimate success depends on the support of the local community and the generosity of the people who donate toys.

You can learn more about Toys for Tots by visiting their website at https://www.toysfortots.org.

Thank You

We owe huge thanks to all of our contributors and fans. We were overwhelmed with fabulous holiday stories. There had to be at least 6,000 submissions on this very popular topic, and we had a team that spent months reading all of them. Elaine Kimbler, Susan Heim, and Mary Fisher found so many "10s" that we made two books' worth of holiday cheer, this one and *Chicken Soup for the Soul: The Wonder of Christmas*, which was published in 2018.

Susan Heim did the first round of editing, D'ette Corona chose the perfect quotations to put at the beginning of each story, and Amy Newmark edited the stories and shaped the final manuscript.

As we finished our work, Associate Publisher D'ette Corona continued to be Amy's right-hand woman in creating the final manuscript and working with all our wonderful writers. Barbara LoMonaco and Kristiana Pastir, along with Elaine Kimbler, jumped in at the end to proof, proof, proof. And yes, there will always be typos anyway, so feel free to let us know about them at webmaster@chickensoupforthesoul. com and we will correct them in future printings.

The whole publishing team deserves a hand, including our Senior Director of Marketing Maureen Peltier, our Vice President, Production and Project Management Victor Cataldo, and our graphic designer Daniel Zaccari, who turned our manuscript into this beautiful book.

Sharing Happiness, Inspiration, and Hope

Real people sharing real stories, every day, all over the world. In 2007, USA Today named Chicken Soup for the Soul one of the five most memorable books in the last quarter-century. With over 100 million books sold to date in the U.S. and Canada alone, more than 250 titles in print, and translations into nearly fifty languages, "chicken soup for the soul®" is one of the world's best-known phrases.

Today, twenty-six years after we first began sharing happiness, inspiration and hope through our books, we continue to delight our readers with new titles, but have also evolved beyond the bookshelves with super premium pet food, television shows, a podcast, video journalism from aplus.com, licensed products, and free movies and TV shows on our Popcornflix and Crackle apps. We are busy "changing the world one story at a time®." Thanks for reading!

Share with Us

We all have had Chicken Soup for the Soul moments in our lives. If you would like to share your story or poem with millions of people around the world, go to chickensoup.com and click on Submit Your Story. You may be able to help another reader and become a published author at the same time. Some of our past contributors have launched writing and speaking careers from the publication of their stories in our books!

We only accept story submissions via our website. They are no longer accepted via mail or fax. Visit our website, www.chickensoup.com, and click on Submit Your Story for our writing guidelines and a list of topics we are working on.

To contact us regarding other matters, please send us an e-mail through webmaster@chickensoupforthesoul.com, or fax or write us at:

Chicken Soup for the Soul
P.O. Box 700
Cos Cob, CT 06807-0700
Fax: 203-861-7194

One more note from your friends at Chicken Soup for the Soul: Occasionally, we receive an unsolicited book manuscript from one of our readers, and we would like to respectfully inform you that we do not accept unsolicited manuscripts, and we must discard the ones that appear.

Chicken Soup
for the Soul

The
Wonder of
Christmas

101 Stories
about the
Joy of
the Season

Amy Newmark
Royalties from this book benefit TOYS FOR TOTS

Paperback: 978-1-61159-982-4
eBook: 978-1-61159-282-5

More Holiday

Chicken Soup for the Soul

A Book of Christmas Miracles

101 Stories of Holiday Hope and Happiness

Amy Newmark
Royalties from this book benefit TOYS FOR TOTS

Paperback: 978-1-61159-972-5
eBook: 978-1-61159-272-6

Joy and Wonder

Chicken Soup for the Soul

for the Soul

Think Positive, Live Happy

101 Stories
about Creating
Your Best Life

Amy Newmark
& Deborah Norville
Journalist and Anchor of *Inside Edition*

Paperback: 978-1-61159-992-3
eBook: 978-1-61159-293-1

Inspiration for

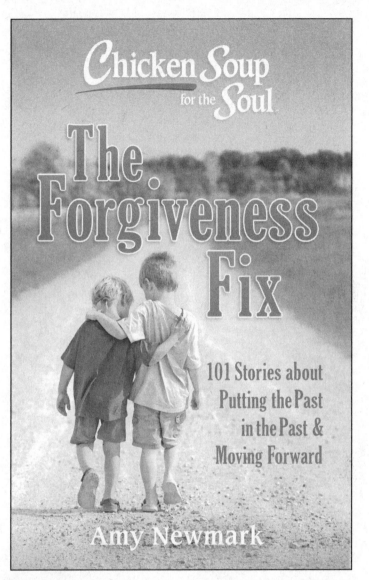

Chicken Soup for the Soul

The Forgiveness Fix

101 Stories about
Putting the Past
in the Past &
Moving Forward

Amy Newmark

Paperback: 978-1-61159-994-7
eBook: 978-1-61159-294-8

a Better Life

Changing your world one story at a time®
www.chickensoup.com